THE WOUND OF THE BORDER

25 years with the refugees

Jesuit Refugee Serv

The Wound of the Border
This is how JRS workers described the situation in the
Thai-Cambodia border refugee camps during the 1980s.

Jesuit Refugee Service (JRS) is an international
Catholic organisation with a mission to accompany, serve and plead the cause of refugees and
forcibly displaced people. Set up by the Society of
Jesus in 1980 and now at work in over 50 countries,
the priority of JRS is to accompany refugees whose
needs are more urgent or forgotten.

© Jesuit Refugee Service, October 2005
ISBN: 88-88126-03-1

Edited by: Amaya Valcárcel
Production: Stefano Maero
Cover design: Stefano Maero
Cover photo: *Indochinese boat people in Hong Kong in the early 1980s.*
                This group of refugees first inspired Fr Arrupe to establish JRS.
                © JRS International

Copies of this book are available from:
Jesuit Refugee Service
C.P. 6139, 00195
Roma Prati, Italy
Fax: +39 – 06.68.80.64.18
international@jrs.net
www.jrs.net

CONTENTS

ACKNOWLEDGEMENTS

'St Ignatius called us to go anywhere we are most needed for the greater service of God. The spiritual as well as the material needs of nearly 16 million refugees throughout the world today could scarcely be greater'. The words of Fr Arrupe in his letter of 1980, which established the Jesuit Refugee Service, have inspired many people to give themselves to the service of refugees.

The Wound of the Border is how JRS workers described the situation in the Thai-Cambodia border refugee camps during the 1980s. This powerful metaphor gives title to this book and reminds us, 25 years later, that it is an accurate description of the suffering of today's 50 million forcibly displaced people worldwide.

The history of JRS is the history of refugees. We want to commemorate these 25 with this memoir. But is this something to celebrate? As one JRS worker said, we can only celebrate on the day JRS comes to an end; this will mean there are no more wars, and no more refugees.

The centre of gravity of this book is not only JRS and its many works, but the refugees themselves. What we celebrate is their dignity, courage and determination to keep hope alive, to choose light instead of darkness. It is not meant to be historically exhaustive, but to bring together testimonies of people who have witnessed the growth of JRS. They offer their experience and vision, share significant events in their regions, the specific challenges and dilemmas they encountered, and the signs of hope.

This book has been written thanks to one priceless resource: the lives and experiences of JRS workers. But many people and organizations have played a vital part in JRS story whose praises remain unsung, a feature of this account I readily acknowledge and regret. To try to write a concise historical account on such a wide range of subjects inevitably leads as well to arbitrary decisions about what to include and what to leave out.

Many friends, in particular Stephen Power SJ and Mark Raper SJ, have provided valuable assistance during the preparation of this book. For comments and editing support I am indebted to Susana Barnes, Jenny Cafiso,

Frances Wall, David Holdcroft SJ and Peter O'Driscoll. And of course I am especially grateful to Lluís Magriñà SJ for having thought of producing the book.

I give thanks, on my own behalf and that of many colleagues who have enjoyed the privilege of becoming companions of the refugees.

Amaya Valcárcel
Rome, September 2005

8

INTRODUCTION

The Arrupe Vision in Action

Jesuit Refugee Service (JRS) was founded on 14 November 1980 by Fr Pedro Arrupe, at the time Superior General of the Jesuits. While Pedro Arrupe gave inspiration and vision to JRS, it was his successor, elected in 1983, Fr Peter-Hans Kolvenbach, who has implemented that vision and overseen the development of JRS until now. During the 1980s, I was Regional Director of JRS in Asia, and from 1990 to 2000 International Director.

Pedro Arrupe remained General from 1965 until incapacitated by a cerebral stroke in August 1981. During one of my visits to Rome in the eighties, Dieter Scholz, then Director of JRS, brought me to the infirmary of the General Curia to meet Fr Arrupe. Though almost paralysed by his stroke, it was clear that Fr Arrupe understood who I was and what I was doing. He wanted to ask me a question but could not find the words, so Brother Bandera, the infirmarian, brought him paper and pencil. With his left hand, Fr Arrupe shakily drew a map of India, then the droplet shape of the island next to it. By pointing to the island clearly he was asking me, 'What is JRS doing to help the people of Sri Lanka?' I am sure Fr Arrupe was doing the only thing still in his power for the people of Sri Lanka, namely praying for them. He would be happy to know that JRS South Asia is still responding in a practical way to his question, by accompanying, serving and defending the victims of the long running civil war and also those affected by the recent tsunami.

I was privileged to meet with Fr Arrupe on a few other occasions as well, each an unforgettable experience. One such was in Manila in early August 1981, about four days before his stroke. During a meeting of only five or ten minutes, Fr Arrupe asked me to work for JRS in Asia. What could I say but 'I will try my best'. A year before, in mid-1980, while he was still active as General, I had been shown to his austere office at 8.00 in the morning, assured that he only had 10 minutes free before leaving for a trip to Spain at noon. In the event, he spoke to me for a good half hour, with vigour, about his vision for the Society's service to refugees. Only later did I discover that his trip to Spain was to deal with one of his most difficult challenges as General, namely to confront a group of Spanish Jesuits who wished to break away from the Society. His dream of bringing the Society to the service of the refugees fired him with a different type of energy.

While Arrupe's vision remains inspiring, it is the close contact with refugees that time and again provides JRS workers with new strength and motivation. This was in fact Arrupe's vision. He knew that the refugees themselves would be a gift to the Jesuits and their companions. When I met him in 1980, I had the temerity to question his assertion that the Society would profit from its service to the refugees. He delighted in reassuring me that he did not mean we should serve the refugees for selfish reasons in order to gain from doing so. He simply wanted to insist that to work with them would be good for us too. During 25 years of watching Fr Arrupe's vision being implemented around the world, I have come to appreciate the wisdom of his prediction. I give thanks, on my own behalf and that of many companions who have enjoyed the privilege of becoming companions of the refugees. What a gift the Lord has given us!

Coming to appreciate refugees as a gift may surprise some, since the stories concerning refugees are often overwhelming and depressing. The Tsunami in 2004, East Timor and Kosovo in 1999, Rwanda in 1994, Somalia in 1992... Every few years a new calamity occurs, with compelling images surfacing that dramatise the stories of anguished people driven from their homes by violence or disaster, and congregated by the tens of thousands in makeshift settlements. To the distant observer, the history of refugees is a succession of desperately similar crises likely to inspire compassion but often defying understanding. New crises may seem beyond our reach or leave us feeling there is little we can do.

In actual fact each new crisis provokes new initiatives. New organisations are born out of concern and devise practical ways to offer assistance. JRS was created in precisely this fashion. Fr Pedro Arrupe, who had himself lived in Asia, was deeply moved by the image of Vietnamese people seeking to escape their homeland by boat. When he voiced his concern to others, he discovered that they were similarly moved by these dramatic scenes. And when concerned individuals responded with diverse, creative and substantial offers of help, he realised that the Society of Jesus was well placed to coordinate coherent international action. Arrupe saw congruence between the Vietnamese refugees' plight and specific characteristics of the community he headed. Moreover, he quickly perceived that the Society could help not only the Vietnamese, but also the refugees then in flight from Somalia and Ethiopia, and also those escaping Cambodia and Laos.

Fr Arrupe established JRS as a unit within the Society designed to communicate the plight of refugees and to act as a 'switchboard' connecting identified needs with offers of assistance. He was sure that the Society could rely not only on the cooperation of its own members and communities, and not only on the parishes, schools and other institutions under its care, but also on the generosity of our many friends, especially religious congregations and lay movements. Arrupe has been proved right. Many JRS projects involve only a tiny contribution by Jesuits but make possible the collaborative efforts of hundreds of volunteers, lay and religious.

At the same time, other less publicised but equally dramatic humanitarian crises were occurring, notably in the disaster-ridden Horn of Africa. In the early 1980s, JRS launched a project to help Tigrayan and Eritrean people displaced by war and famine in north-eastern Ethiopia. A coordinating centre for African initiatives was started in Nairobi, and soon afterwards another in Bangkok for the Asian region.

Although the threefold mission of JRS, namely 'to serve, accompany and defend the rights of forcibly displaced people', acquired this succinct formulation only in the late 1990s, the JRS vision was clear from Arrupe's 1980 letter and in the earliest initiatives of JRS. In the otherwise quite diverse early projects one sees the term 'refugee' interpreted broadly, to mean people forcibly uprooted from their homes and families and livelihoods. Later, more precise terminology would be developed in international law to distinguish internally displaced persons, stateless persons, urban refugees and asylum seekers. This legal terminology remains important in assigning responsibilities among governments and international organisations. For JRS, however, the human experience of forcibly displaced persons of any category is a summons, and Catholic social teaching has always endorsed this broad understanding of 'refugee'.

The service offered by JRS is always pastoral, but the meaning and manner of our pastoral presence changes depending on the beliefs of the refugees themselves. Pastoral care offered to Muslim, Buddhist or Christian people is distinctly different in each case. JRS' 25 years span the pontificate of John Paul II, who consistently spoke of the Church's obligation to offer a pastoral welcome to all who enter our countries, even when the host government brands them 'illegal'. From the beginning, JRS offered support to local Churches, in most cases ill-equipped at first to respond pastorally to the needs of the newcomers. And from the beginning many Church agencies, especially the Caritas federation, became firm and mutually supportive allies of JRS.

JRS teams generally include a significant number of local workers as well as international personnel. They arrive into emergency situations, with fewer resources than most, and they stay longer. JRS personnel have credibility to speak with authority about the world-wide problem of refugees because its field teams are so authentically engaged in listening to refugees in so many places. Communication is at the heart of JRS' success. Its elements include hearing the refugees out, reflecting on experience, and developing effective communication within the organisation and a credible voice beyond it.

Many initiatives by JRS are inspired by what is learnt from refugees themselves. For instance, JRS was an early entrant in the world-wide campaign against the production and use of landmines, strongly supports the education of girl children in Africa, and after assisting victims in so many conflicts, helped start a campaign against the recruitment of children into both rebel and official armies. JRS constantly decries long-term and mandatory detention of asylum seekers, and while campaigning for these policies to be dismantled, works for the release — painstakingly and one by one — of individual detainees.

Now, 25 years later, the face of forced migration has changed and JRS faces new challenges. In 2005 there are 6.4 billion people in the world, compared with 4.4 billion in 1980. More people than ever are on the move today, yet fewer places exist in which a forced migrant can find safety. While the modern society is distinguished by high numbers of migrants, many societies are nonetheless hostile to new arrivals. Harsh border restrictions confront asylum seekers, rational political debate is deliberately undermined, and difficulties are placed in the way of expanding immigration even in countries that have traditionally opened their doors to newcomers. Meanwhile, tens of millions of people displaced by conflicts are unable to cross a frontier and so are left uprooted within their own countries. These are now described as 'internally displaced persons'. Victims of natural disasters are also numerous, though often human action, or inaction, must take some of the responsibility for their plight. In Africa, for example, wars invariably increase the risk of famine. As populations increase, poorer people are pushed into unsafe areas such as denuded hillsides on the edge of cities, or overcrowded valleys in earthquake-prone regions, or to coastal shores of cyclone-vulnerable islands. Thus they are made more vulnerable to natural disaster.

The history of JRS is about the lives and hopes of people we know personally. This personal knowledge constantly transforms our understanding.

12

JRS opens a door — beyond transitory and shocking images — into the inspiring lives of people struggling to defend their rights, protect their families and give their children a future. This book invites you to witness the JRS way of walking with refugees, offering fresh perspectives on world events, while highlighting compassion, understanding and helpful paths to action.

Mark Raper SJ
June 2005

Mark Raper with survivors of the genocide in Rwanda, 1995

Indochinese refugees

Chapter One

ASIA and the PACIFIC

The activities of JRS in the Asia region were dominated at first by the sequelae of the Indochina wars[1]. Most initiatives were set against the background of Cold War ideology and rhetoric. JRS quickly established programs in every camp that housed Lao, Cambodian and Vietnamese refugees throughout the Southeast Asian region. In South Asia around this time large numbers of Afghan refugees had settled inside the borders of Pakistan and Iran. In the late 1980s and early '90s, a small JRS program was started to assist the Afghans in Pakistan. In Sri Lanka, many people were forced from their homes in 1983, when the ethnic Singalese reacted violently to armed campaigns by the 'Jaffna' Tamils. The conflict continued until the cease fire agreements of recent years, displacing many in the process. But through the 1980s JRS mainly worked with the 'Tamil repatriates' who came to India under an agreement between the two governments.

Although Western nations initiated a great deal of propaganda and provided funds in support of those escaping from Communism, JRS gained permission to work in the Southeast Asian countries only through delicate negotiations with governments, and usually with their security agencies. In places where world politics was less dominant, local frontier politics loomed large, as with programs to assist the Burmese refugees in Thailand and in Bangladesh. India's desire to maintain strong influence in Nepal and Bhutan, which are buffer states with China, continues to dominate outcomes for Bhutanese refugees in Nepal.

Although JRS directors were given authority to open programs wherever they identified a need and could find a way to begin, the best initiatives

---

[1] Indochina is a large peninsula in Southeast Asia. It lies roughly east of India, south of China, culturally influenced by both. It comprises the territory of the former (colonial) French Indochina: Cambodia, Vietnam and Laos, and in the wider sense it includes Myanmar, Peninsular Malaysia and Thailand. (The Columbia Encyclopedia, 6th Edition, 2005)

resulted from partnerships with local bodies, such as the local Jesuit Province. An invitation of this kind could open the possibility of matching outside expertise and resources with local knowledge, leading to more effective projects. Without a local community base, or without knowledge of local customs, people and languages, or without an invitation from a Jesuit Province ready to make a commitment, it was often difficult to form an effective team. For such reasons JRS never managed to engage fruitfully with West Papuans who crossed into Papua New Guinea, or with Filipinos displaced by the civil conflicts in the Philippines.

The focus of JRS work in Asia has shifted to respond to the changing circumstances of forced displacement throughout the region. This chapter offers a glimpse of the long history of JRS in that region as seen through the eyes of those who have accompanied the refugees.

THE WOUND OF THE BORDER
Pierre Ceyrac SJ

Fr Ceyrac worked between 1980 and 1993 in the Thai-Cambodia border camps. He has devoted all his life to the service of the poor. For this reason he received the "Legion d'Honneur" from the French Government.[2]

I spent 13 years in the Thai-Cambodia border camps, from 1980 to 1993. Throughout these years I lived one of the deepest and breathtaking experiences of my existence.

The story started with a call from the Thai Church at the end of the 70s. Caritas Thailand had asked Caritas India to send a team of volunteers when in 1979 the Khmer Rouge camps were discovered. India had the reputation of having experienced teams. The Thai Church was very young, without humanitarian experience and teams of volunteers. I had quit my work as national treasurer and I was available to my provincial. One day he phoned me: 'Pierre, are you ready to leave to Cambodia with a team of doctors and nurses?' I answered: 'Of course!'

In July 1980, Fr Arrupe came to Loyola College in Madras. I turned to him to get confirmation of my next destination. He just told me these words: 'Of course, go!' It is good, in our lives as men, to change the gear from time to time... We are attached to so many things (even in India!) and we manage to build our little hole, very comfortable, protected from the strong winds that blow over all the corners of the world. It is good to retake the sail, and have the courage of leaving again.

Two months later, I was leading a group of twelve volunteers: eight doctors and nurses, four Jesuits – Paul Macwan, Noel Oliver, John Bingham and myself. We left towards a mission of six months to Phanat Nikhom, in a camp near Bangkok. After these six months, John and I decided to stay. We went to Rome to meet the Curia and Fr Arrupe together with all his assistants, and during two hours we spoke about the situation. In 1982 Fr Arrupe

---

[2] Reflections are taken from the books *Pélerin des frontieres and Une vie pour les autres, l'aventure du Père Ceyrac,* by Jérome Cordelier.

17

gave us the authorisation to go to the Cambodian border. So we finally went to Cambodia. We fell in love with the Cambodian and Vietnamese people who at times shared the same camps. First we stayed in a camp inside Cambodia, called Anpil. After four years, we were chased out by the bombings which put us at great risk, so we went back to Thailand. It was like a film scene, under the bombs, in the middle of great chaos and in a state of emergency. But it was not cinema. People died. For me it was a deep experience: we touched what is deepest in human distress.

I had met distress is the slums of Calcutta and Bombay. But I think there is nothing comparable to the distress of a refugee. They are uprooted people, cut off and thrown out like the trees that we transplant and uproot. Refugees think that they finally left behind hell but distress continues in the camps and sometimes it follows them in the western asylum countries where some of them arrive, which they call 'third countries.' I recall a Cambodian girl saying to me: 'Father, you are my father, my mother, my brothers and sisters, because I lost my father, my mother, my brothers and sisters.'

I met amazing people. I remember this engineer who had two children and had to flee with them, escaping the Khmer Rouge. He succeeded in crossing the border and staying in Kao I Dang where he was forbidden, so they hid in the tombs and used bamboo sticks to breeth! He told me: 'I cannot live in my country, neither in the border, nor here in Kao I Dang. I have to hide since I am illegal and I am refused by all the "third countries". I visited all the western embassies – France, the US... – and I am rejected all the time. Are we evil people, we Cambodians?'

Rejected: This was the response to all the requests of this sort. Some of the refugees could not stand their exile. I remember the tragic end of a man who hung himself; he left a paper beside the tree where these words were written: 'I am rejected by all the third countries so there is only the fourth country left'.

From time to time I happened to visit a 'third country'. I went to France, the US, Canada to raise awareness about the situation we were living and to ask them to open their borders to refugees. I remember on one occasion a beautiful sentence of the archpriest of Montreal who was responsible for the services to refugees in French Canada: 'For us it is not an obligation to receive refugees but a privilege!'

There is a formidable lesson of courage and dignity to learn from refugees. I remember all the people who had stepped on landmines and had lost an arm or a leg. I went to visit them and many said: 'Father, there is no problem.'

John Bingham and I were the only authorised to stay in the camp, as priests. What a crazy show to take the road towards the place where everything was going to be bombed, and watch the civilian and military cars driving fast the other way.

The refugee population was 225.000 people, 200.000 of them were Buddhists, 20.000 Muslims and 5.000 Christians, Catholics or Protestant. I was very linked to the Buddhist monks. One of their abbots was called Monichenda. He quickly became an extraordinary friend with whom I worked a lot. Under his inspiration, the community of monks developed several humanitarian works. This is not frequent, since it is not in the tradition of Buddhist monks to be present in the world. We made big marches together. Monichenda became a brother and I was always welcomed in his place, in his little house or in the pagoda, with great sense of fraternity. Relationships among communities and between the different NGOs were generally excellent as well as our relationships with bigger organisations such as the International Committee of the Red Cross and UNBRO, which represented the High Commissioner for Refugees. Working together for one cause helps developing deep friendship.

With the mandate of the United Nations, we were responsible for the education of 110.000 children. I led a team of 40 people coming from 16 different countries, most of them young people with a humanitarian feeling. They spent between four and five years in the camp. Together we were able to establish an education system: schools, vocational training, and universities for engineers and lawyers. With little means but great effort we fought for human dignity.

This experience was very strong for all these young people. All of them keep this 'wound of the border', which is a very deep expression we use among us. Three of us were the last ones to leave the bigger camp, Site Two, when it was closed. It was an endless cascade of ambulances driving handicapped people back to Battambang, in Cambodia.

Meeting in Paris some years ago with some 20 young people who had worked with us in the border camps of Thailand, we were evoking some of the great

19

figures we had met there and the joys and sorrows we had shared with them. And we realised, as we were talking, how these joys and sorrows were still deeply alive in us, as a sort of nostalgia in our subconscious, as a wound in our flesh – the wound of the border. I hope and pray that this wound will never close up fully, never completely heal, as long as there still remain refugees somewhere in the world – men, women or children without home and without country.

Every morning Fr Ceyrac takes his crumbling Toyota and drives 60 kms from Aranyaprathet to the refugee camp where he works. The road goes through the rice fields where peasants work with their water buffalos. Before leaving, Fr Ceyrac takes with him food, sweets, cigarettes and magazines. He drives and then stops. He hides the letters in his car, on himself or on the passengers, in their pockets or under their clothes. Further along, three or four soldiers of the Thai army, Task Force 80, stop him at a check point. Fr Ceyrac gives them some cigarettes and magazines.

– 'Thank you, Father!' say the soldiers.

Fr Ceyrac repeats the operation at each check-point along the road.

Fr Ceyrac is a 'postman'. He brings news and money to the families in the camp, and this is known among the refugees. He gets letters from Europe and the United States, changes the money in Thailand and brings it directly to their beneficiaries in the camps. He brings with him thousands of dollars. One day, the chief of a check-point asked him to get out of the car. When they checked the car they could not believe their eyes. The driver was carrying an immense quantity of letters and some twenty thousand dollars. The soldiers confiscated the money and opened all the letters. Fr Ceyrac has to explain his behavior before two generals and a colonel. He was then prevented from entering the camp for one month.

Une vie pour les autres, l'aventure du Père Ceyrac,
Jérome Cordelier, Perrin, p. 191-193

Mark Raper SJ/JRS

Pierre Ceyrac SJ with Cambodian refugees in Site Two camp, Thai Cambodian border, 1986

FIRST REFUGEES IN CAMBODIA
Kike Figaredo SJ

Kike Figaredo worked from the eighties until the early nineties in the Thai-Cambodia border camps and later in Cambodia, when the refugees returned home in 1993. Programmes there were built on many years of experience gained in the camps, particularly with the landmine survivors. As the JRS work in Cambodia was clearly a work of development, JRS became the Jesuit Service Cambodia in 1995. JS Cambodia was, and still is, actively involved in the International Campaign to Ban Landmines, while faithful to its commitment to serve refugees who arrive in Cambodia.

Jesuits first arrived in Cambodia in the seventeenth century, due to persecutions in Japan. So these Jesuits were refugees in Cambodia. The first presence of the Society of Jesus in this little South East Asian country lasted until the suppression. During those years, the Jesuits developed all kinds of mission apostolates.

It was in the late eighties that the Jesuits finally returned to Cambodia, thanks to Fr Arrupe's call, to serve the Khmer refugees who were fleeing from the Vietnamese invasion and from a violent civil war. Our presence and work in the Thai-Cambodia border refugee camps consolidated our knowledge of the Khmer culture and strengthened our friendship with the Khmer people. So, in the early nineties, when the security situation improved in Cambodia, we decided, as JRS, to accompany the refugees back home. The country and its people were broken by war and violence. Once in Cambodia, and after some assessment, we started our work there, hand-in-hand with the Khmer people, the handicapped, the orphans, the widows. This closeness to the people has given light and creativity to the apostolic services provided by the Society of Jesus, the style of life and even the type of communities. This, in many ways, is subtlely different to the presence of the Society in other places where Jesuits have been present for decades.

Together with the refugees we have learnt to understand the lives of those who lack everything. We have learnt to accompany them, listen to them and structure services so that hope comes to their lives, their dignity is built and their voices are heard.

Michael Coyne/JRS

Tun Channareth and Kike Figaredo SJ, Cambodia, 1993

In Battambang, northern Cambodia, we have now a small center to welcome people with disabilities. These people have suffered years of war. Many of them are landmine survivors. This place is called the Arrupe Center. It reminds us of the person who has inspired us to open our institutions to the little ones and those in need. Srey Mau and Tang are two little girls who had a landmine accident in March 2005. Thanks to the inspiration of Fr Arrupe, who made our presence possible in Cambodia through the creation of JRS, these two girls have a place where they restructure their lives and look ahead with joy and hope. We are very grateful to JRS in this corner of Cambodia.

JRS IS A JESUIT MINISTRY
Edward Brady SJ

After refugees began to arrive in greater numbers in the countries neighbouring Vietnam, Laos and Cambodia, some Jesuits offered themselves for pastoral work among them. Ed Brady started to work with JRS in Thailand in 1981. He then moved to Sudan, where he worked among the internally displaced people in Khartoum and other parts of the country (see chapter on Africa).

My direct involvement with refugees first in Thailand and then later in Sudan spans the years 1981 through 1999. For myself it has been a privileged form of Jesuit ministry.

In late 1980, a priest friend who was a senior administrator in the Catholic Relief Service informed me of the CRS initiative to recruit priests to work in refugee camps in Thailand. Given my previous years of ministry in Sri Lanka I found the initiative very attractive. Thanks to Fr General's appeal to provincials for volunteers for the refugee ministry (unknown to me at the time), I had no difficulty in obtaining my provincial's permission to apply for such a ministry, and was happy to be quickly accepted with travel arrangements made to leave for Bangkok early in the new year. On arrival in Thailand, I was posted to be part of the CRS team serving in the Ban Vinai Camp situated near the Mekong River which serves as the border with Laos in the northeast of the country. The camp had been for a number of years hosting the hill tribe Hmong people who had opposed the communist regime in Laos and had at the end of the war been forced to flee across the Mekong into Thailand.

I soon found that I was one of a number of Jesuits recruited from various provinces to serve in the Thai refugee camps as part of the Society's response to minister to refugees. In Thailand it meant not only ministering to the Vietnamese boat people but also to those fleeing Cambodia and Laos as well. We were sponsored by CRS which in turn was serving as part of COERR, the Thai Catholic Relief and Refugee Agency's response to the refugee crisis. In the following months I was happy to get to know fellow Jesuits from the various camps with whom we had periodic meetings to share experiences, etc. Later I was also joined in Ban Vinai by several Jesuit companions.

The experience I want to share regarding the refugee ministry being a ministry very much in keeping with our Jesuit charism was triggered when two of our most experienced men with years of missionary ministry in India had, along with a number of others, not received a renewal of their contracts by the Thai Catholic Agency. These men were working on the Cambodian border and had been requested by the exiled Bishop of Phnom Penh to remain on the border by any possible means, since he and some of his priests, all French missionaries, not only were expelled from Cambodia by the Khmer Rouge, but also were not allowed by the Thai authorities, apparently for political reasons, to reside nearby and minister to their people in the border camps. The Bishop was particularly concerned that the Blessed Sacrament be available to some heroic Cambodian Catholics who would cross over into the camps in order to carry the Eucharist back to distribute to fellow Catholics in Cambodia at the risk of being identified as Catholic and being subjected to imprisonment or worse.

Our two brother Jesuits had several options before them. They could join other NGOs working on the Cambodian border; they could be the catalyst for us Jesuits to form our own NGO and continue our refugee ministry independently of the Thai Catholic Relief and Refugee agency; they could fold their tents on the border and seek to assist refugees in nearby countries. At this point in JRS, we were still working under Fr Arrupe's initial vision that we would not form ourselves into a separate organisation, but be members of an international Catholic NGO ministering to refugees. The matter was referred to Fr Arrupe who in turn said he would stop off in Bangkok himself on his return from a visit to the Philippines in order to sort the matter out.

So it was that all of us Jesuits in the refugee ministry were called to Bangkok to meet with Fr Arrupe. On arrival, he announced he wanted to meet not only with those of us serving the refugees but with all the Jesuits available in Bangkok who, though not many in number, had for a number of years been carrying on mainly an educational ministry to university students, lecturing at various universities and administering a students' hostel, etc.

Fr Arrupe opened the meeting by saying that he wanted to meet with all of us before he met with the Archbishop of Bangkok, who had taken an active interest in the refugee ministry and headed the Catholic Refugee and Relief agency. Father Arrupe wanted to learn if the Archbishop sought the continued services of the Jesuits in the camps and, if so, whether there were any

25

conditions attached. During the course of the discussion, one of the senior Jesuits of the Bangkok community asked: 'What if these people make a mistake?' This was a question which reflected his apprehension regarding Jesuit involvement in the refugee ministry and the possible negative consequences for the Jesuit educational apostolate which had already attracted the criticism of local authorities worried about communist inspired 'student movements'. Fr Arrupe's response was clear. He said he called the meeting of us all precisely to avoid having, as he put it, 'two Societies of Jesus' in Thailand – one serving the refuges and one serving our more 'traditional' apostolates. He went on to say that he had called us together so that we could consider the options before the Society and prayerfully discern what seemed to be the best course of action. He went on to point out that, in discerning together, we were not assured to make a decision that was 'infallibly correct'. In fact the decision may later on prove to be, at least in the eyes of some, a 'mistake'. He said that such a decision should rather be regarded as something that God's providence allowed and one that we should use as a means of improving our service for the future. He pointedly remarked, 'if we make a mistake, we make a mistake together' – and then go on from there.

After Fr Arrupe met with the Archbishop, we again convened to concelebrate the Eucharist during which Fr Arrupe shared that the Archbishop had asked that we continue in the refugee ministry. He and Fr Arrupe also had agreed on some guidelines for our relations with local Church personnel. In his remarks Fr Arrupe expressed his great hope for the Society's ministry among refugees and drew upon his former medical training in his remarks that the initiative in the Thai camps was, in his eyes, the 'birthing' process of a new form of ministry in the Society. It was only after that Eucharist that I realised Fr Arrupe's great hope that the refugee ministry would be of benefit not only to the refugees but also would become an effective means of putting us Jesuits more in touch with the experiences of Ignatius and his early companions in caring for the needy and destitute.

A memorable supper together followed and, hours later, Fr Arrupe took the flight for Rome. Whilst in the air he suffered the stroke that incapacitated him for the rest of his life.

It was Fr Arrupe's firm conviction that the refugee ministry is truly in keeping with the Jesuit charism, an insight I found quite helpful in the early days of JRS when I came upon fellow Jesuits and others who were not as enthused as Fr Arrupe about its true value to either refugee or to we Jesuits.

AT THE THAI-CAMBODIA BORDER, 1984
Virginia Hasson RSM

Virginia Hasson has been working with JRS since the early eighties, both in Asia and Africa (see chapter on Africa), and as a resource person on education issues.

One March day in 1984, I was sitting in my office at Gwynedd Mercy College (GMC) in Pennsylvania when I received a phone call that would greatly broaden and challenge me for years to come. Isabelle Keiss RSM, the President of the college, was asking me to come to her office to meet with Ed Brady SJ. It seemed that Ed, who was working with JRS on the Thai-Laotian Border, had an idea that he thought might interest the faculty of GMC, and also possibly the Sisters of Mercy.

During this meeting I was introduced to two of the hallmarks of JRS that I would see in action many times over the succeeding years. The first of these qualities was: *Listen to the refugees themselves to learn what they want and need.* The Hmong refugees in the Ban Vinai Camp wanted very much to continue their education beyond the six years of primary school permitted by the Thai authorities. Since those working in the camps could not provide post-primary schooling, Ed thought a solution might be to have the teaching done through the mail. Thus was born the Overseas Tutorial Programme. This programme lasted for a number of years and a few students even completed up to beginning tertiary level mathematics. This illustrates a second quality of JRS in its work with the refugees: *Seek a creative solution to what may seem to be an impossible problem.*

In the late 1980's I had the privilege of working with JRS on the Thai-Cambodian Border. Here I learned more about the developing modus operandi of JRS. I say "developing" because JRS was just a fledgling organisation and those working in it were striving to be true to the vision of Father Pedro Arrupe and struggling to apply that vision in volatile and unpredictable circumstances.

Here I saw put into action the principle: *Do your best to understand the political situation while endeavoring to serve all the refugees.* Site Two was the barbed wire enclosed home of more than 140,000 men, women, and children asso-

27

ciated with the Khmer People's Liberation Front (KPNLF). The KPNLF were one of the three factions resisting the Vietnamese occupation of Cambodia. However, the KPNLF were themselves divided. In order to continue to work with the teachers as a whole, JRS arranged for a "neutral" piece of land where the Teacher Improvement Classes could meet. One incident demonstrated how much the teachers themselves wanted to overcome differences. A group of the teachers decided to apply a lesson they had learned in their Community Building Classes. So they came early to class one day to rearrange the seating in the way that they had learned gives participants the sense of being equally involved.

The Cambodia situation provides an instance of another operating principle: *Refugees are vulnerable until they are safely home.* As the Peace Accord was being shaped, JRS became involved in cross-border activity. In Cambodia a team was put in place to advocate for and to assist the returnees once repatriation began.

In the case of Cambodia, another principle was evidenced: *Structure is the means not the end for service.* Those working in Cambodia realized that the Jesuit presence would be needed long after resettlement had taken place. So Jesuit Service Cambodia was initiated and is thriving there even today.

Before leaving my reminiscences of Asia, let me reflect on a learning from Pilau Bidong Camp in Malaysia. Pilau Bidong was an island on which many Vietnamese Boat People were held. Among other services, JRS provided for the pastoral needs of the Catholic people there. Each Saturday evening, hundreds of refugees would gather in the bamboo chapel on the highest part of the island, wholeheartedly participating in the Eucharistic Liturgy. At the conclusion of the Liturgy, the congregation en masse moved outdoors to a shrine built from bits of the many ships scuttled by the guards as the refugees reached the island. With great emotion, the Vietnamese leaders led the people in prayers of thanksgiving for their own deliverance and in supplication for the souls of those who had lost their lives to the sea or at the hands of pirates. The JRS personnel demonstrated that they understood: Giving the refugees the lead often brings us all to the heart of the matter.

This essay is a reflection on a very small portion of my experience since the beginning of my association with JRS. The fledgling organisation that I first met over twenty years ago has grown in complexity, breadth, and scope. However, JRS still struggles to know how to best to accompany, serve, and

Kike Figaredo SJ/JRS

Cambodian boy, 1993

advocate. It is in this struggle and lack of certainty that JRS truly shares in the life of refugees and displaced persons. I thank God that even in a small way I have had the privilege of participating in this struggle.

29

MEMORIES OF BAN VINAI CAMP
Marie Julianne Farrington SSMN

*Sr Marie Julianne worked with JRS during the early eighties in the
Ban Vinai camp in North Central Thailand, with the Laotians and
other refugees from Indochina.*

In 1982, after long service in my Province's administration and some months
of solitary prayer, I began seeking the possibility of service in a more international context. Janet Carroll MM, then working at the Vatican Mission to
the UN, told me that the Jesuits were in the process of organizing a group to
work with refugees. I contacted Dieter Scholz SJ who was in the process of
creating the basic framework of this organisation.

After some correspondence and many conversations, it was determined
that I should be sent to Sudan to help in the situation there. At the time the
Sudanese Bishops were attempting to reach an agreement with the government to grant visas for those coming to work with JRS. It was a long and
frustrating process. I waited approximately six months and when a visa
was not forthcoming, Dieter suggested that I go to Thailand where visas
could be more easily obtained.

In Bangkok, I went to the Jesuit Provincial headquarters where Fr Edward
Brady warmly welcomed me. Ed was in charge of the JRS work in camp Ban
Vinai in North Central Thailand. Ban Vinai was a camp almost exclusively
for the Hmong people from Laos (though there were also some lowland
Laotians present). The Hmong had supported the US in the Vietnam War
and, after the defeat of the US, were now hunted in their country. JRS workers were welcomed in Thailand under the umbrella of COERR, the local
Caritas organisation. Hence we visited their office to get a card that indicated their responsibility for us and which could be presented to the local
civic authorities. Archbishop Renato Martino, then Nuncio in Thailand,
supported the JRS work.

Arriving by bus after a 10-hour ride from Bangkok, Ed and I were met by
Sisters Rosalie and Pierre Marie, French Sisters of Charity, both of whom
had worked long years in the missions of Laos. They had been expelled
when the Communists took control. They spoke Laotian and Thai and were

already at work in the camp. I lived with them during my time there and we communicated in French. Sister Rosalie was working in the beginnings of an education program, and Sr Pierre was especially concerned with a rather large group of lepers, whom she had known in Laos and who lived in a separated section of Ban Vinai. They suffered the discrimination of the other Hmong, who, in ignorance, feared the contagion of leprosy.

The camp, an hour's ride from Chiang Khan, partly along the Mekong River, had already been in existence for seven years in 1982. It accommodated 45,000 people in the most primitive of conditions. For the newcomer, it was like being dropped into an unknown world.

We all lived in Chiang Khan (Loei Province). Workers from many aid organisations, such as World Vision and Concern, also had their housing in this small city and there was a lively, cordial relation among us all. Also, living in a strong, active Buddhist culture was amazing and eye-opening.

The Hmong were an itinerant, mountain people. Even at home, in a more peaceful time, they had had little time for education, practicing a sort of slash-and-burn agriculture. They had been fierce warriors and because of the role they had played with the Americans were eligible to immigrate to the US. However, most wanted only to return to Laos under a non-Communist regime. It took a long time before some of the young men, finally accepting that this would not easily happen, decided to take the US offer. We saw some young families leave for the US. However, most remained and were eventually forced back into Laos.

The camp was a terrible place especially for the men. They had lost all authority and had little to do. The women cared for the children, of whom there were many, and also did their fine sewing craft.

There were up to 20,000 elementary school children in the camp. Fr Brady conceived the idea of identifying young male adults who had had at least a few years of formal education in order to give them some formation in English, math and the most basic science. This was done with the help of interpreters since none of us spoke Hmong. (Only in 1975 had Hmong been committed to a written alphabet.) JRS also gathered classes of elementary school children, which were then taught by the young adult male Hmong. These classes were often located under simple structures such as a roof held up by supports.

There were no books, except an occasional one used by the young teachers. We tried to equip each class with black, painted panels of wood that could be written on with chalk. We formulated, and later refined, the most basic kind of curricula which could be adapted to the needs of the students. The young people were very desirous of education and more sought to take advantage of the opportunity than could be accomodated. We tried to have some contact with the Thai education authorities and once a month I made the overnight bus journey to Bangkok for a meeting with the Education Department.

Most Hmong were animists, while there was also a small percentage of Catholics in the camp. Their religious needs were met by two French Oblates of Mary Immaculate, who were missionaries to Thailand. For the Catholic camp workers and JRS staff, we some days had Mass in the camp, or we would gather in the evening for Mass at the Sisters' house. These prayer times were an important source of strength and grace.

During the year and a half that I was there, we were twice visited by Mark Raper SJ, then the Regional Director. His visits were stimulating in every sense. He had already a wide experience of social ministry in Australia, and was possessed of a deep compassion, and remarkable creative and administrative skills. After a time, he established an Office in Bangkok where a wonderful spirit of community and hospitality was nourished and extended.

During this time there was one regional meeting of all JRS workers in Bangkok. The larger number working in Thailand were those in the camps along the Cambodian Border. There were also, as I recall, representatives from the Philippines, Burma, Indonesia and Hong Kong. I was the only woman present!

The meeting considered many pioneering efforts, all in their early stages. There was also consideration given to the needs of the JRS workers. JRS was gradually developing a philosophy and practice of 'accompaniment' of refugees. There was as yet, little organized attention to advocacy, though some were calling for it.

What I am describing, with the handicap of more than a 20 year lapse of time, were some of the beginnings of the effort by JRS to respond to the needs of refugees. The subsequent amazing spread and development of JRS, fulfilling the vision of Father Arrupe, has been one of the most clearly prophetic achievements of the Church of our time.

JRS ASIA BETWEEN 1983 AND 1989
Andrew Hamilton SJ

Andrew Hamilton SJ has been involved with JRS since its beginnings, working in the Thai-Cambodian border camps and in El Salvador. He has written a 'History of JRS Asia Pacific' among other refugee issues.

I first came to know JRS intimately at the end of 1983, three years after its establishment by Fr Pedro Arrupe. My association with it has always been marginal – originally in the interstices of my teaching commitments: I worked for three summers in the Cambodian Camps on the Thai border, and later spent six months in El Salvador. I have also written on refugee issues, attended many JRS Asia/Pacific meetings, and have had small commitments to the Cambodian, Laotian and Latin American refugee communities in Melbourne.

In South East Asia refugees were created by the aftermath of the Indochinese war. Cambodians had fled hunger and brutality when the Vietnamese army overthrew the Pol Pot regime. Vietnamese had also left, most by boat, and a large number of Laotians had also fled to Thailand. For the most part they arrived in neighbouring countries that had not signed the United Nations Convention on the Status of Refugees. Their situation was therefore precarious. Initially, many refugees were accepted for resettlement by Western nations, but by 1983 most were held in camps where they waited for a long time for resettlement or, as for many of the Cambodians, the opportunity to return safely home. The camps were generally administered and overseen by authorities of the host nation, and funded by United Nations agencies. JRS members were some of only a few of the NGO's and volunteers working in these camps.

The early years of JRS had much in common with the beginnings of other refugee organisations I have been associated with in Australia. The first years were full of individual energy and struggle, as ideals and commitments were given concrete shape. Decisions had to be made quickly and simultaneously about how best to accompany refugees, about priorities in choosing works, about organisational shape and about how to conduct oneself in a variety of working relationships, all in a constantly demanding and complex environment.

In turning Fr Arrupe's commitment to refugees into a reality, JRS had first to recruit people to work with refugees and to place them in the field. Initially, the natural source of workers and local representatives for this new Jesuit commitment was the Society of Jesus itself. Jesuits were also found in many of the nations to which refugees first fled and in which they were later resettled. If these Jesuit resources could be coordinated, they would offer much to refugees.

If JRS was to place Jesuits with refugees it had to commend the commitment to refugees to Jesuits and their publics around the world. The most effective form of commendation is always to tell stories. Many Jesuits who spent short term placements in Asian refugee camps spoke widely about the life of refugees and their own experience when they returned. They created a keen interest in refugees, and often led others to consider working with refugees. Many of us, too, wrote for Jesuit and other Catholic magazines of the lives of refugees. By 1983, *Diakonia*, the newsletter of JRS Asia/Pacific, had begun to appear. It publicised refugee issues and the work of JRS with them for Jesuit publics. These different forms of publicity were very successful in making the service of refugees seem important and attractive to the Jesuit world.

JRS had also to place people in positions where they could serve refugees effectively. This was a complex process. It involved a network of relationships, all of which needed to be negotiated. The normal pattern of Jesuit government is through Provinces. JRS was unusual because it was an organisation that worked across Jesuit Provinces. Their Provincials could commend Jesuits to work with JRS, but their acceptance and placement had to be the responsibility of JRS. Both the local Province and JRS shared a role in their sustaining.

The relationship between JRS and the Province in whose territory Jesuits would work with refugees had also to be negotiated. Ideally, Jesuits in the area would care for refugees, as they would for other people in the country. But this was impossible in most countries to which refugees fled. The majority of Indochinese refugees had fled to Thailand, a country in which there were few Jesuits. To meet the needs of refugees effectively was impossible for the local Jesuit region, so that good working relationships had to be established between the local Jesuits and those working with JRS. The hospitality and support of the Jesuits of the Thai region to JRS were exquisite.

JRS had to build working relationships with Churches and their agencies, and with other non-government organisations. These relationships were crucial in winning acceptance by local Governments of the JRS presence. Governments were sensitive to the presence of refugees on their soil, and in the administration of their policies often failed to respect their dignity. In Asia JRS usually placed people through other organisations. In 1981, a crucial meeting between Fr Arrupe, and the Jesuits in Thailand, including those working with Refugees, decided that JRS workers would be placed with COERR, (Catholic Organisation for Emergency Relief and Refugees), as the Cardinal Archbishop of Bangkok had requested. In Malaysia, JRS workers were placed through Red Crescent, the local counterpart to the Red Cross.

Sometimes large ideas drew fire from a variety of sources. On one occasion, for example, the local JRS workers in the Cambodian camps dreamed of establishing a university of the Forest – a programme that would offer tertiary education accredited by Western universities. It was an imaginative idea with the capacity eventually to benefit Cambodia if and when the refugees returned there. Its originators were surprised to find that local Jesuits and Church representatives were cool towards the idea because such high profile programmes among refugees would alarm the national government. The United Nations representatives were also unsupportive, because they feared that highly developed educational programmes would draw increasing numbers of people to the Border, and create an imbalance between what was available to the refugees and to the local Thai population.

Perhaps the event with most significance for the JRS recruitment policy was the formation of the Mercy Refugee Service in 1985. From the beginning, a number of Mercy Sisters had worked in placements arranged by JRS. The Congregation was therefore encouraged to develop its own refugee service. This form of organisation allowed Religious Congregations to recruit and place their own sisters and volunteers with refugees, and where helpful to cooperate with JRS. It also allowed them to bring their own spiritual vision and the advantages of their local connections to the refugees, while being able to benefit from the organisation and resources of JRS.

Having placed workers, JRS was then challenged to develop a characteristic way of proceeding consistent with the Jesuit ethos. In the Asia/Pacific region, the annual JRS meetings were a particularly important tool. They allowed workers to meet one another, to develop a feel for characteristic JRS ways of working, and to explore connections between their work and the institutions in the developed world.

Refugees rewrite the history of the world, from the point of view of the dispossessed and powerless. They enable people, like myself, to begin to re-configure our own lives.

Refugees reveal the structural sin embedded in the world's contemporary systems. They reveal a task still to be accomplished.

So, my refugees friends, whom I deeply admire for your incredible courage, resilience, creativity and humanity, a huge 'Thank You'. Your retention of your own humanity despite your often appalling treatment and experiences, is, for me, a mystery of the power of God's tremendous loving compassion in your lives, and is a challenge to a world so clearly in need of loving compassion.

David Townsend SJ
September 2005

No boundaries
Herbert Liebl SJ

Herbert Liebl joined JRS in 1989. He worked in Malaysia with the boat people, and later in Zambia, Angola, East Timor and Indonesia. He now works in southern Sudan.

During my first assignment in Malaysia in 1989 I was introduced to the vision of Fr Pedro Arrupe. I saw with great joy that the first disciples in the refugee camps of South East Asia were marked with this great vision. They became for me teachers and examples.

Under the leadership of Frs Mark Raper, Tom Steinbugler, Peter Balleis, Frank Brennan and Dieter Scholtz great strength was passed on to people working in the various camps. I felt this even when I was alone on the island of Palau Bidong in the east cost of Malaysia. I was never left alone or put down.

Fr Arrupe eliminated all boundaries and offered us a very powerful apostolate by connecting different kinds of people with one focus: To accompany, serve and plead the cause of refugees. I have learned so much from teams formed by male, female, religious and lay people, working together. It was for me a tremendous experience and I still draw strength from this vision.

The presence of women in JRS has contributed significantly to the vision of Fr Pedro Arrupe. When I reflect on the dynamics of JRS, it strikes me the way women in the teams make things alive. Their presence and committed work gives depth and direction to the apostolate in a very direct way. Jesus seemed to have no difficulties with women, intentionally women felt his tremendous love.

My first assignment with JRS brought me to Palau Bidong island. With Sr Nancy we were in charge of 1,500 unaccompanied minors, so called "boat people" from Indochina. This tiny island of a span of two football fields gave shelter for up to 20,000 refugees. An estimated 30 per cent of the people had lost their lives while crossing the sea in search for asylum. This experience, together with a lack of food and security, gave the ground for tremendous suffering. This experience was essential for my whole journey with JRS.

My second assignment with JRS was in Meheba refugee camp, in North East Zambia. After the signing of the Peace Accord between Savimbi and Dos Santos, JRS decided to accompany the Angolan refugees back to Angola. In Cazombo, Angola, we were a very strong team of four Jesuits from Venezuela, Belgium, Austria, India; sisters from USA, Ireland and Australia; and lay people from Ireland, Scotland and Japan. In this team I felt a very powerful dynamic which was rooted in helping the refugees to go back and rebuild their homeland.

In 2000 I went to work in East Timor, initially as an administrator for JRS in the country office. Frank Brennan SJ was our Country Director. I later went to work to West Timor and this was a real turning point for me. What I encountered there was a shock and I felt JRS was not ready for this tremendous difficult task. The militias linked to the military of Indonesia were life threatening to the refugees who were trapped in this situation.

In these circumstances, the implementation of Fr Arrupe's vision 'a call to all Jesuits regardless of nationality, province or countries to join the refugees' would have been of tremendous strength. What appears now is that there are fewer Jesuits in the field. We became actors from afar. Fr Arrupe wanted us Jesuits to get involved in the misery of people and get our minds and hearts renewed.

In my experience, every situation is unique and not comparable from place to place. We are called to be in constant reflection to match our service with the real needs of the refugees. It can either be material support – building houses, supplying food or learning tools for the children – or helping people to rebuild their inner trust, as in East and West Timor where our task was to build bridges between people in order to bring back confidence among them. This encouraged them to return back home. The church had in all these situations a tremendous role to play.

F. X. Sumaryono

Refugees from East Timor go back home from West Timor, 2000

ACTING TOGETHER: MERCY REFUGEE SERVICE AND JRS COLLABORATION IN ASIA

From the early 80's, a number of Mercy Sisters had worked in place-ments arranged by JRS. The Congregation was therefore encouraged to develop its own refugee service. An event of great significance for the JRS recruitment policy was the formation of the Mercy Refugee Service (MRS) in 1985, with Mary Densley as its first Coordinator. In dialogue with JRS, Mary put in place many procedures for recruit-ment, screening, and placement, for their support while in the field, and for their de-briefing on return. The rationale and procedures that JRS and MRS developed in those years became the model for JRS' partnerships with at least 50 other congregations around the world.[3]

Malaysia

The first fieldwork collaboration between these fledgling organisations be-gan in October 1983 in the refugee camp of Pulau Bidong in Malaysia, where the Mercy Sisters worked, teaching and caring for over six hundred Vietnamese primary school students.

Joan Campbell had first been sent to Malaysia by the Australian Red Cross, on a six month contract. Later in 1984 she switched to JRS and stayed on for 10 years. Carole McDonald joined her in Pulau Bidong in 1985. Both were assigned by Malaysian Red Crescent to teach English as a Second Lan-guage to adults, but when they saw the hundreds of children roaming wild, they persuaded the authorities to let them set up schools, Joan for primary and Carole for slightly older children. Classes ran throughout the day and at night they prepared the teachers, all recruited from the camp population. Basic literacy was useful for refugees' resettlement opportunities.

Joan and Carole instinctively identified greater needs in the camp, and call-ing on their years of experience and training as teachers and school admin-istrators they gave meaning to the lives of thousands of children, to their

---

[3] Taken from reports by Mercy Sisters and from Mark Raper SJ, *Mercy and the National Interest*, Keynote address for the National Conference of Mercy Refugee Service, 22nd November 2002. The Academy, Melbourne.

parents, and to the young people they recruited as teachers, all of whom would otherwise be sitting miserably in their shacks or running feral across the island. That method of work, teacher training, that was pioneered by Joan and Carole and then taken up by Maureen Loghrey, has been the classic JRS way of running education activities, at least in Asia and Africa.

> There is also a sense of quiet, almost lethargy, despite the activity of cooking and washing of clothes that takes place in the compound for all to see. This new feeling of hopelessness was borne out when I spoke with some of the adults in addition to the unaccompanied minors. The chief of Police said he felt that the spirit of the people had been broken and both of us felt that this was an extremely sad situation. Everyone was just waiting for their turn to be told they will be on an Orderly Repatriation List and then many of them would volunteer to return home rather than lose some of their assistance money. More than half of these people have had their names cleared by the Vietnamese Government for return.
>
> Carole McDonald RSM, *The Ending of a Long Story*, 1996

By 1988 two more Sisters of Mercy had begun work with JRS in Malaysia, in the Sungei Besi Transit Camp. By the end of 1988 another had arrived to continue the running of the Junior High School program in Pulau Bidong.

1989 was a watershed year in the handling of refugees in these Asia Pacific countries of first asylum: Hong Kong's government decided that, from June of 1988, it would no longer give future refugee arrivals automatic refugee status. The new policy was soon implemented by other ASEAN countries and applied to all refugees arriving after the 14th March 1989. Carole McDonald RSM recalls:

'When large numbers of refugees and in particular children were rejected for resettlement, we had to cope with groups of very severely depressed people who sometimes tried to harm themselves. It was difficult to rejoice with those who were successful, encouraging those still to go through the process or actually going through it and at the same time to be sympathetic and give hope to those who had failed in their application. Many saw the decision they received, rightly or wrongly, as a matter of life or death so the stakes were fairly high. For us it was very stressful personally, especially if you were present when individuals and groups received the news'.

After a few months Mercy Sisters became responsible for the supervision of unaccompanied minors and the social work in the camp. Others continued their educational work with JRS in Pulau Bidong until its closure in November of 1991; they were the last foreigners to leave. Work continued at the Sungei Besi Transit Centre. Still others left to begin work at Sikhui in Thailand in December.

Thailand

In the early 80's, popular sentiments provoked many initiatives of assistance, in particular for the Indochinese boat people. But by 1984 and 1985, when the first Australian Mercy Sisters went to the field, things were getting tougher.

Bernie Evens wrote[4] of her first impressions of Phanat Nikhom camp: "I remember how I hated the barbed wire fences and the guards. Not the individual guards, who often enough were pleasant young men, but the principle of having guards to keep innocent human beings behind barbed wire fences – guards, who, if they were unpleasant young men as they sometimes were, exercised such power over the defenceless people inside. I hated the indignities to which the stateless, dependent people were subjected."

In Phanat Nikhom and Sikhui, Mercy Sisters worked with Laotians, Hmong, Cambodians and Vietnamese refugees and began a program to train English teachers. Initially Fr Neil Callahan coordinated the school at Phanat Nikhom; he later left as a result of deteriorating health and was replaced by a Thai woman named Meo.

All JRS placements at this stage were coordinated through COERR (Catholic Offices for Emergency Relief and Refugees). It was not until 1985 that Mark Raper SJ established the JRS Asia Pacific Office in Bangkok. Over the years two Mercy Sisters worked in the JRS Asia Pacific office under Tom Steinbugler SJ and Quentin Dignam.

---

[4] Quotation is taken from *The Life We Share*, Reflections from the Mercy Refugee Service Australia, edited by Rosslyn von der Borch, Sydney, 1992. Rossi was herself a Mercy associate serving with JRS Asia Pacific in the Bangkok office.

Following the second annual meeting of JRS Asia Pacific at Xavier Hall, which was attended by Patricia Pak Poy RSM, the decision was reached at the ISMA (Institute of the Sisters of Mercy Australia) Plenary Council to establish the Mercy Refugee Service.

During this period JRS faced the challenges of working in Khoa I Dang camp near Arunayprahet on the Cambodian border. Here were three camps dedicated to civilians from three distinct political factions, the Khmer Rouge, KPLNF (with whom the Mercy Sisters worked) and the supporters of King Norodom Sihanouk. There were also camps at Ban Vinai in northern Thailand for the Hmong and other mountain peoples from Laos – one for lowland people at Nong Kai and one for Karenni people on the Burmese border. During a turbulent political situation JRS still managed to keep good relations with the various factions. Security was often tight around the camps, with even mail being forbidden to those within, leaving several MRS workers with the precarious task of smuggling mail into the camps past over-zealous guards.

JRS also had a small presence in the refugee camp of Sikhui from 1994 onwards, running education and social service programs. In particular they worked with unaccompanied minors within the camp and with *boat people* who had been the victims of violence and piracy during their journey from Vietnam.

Philippines and Hong Kong

Throughout the late 1980's JRS and MRS worked at detention centres in Hong Kong such as Chi Ma Wan, Whitehead and Tai A Chau (on a small island off the bustling city of Hong Kong). The slowing of resettlement by Western countries, and what became the new policy of repatriation as a direct result of the 'Comprehensive Plan of Action', made the situation in the late '80s in Hong Kong often seem hopeless. Compared with those of Thailand, the memories of Hong Kong are frightening, the camps there being much more prison-like than their Thai counterparts. Still the people were coming...

During 1989 Mercy Sisters worked in counselling situations at Whitehead detention centre. This experience brought to light the frustrating nature of immigration bureaucracy that was exceptionally bad in Hong Kong at the time. During this time there were riots and often brutal violence. The Sisters' office was looted. Mercy Sisters also worked collaboratively with JRS in education and the provision of care and social services for Unaccompanied Minors in the Chi Ma Wan and Tai A Chau Detention Centres.

In 1996 the situation at the Tai A Chau detention centre changed considerably. Six thousand refugees still lived in the camp within a fenced enclosure of three story tin huts. While some still clung to the hope of resettlement most were beginning to accept the grim reality of repatriation back in Vietnam.

In the Philippines, Palawan camp for Vietnamese boat people saw a succession of MRS mid-wives from September 1993, such as Lizzie Finnerty and Anne McDonnell, and then lay associates Ann Back and Meg Hicks. One mother simply refused to acknowledge her child. So Lizzie had no choice but to take this baby home, name him (she called him Minh Tri) and care for him for 3 or 4 months, until she could then deliver the baby for adoption in the US.

Thai-Burma border

Since 1997 MRS and JRS have been particularly active on the border of Burma and North Eastern Thailand near Mae Hong Son. Maureen Lohrey and Margaret Tallon worked with JRS in developing education programs with Karenni refugees who had fled Burma fearing the violent offensives of the SPDC (State Peace and Development Council, formerly the State Law and Order Restoration Council). Beginning as a small-scale education operation in 1997 the JRS project had tripled its capacity by 2000. In January 2002 Barbara Anderson replaced Sr Maureen as coordinator of this combined JRS/MRS program, with Sr Margaret also returning to Australian a few months later. In 2004 the position was once again handed over to another MRS volunteer, Gaye Lennon RSM, who continues to carry out MRS and JRS' long-term commitment to the Karenni people of Burma.

Nepal

MRS was involved in JRS' regional program in Nepal, assisting Caritas Nepal in its implementation of a secondary education program with Bhutanese refugees. This work was done in collaboration with PS Amalraj SJ and Tomy Joseph SJ, and music teacher Matthew Daz. The challenges faced in this task were massive, with a refugee population of over 95,000 stretched across seven separate camps, all between half an hour and an hour's journey from Caritas' field office in the village of Damak.

During October 1998 the director of the Bhutanese Refugee Education Program unilaterally decided that the program should become part of the wider Nepalese education system. It was feared by all that this would be of detri-

The situation for the refugees in the camp is protracted. Many have been living in this restricted environment for more than 15 years. They are endeavoring to build a strong democratic civil society in the hope of eventually returning to their home-land, where the infrastructure can be reassembled and thereby giving hope to ethnic people who have had no previous opportunities for socio-economic development inside Burma.

Gaye Lennon RSM,
Project Director in Mae Hong Son, Thai-Burma border

Maureen Lohrey RSM/JRS

UNHCR registration point at the Thai-Burma border

ment to the students as it meant a shift to the Nepalese curriculum which was of notably lesser quality than that which the Bhutanese formerly used. At the same time, plans to bring sisters from India who were fluent in Nepalese brought a glimmer of hope. They were to become a valuable aid for the counselling and social work services.

East Timor

From March of 1999, JRS assisted with providing immediate protection and relief for over 250,000 displaced people who fled the country following the violent reactions to the independence ballot of 30th of August. JRS' involvement was hampered by the violent death of JRS director Karl Albrecht (who was gunned down on 11th September 1999) and that of an Indonesian Jesuit assigned to East Timor, Tarcissius Dewanto SJ.

MRS joined the JRS team in Dili offering expertise in education and assistance with curriculum planning, teacher resources and training, all under the auspices of the local church. This collaboration also endeavoured to provide education and health care training in country areas including the districts of Maliana and Luro. MRS was also involved in health care, an integral part of JRS's operations in East Timor following the systematic destruction of health care facilities by Indonesian sponsored militia and departing troops after the independence ballot. JRS eventually withdrew from East Timor, with one MRS worker staying on to continue the education programs with the Marist Brothers.

Australia

Mary Densley, and her successors, Bernie Evens and Marg Moore, involved Mercy communities and congregations in Australia too, through twinning, partnerships and various educational activities. They are involved in local community resettlement activities, welcoming families to parishes and schools, teaching English to refugees or helping in whatever are their needs, and in programmes for training lay volunteers.

There is a risk in naming anyone, because that means we leave out the others: Marlene Flaherty, Mary Keely, Joan Kelleher, Sandra Smolenski, Loreto Conroy, Nicole Rotaru, and countless others have proven an immense capacity to identify the needy individuals and respond personally to them, and to set up practical programmes that encompassed the greatest possible number of people.

MEMORIES OF A BAN-LANDMINE CAMPAIGNER
Patricia Pak Poy RSM

Patricia Pak Poy has been a close friend and tireless worker of JRS since its foundation. She was involved in setting up the Mercy Refugee Service in 1985. She has a key role in the International Campaign to Ban Landmines, where she has been very active since JRS' official involvement in 1994.

Australia has been a country of indigenous people first then migrants, exiles, refugees and asylum seekers. In 1975 with the fall of Saigon thousand of refugees from Vietnam fled to camps and the issue had been taken up by the Asian Bureau Australia (ABA) founded by the Australian Jesuits – Peter Dwyer, Mark Raper, Michael Kelly and others – for the better understanding of Asian realities by the whole of the Australian church and society in 1972. My contact goes back to those days.

ABA was right there moving on the refugee concerns when Fr Arrupe called on the Society to put itself very deliberately at the service of refugees and displaced people. Some Sisters of Mercy helped provide the 'woman-power' for JRS in the camps.

In 1984 Mark Raper the then Director of JRS Asia Pacific invited me to help facilitate a regional meeting of JRS-Asia Pacific in Bangkok after its first five years. It was a group of highly talented, dedicated and, I may say, highly individual men and some women from France, Belgium, the US, Australia, Germany and elsewhere, who did not need 'facilitating', but whose life-experience in the field needed to be heard, shared and coordinated for action – a huge challenge.

I had watched the development of Fr Arrupe's vision as it was put into action, and was inspired at the clarity of the principles of love, service and accompaniment that were being lived out in the difficult, highly political and sometimes violent atmosphere of the camps. Always the people and their needs came first, and the people trusted the JRS constancy.

For me there was an even greater challenge. I had been able to visit some of the Vietnamese, Lao and Cambodian communities in border camps in Thailand, and had met refugees from Vietnam in Australia. I had worked with the

47

Australian Sisters of Mercy in forming the Australian Institute of Sisters of Mercy. Now was the time for us to consider the commitment to a Mercy Refugee Service. This proposal was discussed by the Plenary Council of the Sisters at the end of 1984 and enacted early in 1985.

I myself have not worked any length of time in the camps, but have kept a close contact with JRS Asia Pacific over the years when I was in the leadership team of my congregation in Australia. I was able to have a six month placement in the Asia Pacific office in Bangkok in 1990, working with Tom Steinbugler SJ, Kep, Ah, Took and the team at the office. Out of that experience came my impulsion into action for a total ban on antipersonnel landmines.

While I was in Bangkok one of Bob Maat's friends was injured by a landmine – a Thai farmer from near the border – not a soldier, not in a country at war. At the time Denise Coghlan RSM and Noel Oliver SJ were planning Banteay Prieb (House of the Dove), the rehabilitation centre in Phnom Penh. In 1993, JRS formally joined the International Campaign to Ban Landmines. Denise, together with JRS internationally, has made a critical and crucial contribution to the work and success of the campaign.

These 25 years with JRS have been for me rich and graced beyond words. The gift is in those fragile but courageous people forced to leave their home and country, and it is in knowing the love, service and accompaniment that are the work of JRS, with special thanks to Dieter, Mark and Lluis who have fostered it. I celebrate the 25 years with thanksgiving and rejoicing.

Sr Patricia Pak Poy on her way to a village in Cambodia, 1993

Don Doll SJ/JRS

Although I am the Youth Ambassador for the International Campaign to Ban Landmines, I am still in grade 11, because after the war it was difficult to go to school and many of us spent three years in the first class. I used to be shy and ashamed but now I want to do something to make the world a better place for people.

When I was 12, I went to the United Nations in Vienna and asked them to ban landmines. They did that in Ottawa in 1997 and I celebrated there, and also in Oslo when i saw Jody Williams and Tun Channareth receive the Nobel Peace Prize on behalf of the International Campaign to Ban Landmines.

There is still much to do to implement this Treaty, to clear the mines from countries like Bosnia, Cambodia, Angola, Afghanistan and Iraq. In Nairobi, Kenya, at the first Review Conference of the 1997 Mine Ban Treaty, in 3 December 2004, a new action plan for assistance to mine affected countries for five years was adopted.

Many people victimized by the mines have no house, no water close to their homes, no jobs, no opportunity for their children to go to school, no affordable health care. We need to campaign for their rights, especially the rights of the poorest ones.

Song Kosal, Youth Ambassador,
International Campaign to Ban Landmines

Taken from *Surviving Landmines.*
Personal accounts of child Bosnian
landmine survivors. JRS, 2004.

Kosal works very closely with Jesuit Service
Cambodia, defending the rights of landmines
survivors in Cambodia and all over the world.

LIFE IN PHANAT NIKHOM AND SITE TWO, THAILAND

Bernie Evens RSM

Sr Bernie worked between 1984 and 1987 in Site Two and Phanat Nikhom, two refugee camps in Thailand which sheltered refugees from various parts of Indochina. From 1987 she worked with resettled refugees in Australia and in 1992 she became the Coordinator of the Mercy Refugee Service.

I joined JRS in May 1984. Joan Campbell RSM from Melbourne was the first Australian Mercy Sister to join and she had been working in Malaysia at Palau Bidong for some months prior to my going to Thailand.

Fr Alfonso de Juan at Xavier Hall was the JRS Coordinator in Thailand. The Asia Pacific Regional Office had not yet been set up. In keeping with JRS policy I was employed by COERR, the Catholic Office for Emergency Relief and Refugees, which was set up and run by the Catholic Church in Thailand. Fr Bunlert was the Director.

My first appointment was to the English School at Phanat Nikhom camp, a camp where refugees, who had been identified for resettlement to a third country, were sent for orientation and language studies.

Coming from comfortable, clean, spacious Australia the crowded camp at Phanat Nikhom was quite a shock to me. The refugees were people from Vietnam, Laos and Cambodia. Though we grieved with the people the loss of their homeland, most of their possessions and often family members, we also had a lot of fun with the refugee teachers whom we trained to teach English to their own people. We became good friends with them.

There were other camps in Thailand at this time – the famous Khao I Dang Camp near Aranyaprathet for Cambodian and Vietnamese refugees who were to be resettled. On the Border with Cambodia, there was Site 8, a camp for Khmer Rouge 'civilians'; Site B, for followers of King Norodom Sianouk and Site 2 for followers of the KPLMF. The people in the last three were not technically refugees and were under the protection, not of UNHCR, but of

UNBRO – the United Nations Border Relief Operation. There was also a camp at Ban Vinai in the North for the Hmong and other Mountain people from Laos and one for Lowland Lao people at Nong Kai. Lastly there were also camps on the Burmese Border for the Karen people.

While I was at Phanat Nikkom I used to travel to Khao I Dang some weekends with a woman from the French School who used to work in Cambodia before the Khmer Rouge took over and who spoke Khmer fluently. We used to go the Cambodian Mass, which had a small Congregation as the vast majority of the people were Buddhist. After Mass people would come to meet us in the Church to collect letters that we had smuggled into the camp for them and to give us letters to take out for them. Fortunately we were never searched!

In November 1984 the second meeting of JRS workers in South East Asia was held at Xavier Hall. Patricia Pak Poy RSM was invited as a resource person. When she returned to Australia she attended the Plenary Council meeting of the Institute of Sisters of Mercy Australia and as a result the Mercy Refugee Service was formed to work in collaboration with JRS.

JRS held an annual meeting for all its workers in South East Asia and each year the numbers attending grew. They came from Hong Kong, the Philippines, Malaysia and Indonesia. In 1985 a Regional Office was set up in Bangkok with Mark Raper SJ as the Director. He was instrumental in much that happened in the region in those early years.

After a holiday in Australia at the end of 1985, I returned to Thailand to work at Site Two for the next two years. I could write a whole book on this experience! There I worked with Virginia Hasson RSM, training Primary School Teachers for the many thousands of Khmer children in the schools at Site Two. Phanat Nikkom had seemed sad and daunting but Site Two made it look like a picnic.

At the end of 1987 I returned to work with resettled refugees in Australia. In 1990 I was invited to work with the JRS Coordinator Australia, Peter Hosking SJ, and in 1992 I became the Coordinator of the Mercy Refugee Service. Also in 1992 I was invited by Sister Virginia Hasson, who was by now working with JRS in Africa, to go to Ethiopia and Uganda with her in July and August. So I thought that working with refugees in South East Asia was hard? I found most everything in Africa difficult – except the people! I visited East Africa twice during my time as MRS Coordinator.

Mark Raper SJ/JRS

Phanat Nikhom camp, in Thailand, hosted Laotian, Hmong, Cambodian and Vietnamese refugees. JRS set up education programs there throughout the 1980s.

The things that really impressed me about the way JRS worked in the years that I was associated were:
- the emphasis on our "walking" with the refugees, doing our best to find what they wanted from us and not imposing what we thought they needed;
- that there was time and personnel provided to enable the field workers to reflect theologically on their experiences; and
- that there were those who met with field workers and listened to their stories and who had the knowledge and expertise to then be placed in positions where they could affect policy making.

THE 1989 COMPREHENSIVE PLAN OF ACTION FOR VIETNAMESE ASYLUM SEEKERS

Paul White

In the late eighties the governments involved in giving shelter to Vietnamese refugees had decided to bring the crisis to an end by instituting a screening process, the Comprehensive Plan of Action (CPA). 'Screened-out' asylum seekers were to be repatriated. JRS established programmes of legal and social counselling. Many young lawyers volunteered their time and expertise to help refugees. Paul White, an Australian lawyer, worked with JRS in Hong Kong and the Philippines.

Throughout the eighties, JRS provided assistance and support in the camps that developed around Asia, building a solid reputation amongst asylum seekers. Teachers, nurses, pastors, social workers and others were with the Vietnamese while they waited in the camps for resettlement to a Western country. Lawyers are not the first to be called upon in a humanitarian emergency and this was no exception. The resettlement process was straightforward for many years so there was no need for lawyers.

In 1989 things changed. The Boat People were still coming but many Vietnamese were incarcerated in their places of asylum, primarily in Hong Kong, the Philippines, Thailand, Malaysia and Indonesia. The number of resettlement places began fall off. Resettlement countries insisted on a different approach for those who continued to depart from Vietnam. Many were considered not to be in need of international protection and were said to be taking advantage of a situation to seek better economic opportunities in the West.

The 1989 Comprehensive Plan of Action for Vietnamese Asylum Seekers (CPA) was signed by many Western and Asian countries who shared the responsibilities for its implementation with the United Nations High Commissioner for Refugees (UNHCR). The effect of the CPA for Vietnamese asylum seekers was that only those who were found to be refugees after going through a legal process in accordance with international law would be deemed eligible to be resettled; the others had to return to Vietnam.

The CPA was a new and innovative way for governments to deal with such a situation. However, to arrange a fair legal process for up to 100,000 people living in five countries when not one of the asylum states had signed the Refugee Convention or had significant experience in a legal process of this nature created enormous problems. UNHCR had a dual role of supervising the process and assisting with the voluntary repatriation. Some parties considered that this created a conflict of interest for UNHCR so independent lawyers were needed to assist.

JRS Asia-Pacific was quick to understand the implications of the change and to respond, albeit in a small way. The dynamics of the CPA were such that without their own lawyers the Boat People were at the mercy of officials, who had limited knowledge about refugee law yet were responsible for the decision about who was a refugee and who was not.

JRS was the first NGO to provide lawyers to assist asylum seekers and responded firstly in Hong Kong and later in the Philippines. An idea arising out of a report of the project officer led to a meeting that quickly turned into a project! Tom Steinbugler SJ (Director JRS AP) and Peter Hosking SJ (Director JRS Australia) and the five or so lawyers who met in Sydney one night to discuss an idea were all surprised that the short meeting continued throughout dinner and then well into the night. By midnight the weary but excited group was confident that a project would develop to provide at least some assistance to some of those in need of legal assistance in the camps in Hong Kong.

Generous lawyers and other donors were quickly found but it was not all smooth sailing. Supporters in Hong Kong included Louis Robert SJ. He wrote an airmail letter (letters were still handwritten in those days) detailing many potential difficulties, the first of which was gaining access to the people in detention. His lengthy experience in the Hong Kong camps and astute observations ensured that there was an opportunity to study any potential difficulties before speaking with officials. After much persistence and tactical advice from JRS workers in the Hong Kong camps, from JRS friends in UNHCR and from Hong Kong residents, a legal project with Australian lawyers and interpreters was born.

The project in Hong Kong provided primarily Australian lawyers and interpreters to assist Boat People to prepare their claims before they were interviewed by Hong Kong Immigration officials. A year later in the Philippines, with the help of the Jesuit-run Ateneo University Human Rights Centre and lawyers from many countries, including the Philippines and the USA, JRS assisted asylum seekers on Palawan appeal against the rejection of their claim by the government of the Philippines.

The legal projects operated for several years and assisted thousands of Boat People understand the process and prepare for interviews that would change the direction of their lives. JRS connections ensured that there was little difficulty finding lawyers, interpreters and administrators to volunteer their time for this valuable work.

Lawyers, interpreters and boat people in the camps often felt at one in their frustrations with the system. Some relationships formed through the project still endure. JRS worked at many levels and advocacy based on solid research became more important as the process was coming to an end. Stateless people were at risk of being left behind as they did not fit the process so JRS took up their cause.

None would say this project was perfect. It was a humble beginning but the experience of JRS lawyers and interpreters in touch daily with asylum seekers led to better understanding of their needs. The Regional Office in Bangkok developed its research and advocacy capacity as well as providing individual assistance. A legal project was established in Cambodia to assist asylum seekers in their dealings with the government and UNHCR that endures today.

WELCOMING RESETTLED REFUGEES IN AUSTRALIA

Celso Romanin SJ

Celso Romanin was the first JRS coordinator for Australia in 1985. In 1993 he moved to Uganda where he worked with Sudanese refugees.

JRS Australia began in 1985 when Mark Raper was appointed as regional director of JRS Asia Pacific, and moved to Bangkok. I was appointed then by the provincial as JRS coordinator for Australia.

Australia at that time was one of the countries which took most refugees for resettlement. My way of working was largely to meet with Jesuits and Jesuit institutions with a view to animating them to welcome refugees and help with resettlement. The result was that many small groups around Australia took the challenge and became friends to refugees as they settled.

JRS quickly became a focus for other religious congregations who wanted to become involved with work among refugees and provided a means for them to send personnel into camps with their particular expertise, especially in education.

So JRS Australia became a recruiting agent for work amongst refugees in camps and a means to educate people about the world of refugees. JRS became a member of the Refugee Council of Australia, and worked hard to set up a Refugee Advice and Counselling service based in Melbourne. This was housed in our home and provided an advocacy service to those who sought refugee status.

Gradually the mood in Australia changed and the main work of JRS became one of advocacy. We were often critical of Government policy, which in turn became more hardened.

At the end of 1988, I left JRS Australia, went back to Parish work and JRS changed direction because of the growing difficulty of representing refugees.

In 1993 I then went to Uganda as country director, where the work was one of education. JRS in Uganda provided mainly primary and some secondary education. We also saw the need for nurseries, where some minimal education began, but they were also a means to improve the health of small children, who were rather malnourished, with the provision of some porridge. We also endeavoured to provide some literacy and numeracy for women who had not had the opportunity for any education. Our presence there gave us the opportunity to help the local church with some pastoral work.

The great contribution we were able to make at that time was to enable young people to become qualified teachers. We endeavoured particularly to single out promising, young women who would become role models for girls of a different life than the soul-wrenching, hard work of gathering wood and water.

This was a most satisfying time because of the close contact with refugees themselves and in seeing the difference education made to their lives.

Once again, JRS provided the means for other congregations and lay people to work among refugees by providing infrastructure, placement and support. In Uganda, religious of five different congregations and lay people from five continents were able to live harmoniously together, praying and discerning in a very refreshing, new way. The work there became ever more difficult with rebel attacks and in many cases refugees were dispersed. Some of our projects had no option but to close.

There is no call to appear strong by attacking the weak. To attack the most vulnerable people on earth is not strength, it is cowardice. In fact the strength of any society is shown by how it protects the weak. Refugees and migrants have been this country's history. They may for a time appear weak. But in the long term they are the strength of our nation.

Mark Raper SJ
Is there not a better way? First published in
Eureka Street magazine, Australia, April 2002.

AMONG THE VIETNAMESE CHILDREN IN MALAYSIA AND THAILAND

Patricia Lynch RSM

Patricia Lynch worked in Sungey Besi camp, Malaysia, between 1992 and 1994. She then moved to Sikhui camp, in Thailand, where she worked until 1995 in a counselling program with Vietnamese children.

JRS was already a very strong force for good in the refugee camps of Asia when I went to relieve Marleen Flaherty for three months in Sungei Besi Camp, just out of Kuala Lumpur in Malaysia. Little did I know, as I left Australia on August 14, 1992, that I would actually stay the best part of three years in Malaysia and Thailand.

Already in Sungei Besi were Srs Joan Campbell, Joan Kelleher, Mary Keely and Marleen Flaherty, all Mercy Sisters from Australia. Present too were Jesuits, David Townsend, Br Heiner, and later Harry Geib. The team was very supportive of each other and their love for and commitment to the refugees was truly inspirational to me.

Probably what sums up for me the presence and the influence JRS had in the camp was an experience I had in my early days there. One day, as I walked through the camp with Yen, my interpreter, a small child ran out from one of the houses, threw her arms around me and hugged me. I was taken by surprise, as I did not know her, but Yen said simply, "She knows who loves her here. It is the Sisters and the Fathers". It stuck me then that the people were very aware that we were with them because we really wanted to be. They knew that we tried very hard to make a difference for them. I also became acutely aware that my warm and immediate acceptance by the refugees in the camp happened because I followed in the footsteps of the JRS workers who had gone before me. For me this said so much about the impact the JRS/MRS presence had among the people, and of the high level of respect and trust that had resulted from it.

My work in Sungei Besi was with the Red Crescent in Social Services. I supervised a Minors' Centre and a Day Care Centre. The former, under the direction of many talented and generous Vietnamese volunteer workers, provided activities for the children when they were not at school. In Primary School there were so many children that the hours had to be staggered, each group receiving two hours of schooling a day. This made the Minors' Centre essential and we had as many as thirteen different activities for the young ones to take part in. We had a lot of fun in a situation that was often tense and oppressive.

My move across to Thailand in 1994 was a different story and I was very much affected by the happenings in the camp there. I worked with Social Services again at Sikhui, just outside Packchong. I was there with Joan Kelleher RSM, who had successfully implemented a primary school programme, as she had in Malaysia. Joan and I were the only JRS presence in Sikhui at that time and I remain grateful for the support given to us from the JRS Office in Bangkok. The situation was stressful as the authorities worked to force the Vietnamese home. In Sikhui, I was responsible for the welfare of the unaccompanied minors as well as for counselling thirteen of the survivors of violence from boats attacked by pirates on the way to freedom. At first there were one hundred and thirty-six minors. Five volunteer workers helped me to make sure they were well cared for, safe and going to school. There were so many that it took me five weeks to talk to each one individually. That was a challenge. Many returned home, and by the time I left the camp only about thirty-eight remained. With the lessening numbers, I was asked to see more of the survivors of violence as one of our colleagues had left the camp. Before returning to Australia, I visited Vietnam to see as many of the returned minors and their families as I could manage. There are many stories to tell, but they would fill a book!

I think if JRS had not been present in the refugee camps of Asia, the plight of the refugees would have been much darker and sadder. Somehow, because we were there the people were able to cope with life better, and even find some joy in an impossible situation. It has always been my belief that all over the world wherever the Vietnamese refugees now live, the names of the JRS workers would still be mentioned with deep affection.

When I left JRS in 1995, the numbers of workers had begun to lessen as the authorities asked the foreigners to withdraw. Many JRS/MRS workers went on to other great work among asylum seekers in other parts of the world. I came home to stay, but my experience has held me in good stead, particularly in my efforts to be with the underprivileged in Australia – street kids, asylum seekers and the underclass of the inner city.

Congratulations to JRS on a dream well realised and still very much alive. I am so happy I had some time playing a small part in the wonderful scheme of things.

UNHCR

Refugee camp for Vietnamese refugees in Hong Kong in the early 1980s

WITH THE UNACCOMPANIED MINORS IN BATAAN, PHILIPPINES

Chris Boles SJ

Chris Boles worked with refugees in England in the late eighties and joined JRS in 1992. He worked in the Regional Refugee Transit Centre in Bataan, Philippines, a camp of first asylum for Vietnamese boat people. He then joined JRS in the UK and simultaneously assisted the International Office in Rome, acting as secretary for the annual Regional Directors meeting. He is the contact person for JRS in Scotland.

My work with refugees began in 1987 as a first year Jesuit novice in Birmingham, England. An organisation there provided assistance to Vietnamese and other refugees newly arriving into the city and my work was with the housing department of that organisation, preparing houses and apartments for new arrivals.

It was an excellent introduction to the world of refugees and got me interested, early in my Jesuit life, in the work of JRS. In the second year of the Jesuit novitiate novices of the British province do a three or four month placement and I had hopes of doing that placement with JRS somewhere.

Thus at the end of my first year novitiate I met with Mark Raper, who was then still director of JRS Asia-Pacific, to ask if I could do my placement in his region. To my great surprise he said no! I hadn't contemplated being told no, so it was a shock! But actually his reasoning made great sense, namely, that a short placement of only a few weeks is of very little help to refugees, who require people committed to long term service and accompaniment.

Mark suggested I prepare myself for a 'regency' with JRS, a period of time where Jesuits in formation take a break from study for two years or so to do pastoral work of some kind. So in order to prepare myself as best I could for a regency with JRS, I began a long and pleasant association with the 'Refugee Studies Programme' (RSP) at Oxford University, where I went after novitiate to study philosophy (and play rugby!). That was an excellent preparation and in the course of my time there I was able to represent JRS to RSP, which eventually led to the establishment of the 'Pedro Arrupe Tutorship' at the University.

Regency came in 1992, with a placement in the Regional Refugee Transit Centre in Bataan, Philippines, a camp of first asylum for Vietnamese boat people. I was responsible for a programme which looked after unaccompanied minors, all those in the camp under 18 who were there alone without any parents or older siblings. The normal way for JRS to work in the Asia-Pacific region, at the time, was to second JRS staff to work with other agencies in the camps, which allowed for a good variety of placements in camps throughout the region.

I worked there nearly two years and found it very gratifying though very difficult and very emotionally draining. A refugee camp is no place to go through childhood, but it is remarkable how many of those children are now settled into good living situations in countries throughout the world.

I often described my work in the camp as 'hanging out' with the children because that is essentially what I did. They were in it for the long haul. No country would resettle them until they were 18 years old, even though they were spoken of as 'first among the first' for care and for resettlement. So I did what I could to make their life in camp more bearable and pleasant but, in reality, I did very little except spend time with them. I was happy to do so.

I was the only JRS worker in that particular camp and my nearest neighbour was on an island very far away. I depended then on the regional office in Bangkok for my support and for news. I was able to make visits there about twice each year which was very important.

I left the Philippines in 1994 with many of the children still there and it would be three more years before the camp was finally closed and any remaining refugees resettled or returned to Vietnam.

More studies followed for me. This time they took place in Toronto, Canada, and again I was able to combine study of theology with practical work. I was a permanent volunteer in the JRS office in Canada, part of the 'Jesuit Centre for Faith and Justice', which gave me a good experience of seeing JRS work in the context of a larger social centre.

I was happy to be there because I knew already my next assignment after studies would be to JRS in the UK, working with our growing team in London.

62

These different experiences of JRS gave me a good overview of at least some of the world of JRS and that was further expanded by annual work in the International Office in Rome, acting as secretary for the meeting of the Regional Directors of JRS each summer. There I was able to see the global scope of JRS which seemed very different from my early days and my time in Bataan. For one thing, projects and regions in Africa were being greatly expanded while at the same time projects in Asia-Pacific were trimming down because of the final closing of camps.

I finished working with JRS full time in 2000, when I came to Edinburgh to work in the justice and peace office of the archdiocese, a job I enjoy and which my time with JRS has prepared me for well. I remain a contact person for JRS in Scotland and always look forward to visitors!

In 1981 Pope John Paul II visited the camp in the Philippines where I would later work for two years. Following that visit he was moved to write to the UN High Commissioner for Refugees to describe the global refugee situation as a shameful wound of our time. Only one year earlier, in his letter which established the Jesuit Refugee Service, Fr Arrupe said the following: 'St. Ignatius called us to go anywhere we are most needed for the greater service of God. The spiritual as well as the material needs of nearly 16 million refugees throughout the world today could scarcely be greater'.[5] These words have inspired many Jesuits and others to give themselves to refugee ministry.

Chris Boles SJ, *Justice and ethics in ministry to refugees*, 1997

---

[5] Letter of Fr Pedro Arrupe, in *Acta Romana 1981.*

Repatriation to Cambodia and major events between 1990 and 1993

Tom Steinbugler SJ

Tom Steinbugler was the JRS Country Director in the Philippines in the mid eighties. In 1990 he replaced Mark Raper SJ as Regional Director in Asia Pacific. As the screening process concluded and the Vietnamese asylum seekers were either repatriated or resettled, he handed over to Quentin Dignam as Regional Director early in 1994.

My first association with refugee work was in 1985 when Mark Raper SJ, then Regional Director in Asia Pacific, invited me to the new Bangkok offices to help with the financial records. Mark kindly invited me on other occasions also, and I used to sit in on his consultations and annual meetings. Also, he asked me to be the Philippine country director, keeping an eye on the Vietnamese arrival camp in Puerto Princesa and the Bataan Processing Zone, the departure area for those going to USA.

Eventually Mark was called to Rome to replace Dieter Scholtz and, since nature abhors a vacuum, I got sucked into his big pair of shoes in January 1990.

The Asian refugee scene was shifting. The civil war in Cambodia wearied everyone, and people longed for an end to it – so also the ever-increasing flow of Vietnamese refugees, arriving by land or boat, which was by now exhausting the patience of the receiving countries. The search to find sponsors for those automatically considered refugees shifted to an emphasis upon refugee status determination as both the first world countries and the UN tried to plug the pipeline. The processing was slow, the camps were miserable, and word gradually seeped in, "Don't come!"

Of the other two main refugee groups, the Hmong from Laos continued to enjoy automatic acceptance by the US, while the Burmese minorities were not going anywhere: unwanted at home, unrecognized in Thailand, they languished in jungle camps where they can still be found.

The Khmer Refugees were mainly in camps just inside Thailand. FUNCIPEC followers were in the enormous Site Two Camp, and others. Pol Pot's peo-

By the end of 1989 we had reached a crunch situation in the border camps for Cambodians. So the 30 members of that JRS team working with COERR (Catholic Office for Emergency and Refugee Relief) entered a serious discernment. Should we stay? Or should we quit the camp, denounce the exploitation of these innocent people and transfer to work in Cambodia? After a six week reflection process our vote was equally split: 15 for staying, 15 for going. We opted for a different strategy: a cross border operation, taking reconciliation, reuniting of families as a priority, while pushing the UN to work for a safe and voluntary repatriation. Denise Coghlan went with a new JRS team to Cambodia. Not knowing which government would ultimately win power in Cambodia, but sure that the poorest would always need care, we opted to work with the war wounded, the land mine survivors, the illiterate peasant people everywhere recruited to fight today's wars.

Denise's work with land mine survivors has built into one of the most successful NGO campaigns anywhere. She mobilised involvement in the campaign by more than 30 JRS country programs. And that movement is deeply embedded in and owned by the people who are being served. Who received the Nobel Prize on behalf of the land mine campaign? It was Tun Chunnareth, one of Denise's team leaders.

I also think of her accompanying Richie Fernando's body home to the Philippines and then welcoming Richie's mother when she could finally bring herself to visit Banteay Preab where her son had been killed by a handgrenade.

Denise is the director of Jesuit Service in Cambodia and interprets the Ignatian mission through her leadership there.

Mark Raper SJ
Mercy and the National Interest, Keynote address for the National Conference of Mercy Refugee Service, 22nd November 2002. The Academy, Melbourne.

ple were in more secluded camps closed to the NGOs (to write that sentence is to recall the hotly-debated question: Were these refugee camps or base camps for the war effort?). Vietnamese 'land' people were in Thailand. Boat people could be found in Hong Kong, Thailand, Malaysia and Indonesia.

The Hmong and Burmese were both in Thailand. JRS Asia Pacific was everywhere. The Bangkok Office grew from one house to two to three, holding offices, a guest house, chapel and an inexhaustible kitchen run by the famous Pi Chan. Burmese refugees found a home here.

Two major developments began in the first half of 1990. In anticipation of the Khmer cease-fire and eventual refugee return, Mark Raper had prepared the ground for a JRS footing inside Cambodia. '*We want to be there to welcome the refugees home*'. Our calling card was to be a technical school for the handicapped, similar to the one in Site Two.

In February 1990, Sr Jeanne Marie Ath, Sr Denise Coghlan and Br Noel Oliver SJ flew for the first time from Bangkok to Ho Chi Minh City and then back to Phnom Penh, at the invitation of the Quaker Society. Eventually the school was established with Br Noel as its first Director, and Sr Denise became the Team Leader for Cambodia, as she is today. Sr Ath pioneered rural cooperation in hundreds of villages in Kandal Province.

The work so well begun by these pioneers has continued, expanded and now constitutes the backbone of the Jesuit Service Cambodia. Sr Denise and Sr Ath remain, along with a number of others from JRS days.

Meanwhile, to assist the Vietnamese in the determination of their refugee status, UNHCR called for proper legal assistance to be supplied by the NGO Group. Louis Robert SJ, working in Hong Kong, attended the initial meeting in Geneva. A group of Australian Lawyers were interested. Peter Hosking SJ hosted a six hour meeting with a 29 item Agenda, and the Hong Kong Lawyers Project was born, under the leadership of Paul White. For three years this project fielded an uninterrupted flow of lawyers assisting refugees to understand the law, enabling them to present their situations in the fairest manner. The project ended when the camps began to close.

A third, less public, service commenced just when Mark was leaving Bangkok. He was caring for a Burmese lass who slowly died, almost literally, in his arms. A group, which had been formed to help her, remained together after both YeYe and Mark were gone. They were young students, driven from Burma, who passed their time in the forests and then came to Bangkok to continue their struggle for independence. Being illegal, they lacked security, jobs, income and proper housing. JRS helped the Bangkok-based people as much as possible. Meanwhile, the Burma Border Consortium, of which JRS was a member, offered modest assistance to the camps along the Border, with the tacit tolerance of the Royal Thai Government.

Another unusual program served the Immigration Detention Center in downtown Bangkok, where many refugees and others were crowded together in terrible conditions. JRS sought the release of these men and women, and their return home.

The danger, in mentioning these highlights, is to overlook the bread and butter JRS work. In so many camps, schools were organized and administered, the sick cared for and counseled, the elderly nourished and supported, babies delivered, mothers cared for, leaders trained... Many volunteers came from Australia, US, Europe and India. Mercy Sisters and other religious women, Jesuit scholastics, brothers and priests, lay volunteers, married and unmarried, young and old. One has to mention Pierre Ceyrac, Vincent Dierckx and John Bingham from India, who came first and left last, Alfonso de Juan who led the very large COERR Team at Site II, Paul White and Tang Lay Lee from the Hong Kong Lawyers Project, Anne McDonald, Lizzie Finnerty and Meg Hicks, midwives at Palawan, Louis Robert and Carole McDonald, who served in several countries, Joan Campbell, who stayed on and on with the Vietnamese in Malaysia and Alan and Denise Nichols, a Protestant Minister and his wife, who left Australia to brave the Catholic world.

Just before leaving, in 1993, I could support Mark in his effort to revive JRS in India, to serve the Bhutanese refugees camped in the mud of Nepal. By this time, the Vietnamese pipeline was clogged, and their camps were closing around the region. The Khmer war was over and the refugees were returning, their problems not yet over. The Hmong flow gradually dried up. And the Burmese? Tragically, they are still there.

The repatriation of Cambodian refugees in time for the well attended May 1994 elections was organised by UNHCR, and was an integral part of the United Nation's efforts to institute democracy and to place a new government in Phnom Penh. Some of the repatriates had been 12 years in exile. UNHCR brought home more than 367,500 Cambodians.

UNTAC (United Nations Transitional Authority for Cambodia) was successful in some of its goals. However, it failed to disarm the forces active in Cambodia or to de-mine the country. In addition, as numbers of returnees increased, UNTAC lost some control over tracking them and monitoring their safety.

UNHCR has had difficulty in giving useful repatriation assistance to returned refugees in Cambodia, especially in regard to securing land for cultivation. Many of the returnees had to choose what came to be known as 'option C' from UNHCR, or cash and food but no land.

The Cambodian case cleary illustrates the need for significant investment in de-arming, de-mining and development work before, during and after the repatriation process. It also points to the need for other organisations (if not a newly mandated UNHCR) to get more significantly involved in helping internally displaced persons. If these elements had been better secured by the UN or others in this operation, it might have been a real model for repatriations for the future.

Mark Raper SJ, *Repatriation in South East Asia*, 1995

'WHAT IS JRS DOING TO HELP THE PEOPLE OF SRI LANKA?'[6]

Sebastian Maria Anthony SJ

Sebastian Maria Anthony worked with the internally displaced of Sri Lanka and in 1998 he was appointed Country Director there. He is presently Provincial of Sri Lanka.[7]

The 1983 riots in Colombo and in other parts the country saw Tamils fleeing towards Jaffna in the North and Batticaloa in the East. Schools, Churches and temples were converted into camps in the capital Colombo and in other parts of the country. In 1993 Fr Vincent Mooken took over the responsibility of first Regional Director for the South Asia Region. He made an exploratory trip to Sri Lanka in 1994. At the time many Srilankan Jesuits were serving refugees commendably in the East but they could not reach the war torn North. Jesuit residences and buildings were often used as refugee camps.

In the beginning, Jesuits from Srilanka actively participated in the meetings of JRS Asia Pacific: Frs Peter Kurukula Aratchi, Nissanka, Anthony Pillai and myself all participated in JRS Asia Pacific meetings in Bangkok as province contact persons or co-coordinators. JRS Asia Pacific responded with visits by Mark Raper, Rossi, Buddi, Suzi Coreford, Adrian Lyons, Andrew Hamilton, Quentin Dignam and Jon Greenway. They visited many affected parts and shared their concerns with JRS International. In this way, Jesuits and the JRS community all over the world became supportive to the Srilankan province.

The exodus from Jaffna happened in October 1995. Nearly 450,000 inhabitants of Jaffna crossed the treacherous Kilali lagoon within two days and sought refuge in the jungles of Vanni. Moved by their stories, in November the Srilankan Jesuits decided to send two Jesuits, Frs Joel Kulanayagam and Alfred Gabriel on an investigative trip.

---

[6] "With his left hand, Fr Arrupe shakily drew a map of India, then the droplet shape of the island next to it. By pointing to the island clearly he was asking me *What is JRS doing to help the people of Sri Lanka?*", Mark Raper SJ, see introduction.

[7] Taken from *20 Years of Service to the Refugees*, by JRS South Asia, 2000.

Don Doll SJ/JRS

Tamils fleeing Sri Lanka towards South India, 1994

By December it was decided to send a JRS team on permanent placement to the war-ravaged Vanni region. The Bishop of Jaffna allowed JRS to work in the Mullaitivu district where the team assisted the displaced people with relief, shelter and educational programmes.

The two priests took their abode amidst thousands of displaced persons in the Mankulam area. Since then they have been displaced twice, moving to Mullaitivu, the epicenter of the conflict. Frs Joel and Alfred Gabriel lived there in mud huts like all other displaced people, as true witness to the mission of accompaniment. Aerial bombing and shelling were common. Life was dangerous but one of them said: "We accompany these people in their Way of the Cross with the hope of witnessing their resurrection in a land of peace".

In 1998 I was appointed as part time Country Director of JRS and the work was expanded. I established the National office in Colombo. Fr General blessed the house in 1999. Apart from co-ordinating the work in the country, the National office kept itself busy with human rights activities and in attending to the needs of the detainees under the guidance of Fr Yogeswaran. Further the national office also has a documentation unit.

JRS served the border towns of Vavuniya, Polanaruwa and Batticaloa through education and assistance to widows. Frs Navarathnam and Jeyabalan Croos from Mannar Diocese were the main power behind our work in Vavuniya. In Suriady, Sr Salette FMM took care of the work while Fr Joe Mary organized the Kokkadicholai project for poor children with monitoring by Mr Alphonse Mary. In the Polanoruwa district JRS worked for the Sinhalese displaced people with the help of Jayantha Pinnavilla OMI. Activities included education of children and income-generation for widows. In Trincomalee district JRS assisted the peace home for orphans run by C. P. Rajendram SJ. The decade between 1990 and 2000 saw the work of JRS expanded and it is hoped to expand it still further, bringing more people under its care.

Don Doll SJ/JRS

Displaced Tamil in northern Sri Lanka

Accompanying Tamil refugees in Tamilnadu, India

Paul Newman

Paul Newman joined the JRS South Asia team in 1998 and since then has been closely following the situations in Sri Lanka and Bhutan. He works as Information and Advocacy Officer and is based in Bangalore.

The story of Sri Lanka is a story of human brokenness. 1983 saw a massive exodus of refugees from Sri Lanka. Around 450,000 were internally displaced and some 230,000 fled to India. India was sympathetic to the refugee cause and many NGOs were requested by the Indian government to render help. JRS maintained a strong pastoral presence at the transit camp in Mandapam.

Robert Cutinha SJ concentrated on refugee rights and undertook a risky trip to the war-torn Jaffna peninsula in 1988, during the period of the Indian Peace Keeping Force (IPKF) He sought the help of other Jesuits to respond to this new challenge of protecting the displaced and the refugees.

The Indian Peace Keeping Force (IPKF) returned home in 1990 and a temporary ceasefire was signed between the government and the Liberation Tamil Tigers Eelam (LTTE). In spite of strong apprehensions almost all of the refugees returned home to start a new life. Life was tough after the accord.

Within two months a full scale war exploded in Sri Lankan between the militant Tamil Tigers and the Sri Lankan Army. Once again, the refugees fled to India. But this time the Indian government was less sympathetic. In the absence of JRS, the Madurai province sent C. Amalraj SJ to assist the refugees at the sea shore.

In June 1990 some 123,000 boat people reached the shores. The journey was arduous, with occasional accidents. The small Jesuit team was overwhelmed. Their work started around 2 am daily. Hordes of frightened masses huddled together in rickety boats reached Indian shores every day. Some brought their sons and daughters, wounded during the aerial bombing and constant shelling.

After the emergency period of landing, the Indian Government shifted the refugees to 133 camps. The camp sites were often poultry yards, market places or even open toilets. The Madurai Jesuit Province provided a full time Jesuit for JRS, Fr C. Amalraj and an office was set up at Dindigul. JRS was also assisted by Br Joe Natarajan, Fr Elais and Fr Arulanandam.

For JRS it was challenge to enter the camps after the killing of former Indian Prime Minister Indira Ghandi in 1991, allegedly by a militant suicide bomber from Sri Lanka. NGOs disappeared from the scene and intelligence agencies took over the camps.

The government imposed a ban on education of the refugees. This lasted until 1996. Despite this, refugees created the Organisation for Eelam Refugee Rehabilitation (OfERR). JRS collaborated with them and tirelessly trained its volunteers to make the projects more participatory with the emphasis on empowerment of the refugee community. JRS projects focused on formal education, technical education and community based projects. The untrained human resource available in the camps was tapped and trained as teachers while women's programs brought in some semblance of a community. Life was miserable but the refugees, to their credit, brought hope for the community.

In 1994 the Indian Government repatriated the refugees with the assistance of UNHCR as a short ceasefire was proclaimed. Human rights organisations advocated against this repatriation. During this period three JRS members visited the war zones: Frs C. Amal, Vinny Joseph and Jerry Rosario.

In April 1995, war broke out with full intensity between the LTTE and the Sri Lankan Army. This time the refugee flows to India were estimated to be about 20,000 people. C. Amal was appointed as the Regional Director of JRS South Asia that same year.

In 1996, Vinny Joseph became the Director of JRS Tamilnadu. Fr Vinny's vision was *empowerment through education*. Parents and students appreciated of the Sri Lankan Refugee community appreciated his concept of building the community through education. JRS began to expand its projects into these 133 camps.

In April 2001 Francis Sales SJ was appointed as the Director of JRS Tamilnadu as Fr Vinny became the Country Director of JRS Sri Lanka. Fr Sales consolidated the works of Fr Vinny and in 2004 Fr Singarayar SJ, the

JRS transit camp Pastor at Mandapam, became the Director of JRS Tamilnadu. In June 2005 Fr Prem Kumar SJ took over as the Director.

In 2003, C. Amal SJ moved over to Liberia as Country Director. PS Amalraj SJ took over as Regional Director of JRS South Asia.

One of the specific marks of JRS Tamilnadu has been its partnership with religious congregations and lay people in this service for the refugees. Today there are 25 volunteers comprising Jesuits, religious from other congregations, lay people and refugees. There are 224 teachers in the various education projects.

The hope of JRS Tamilnadu is that all refugees will go back to their homes with the resources they have acquired in exile, so that they can rebuild their motherland.

Don Doll SJ/JRS

Camp for Tamil refugees from Sri Lanka in Tamilnadu, India, 1994

My journey with the refugees
Varkey Perekatt SJ

Varkey Perekatt was formerly provincial of India, and helped to set up JRS South Asia. He worked with the Bhutanese refugees in Damak region, Eastern Nepal, first between 1998 and 2000 and then again in 2003.[8]

My journey with refugees began in 1970 when, as a scholastic, I volunteered to work with Bangladeshi refugees. An outbreak of cholera, claiming 17 people in one day, remains a vivid memory even after 35 years. That exposure enkindled in me a deep concern for these helpless people who become 'nobodies' through no fault of their own.

When Fr Pedro Arrupe SJ announced the birth of JRS on 14 November 1980, my experience with Bangladeshi refugees ten years earlier rang a bell. It prompted me, as Provincial of India, to set up JRS South Asia in 1992. Later, in 1995, I was present at the 34th General Congregation which reaffirmed the contribution of JRS in different parts of the world after 15 years of service, appealing 'to all the Provinces to support the Jesuit Refugee Service in every possible way' (GC34, no.16). My interest in the cause of refugees grew deeper, leading to my decision to spend a sabbatical year with the Bhutanese refugees in Nepal.

Caritas Nepal is responsible for formal education in the Bhutanese refugee camps in Eastern Nepal. This programme is the largest educational program for refugees anywhere in the world. Over 42,000 students, from pre-primary to post-secondary levels, are educated through the voluntary service of more than 1,200 refugee staff, nine national staff and six JRS volunteers. In 1998, PS Amalraj SJ was the project director. I was appointed as his assistant for the year.

In addition to administering the Bhutanese Refugee Education Programme (BREP) and a vocational training project, Fr Amalraj and I began to pay more attention to advocacy. Bringing together scattered refugee leaders un-

---

[8] Taken from *20 years of service to the Refugees*, by JRS South Asia, 2000.

der one umbrella proved to be a marathon but necessary task and enabled them to take up the refugees' cause of repatriation in a more united manner. What began for me as a year's stay extended to another, because of my deep involvement in building a unified leadership in the refugee community.

On 30 April 2000 I bad farewell to the Bhutanese refugee community and returned to Delhi. I little dreamt that, through God's providence, I would find myself soon after once again in Nepal on the BREP.

In June 2003, I returned to serve the Bhutanese refugees, this time as Project Director. I came back with enthusiasm, as there was great hope of starting a repatriation process after years of waiting. Our euphoria was short-lived, however. Despite waiting for the 13 years, a permanent solution remains elusivee.

It is a challenge for me to be constantly alert in the day-to-day running of BREP while at the same time keeping in touch with what goes on in the community among refugee leaders, in the host country and in the international community. However, the most satisfactory part of my journey with refugees is being a sign of hope in a hopeless situation and a voice for the voiceless.

As leader of the JRS Nepal team, I am pleased to record that JRS does its best to carry out its three main objectives – accompaniment, service and advocacy. There are ample reasons to be grateful to God, to the team members and to every refugee for all that is being accomplished.

Travelling the long road together: JRS with the Bhutanese refugees in Nepal

PS Amalraj SJ

PS Amalraj worked with the Bhutanese refugees in the Eastern Nepal camps since 1997, as Country Director. In 2003 he was appointed Regional Director in South Asia, a region covering Sri Lanka, India and Nepal.[9]

In 1991, the government of Bhutan expelled some 90,000 southern Bhutanese people into the dry Mechi River. Despite living under appalling conditions, these people attracted no international attention until infant mortality rose to alarming heights. The former Caritas Director met them at the river. He responded to their emergency needs and appealed to the JRS International office for help. Tony Fernandes SJ had been a pionner with the Bhutanese people and worked out the infrastructure for a schooling system. Vincent Mooken SJ, then JRS Regional Director in South Asia, tried to bring in more people.

Caritas Nepal again appealed to JRS to send a volunteer to take up the responsibility of Field Director of the Bhutanese Refugee Education Programme. In May 1995, David Townsend SJ was sent to Nepal in response to the appeal. Fr David played a very supportive role in the AMCC (Appeal Movement Coordinating Council). He established and maintained contact with the Bhutanese support groups abroad. In July Stephen Power SJ was sent to assist David in the scholarship programme. Later, in January 1996, at the request of the Caritas Executive Director and the Field Director, JRS sent Joan Kelleher RSM to join the team, while in March Mary Lou Moorhead RSCJ took up the roles of Scholarship Coordinator and Assistant Field Director.

In January 1996 Tang Lay Lee, an Australian lawyer, began a research in the camps on the Bhutanese Citizenship Act of 1985, its validity and consequences. This research highlighted the Bhutanese Refugees' cause in international circles.

---

[9] Taken from *Refugees from the last Shangrila*, 2000.

In 1997 I became Project Director. The following year, Tomy Joseph SJ joined the team on a temporary basis. During his short term of service, Fr Tomy initiated the Vocational Training Programme for school dropouts, which continues today. From 1998, JRS South Asia took over full charge of Nepal operations from JRS Asia-Pacific.

In August 2000, together with a group of refugee representatives, I attended the fifty-second session of UN Sub-Commission on Human Rights in Geneva. This group, together with Elizabeth Janz of JRS and Peter Prove of LWF, worked towards securing the chairperson's statement of the year 1999 on the Bhutanese refugee situation. The presence of the refugee leaders at the meeting made the Bhutanese refugee problem more alive.

At the end of April 2000, Varkey Perekatt SJ completed his contract with JRS and left for Rajasthan. His work in education has been pervasive, however the emergence of BRRRC (the Bhutanese Refugee Representatives' Repatriation Committee) crowned his efforts.

The visit of UN High Commissioner for Refugees, Sadako Ogata, to the Camps on 1st May 2000, was perhaps the biggest event of international importance for the Bhutanese refugees at that time. It gave all possible assistance to the various refugee groups in carefully formulating their independent statements to be presented to the UN High Commissioner. I presented a statement on behalf of the implementing partners. C. Amal SJ, JRS South Asia Director, was present on the occasion. He later met Ms Ogata privately in Delhi, and they discussed important issues connected to the Bhutanese refugee problem.

On 3rd May 2000, Kuruvila Cherian SJ, joined JRS Nepal. He was appointed Assistant Project Director of the educational programme. Soon after, Elizabeth Janz, at that time JRS Representative in Geneva, visited the camps. She had been the advocate of the Bhutanese cause in the international forums and had been responsible for securing the UN Subcommission of Human Rights Chairperson's statement in favour of the Bhutanese refugees in 1997 and 1998.

The history of JRS involvement in Nepal is a picture of varied hues and shades. We see a long line of men and women who gave themselves in service to the refugees. Though the abilities and talents of these people vary in kind and extent, all were put to one purpose, namely, the service of the refugees. Those who came in later enjoyed the benefit of the labour of those who had gone before. This attempt at depicting the history of JRS Nepal is primarily an attempt to pay tribute to those who bore the heat and labour of those days.

Mark Raper SJ/JRS

Bhutanese students in Nepal refugee camp, 1999

80

JRS ASIA PACIFIC BETWEEN 1996 AND 2000
Steve Curtin SJ

Steve Curtin worked with JRS in the Philippines in 1991. He took over from Quentin Dignam as Regional Director in January 1997, until November 2000. Steve continued the work that Quentin had been doing to strengthen JRS programmes with refugees from Burma taking refuge in Thailand. In 2000 with new and massive forced displacements in Indonesia and East Timor JRS launched new programmes in both those countries.

My first assignment with JRS was in the Philippines in 1991 before I was ordained. Tom Steinbugler was the Regional Director of JRS-AP at that time and I was seconded to a Philippines mental health NGO (Community and Family Services International) in the Philippines First Asylum Camp (PFAC) in Palawan. Most of the asylum seekers in Palawan came from Vietnam. This was the time of the Comprehensive Plan of Action (CPA) when countries of the region sought to 'stem the tide' of refugees from Vietnam by 'screening' them against the refugee definition in the Convention before offering resettlement only to those 'screened in'. This was a difficult time in the camps since those 'screened out' faced forced repatriation to the countries they had fled. After many years of automatic resettlement for refugees from Indochina the CPA and screening was a significant change.

I lived at the Catholic parish inside the camp with the chaplain, Fr Bob Crawford. He was a Vincentian priest who had been a missionary in Vietnam before 1975. He was also an interesting fellow to live with. Anne McDonnell was the Mercy Refugee Service midwife with IOM in Palawan at that time and she helped to keep me sane. A Vietnamese American Jesuit, Fr Joseph Tuoc, was also there.

My second assignment with JRS was from 1996 to 2000 with JRS Asia Pacific in Bangkok. I went to assist Quentin Dignam with Thailand programs and to assist in the Regional Office just as the Comprehensive Plan of Action was coming to an end. Quentin had taken over from Tom Steinbugler as Regional Director. Quentin's time as Regional Director was tough because it was the time when camps all over the region were being closed and 'screened out' asylum seekers were being forcibly repatriated. Quentin's last year as Regional Director was especially sad because of the death in Phnom Penh of Richie Fernando SJ.

I was making my first visit to Burma in 1996 when I learned from Quentin that Richie had been killed. Then later that year Gil Carrol, one of our young volunteers from the USA, had a stroke in Bangkok and had to be medivacced home to face a long rehabilitation.

When Quentin finished in Bangkok at the end of 1996 I became the Regional Director. I represented JRS in 1997 at the closing of Sie Khieu, the last camp for Indochinese in Thailand. That really was the end of an incredible era.

With the closure of the Indochinese refugee programs around the region, most of my five years in JRS Asia-Pacific were concentrated in Thailand itself with programs in Bangkok and on the Thai-Burma border.

The JRS Karenni Education Programme based in Mae Hong Son was just beginning when I started in 1996. By the time I finished it had grown considerably. Prior to the work in Mae Hong Son, a lot of the JRS work with refugees from Burma was focused on the students who had been involved in anti-government protests in Rangoon and other cities. Some of the students had subsequently fought against the Burmese army in the jungle on the border and had later moved into Thailand to seek refuge and resettlement. The JRS Border Project Officers did an enormous amount over many years to provide assistance to the students, many of whom had been deeply traumatised by their experience. In Bangkok Oliver Morin and Dee Garcia did wonderful work in the immigration detention centre and our legal officers did some very important casework with asylum seekers.

We had some great information officers and editors of *Diakonia*, *Light and Dark*, and *News from the Field*. They helped the refugees to tell their stories and helped JRS workers to reflect on their work.

I have very happy memories of JRS parties and the *happy hour* gatherings at the office to celebrate birthdays, engagements, welcomes and farewells. Another happy time each year was our annual meeting at Hua Hin. I especially remember some hilariously funny concerts at the end of these meetings. Another meeting each year that I found especially supportive was the meeting of Regional Directors in Rome. Mark Raper was a great 'boss' and I never ceased to be amazed by his capacity to travel and keep in touch and keep on top of so much information.

I also have special memories of times we prayed together at Hua Hin, at the office, in the camps and on the road. I found that the Eucharistic food was the real food for the JRS faith journey.

There were also times when we JRS workers hurt one another just because we are vulnerable and limited human beings and we are working under pressure, sometimes without as much training or preparation as we might like to have. The good God who inspires our work also works in us to heal the wounds that are given and received along the way and God leads us to forgiveness and reconciliation. The times we prayed together were also occasions to pray for one another.

It was during my time as Regional Director that the JRS programs for Bhutanese refugees in Nepal were moved into the care of the newer JRS region of South Asia. I was back in Nepal for a JRS meeting in September 1999 when the post election militia violence in East Timor caused so much death and destruction. I remember rushing back to Bangkok and going on to Jakarta where I was able to maintain some contact with the Jesuits who had remained in Dili sheltering refugees. I was in Jakarta when I learned that the JRS East Timor Director, Fr Karl Albrecht, had been killed on September 11th. Fr Tarcisius Dewanto had been killed in Suai a few days earlier on September 6th.

My last year as Director was a sad year in many ways especially because of those two deaths. This was also my busiest year with major new programs in East Timor and West Timor. At the same time the JRS Indonesia Director who was to succeed me as Regional Director, Andre Sugijopranoto SJ, was starting new programs in parts of Indonesia where people were being displaced by communal violence.

Before I finished as Regional Director at the end of 2000 I went to Mae Hong Son to celebrate Christmas Mass in one of the camps there. On my way back to Bangkok we detoured to Chiang Dao to visit the home of one of the Regional Office staff. A surprise farewell party had been organised for me.

Vilaiwan (Kep) Phokthavi, Tawatchai Hoonghual, Rachanee (Took) Sareechaithaweepong and Emilie Ketudat were the most wonderful people to

Displaced people in Indonesia

work with. These long-term office staff, along with Chan the cook and the various others who came and went, were the core of the incredibly loving and loyal community at the heart of JRS. This included quite a few young, committed and incredibly gifted refugee staff. My time with JRS was a special time in my life. I continue to keep in my prayers the work of JRS and I remember with love all those people whose lives touched my life in those years.

84

RESPONDING TO THE REAL NEEDS
OF THE REFUGEES

Andre Sugijopranoto SJ

Andre Sugijopranoto worked with JRS in Cambodia between 1995 and 1997. In 1999 he joined JRS again setting up the work of in Indonesia. He took over from Steve Curtin as Regional Director in 2001. In September 2005 Andre was replaced by Bernard H. Arputhasamy SJ.

I started working with JRS in Cambodia in July 1995 as a Jesuit regent. My superior did not mention JRS at all when he appointed me. I only knew that I would work in a new Cambodia mission with other Jesuits. At that time, JRS had just handed Cambodia over to the Jesuit Mission.

The real JRS works were legal assistance in Phnom Penh, the displaced persons programme, and the campaign to ban landmines. I worked in Siem Reap, taking care of about 100 displaced persons' families from the Battambang province. My other work consisted in offering services to landmine survivors in Siem Reap, by giving them wheel chairs or crutches and providing loans to the landmine survivor families, among other things. At that time the international director was Mark Raper and the regional director was Quentin Dignam, who was later replaced by Steve Curtin.

In 1996 I attended a JRS in-service seminar in Kigali, Rwanda. I learnt much about JRS spirituality and its mission. When I left Cambodia in 1997, the displaced persons were all settled in a new place thanks to the collaboration between JRS and the Cambodia Red Cross. The Campaign to Ban Landmines was growing and the demining groups were actively demining the land. The legal project also continued in Phnom Penh.

I joined JRS again in 1999 when the Jesuit province in Indonesia decided to work with East Timorese refugees in West Timor. In February-March 1999, the Jesuit Province of Indonesia set up JRS Indonesia in Jakarta. JRS then set up an office in Dili, East Timor, in close collaboration with the Canossian sisters, to help the internally displaced people (IDPs) in East Timor. At this time, everybody working with the IDPs in East Timor was suspected of being pro-independence.

In September 1999, JRS Indonesia started in West Timor. On 7 September the director of JRS East Timor was shot dead. At that time, there were about 280 thousand refugees in West Timor. I set up a new JRS office and activities in Kupang, West Timor. There were no Jesuits in West Timor so I started by working closely with the local diocesan team. We provided medical help for the refugees and gave emergency assistance (rice, water, etc). Later on, after UNHCR came to West Timor, JRS separated from the diocesan team. We wanted to concentrate on the repatriation programme. We also ran an education programme ourselves. When I left West Timor in 2000, we had three offices in West Timor, in Kupang, Atambua and Betun. About half of the refugees returned to East Timor. The militias were wildly opposed to NGOs because they did not want people to return to East Timor.

While I was country director of JRS Indonesia, we also expanded our programme to the Moluccas. Again there was no Jesuit in Ambon, in the Moluccas, so in March 2000 we started working in these with the diocesan team. The problem in the Moluccas was the religious conflict between Moslems and Christians. JRS worked with both sides. We provided emergency assistance, wrote many articles of advocacy, visited both Moslem and Christian IDPs and organised reconciliation activities between Moslems and Christians.

When I left JRS Indonesia in 2000, our team had withdrawn from Ambon because of the conflict. Many people had been killed, even in front of our office. The team moved to West Timor waiting for a more secure situation in order to return. They merged with the JRS West Timor team working with the East Timorese refugees.

In January 2001, activities in Ambon started again. Later, we expanded the programme to Buru Island, Seram Island and lastly to Langgur Island. In March 2001, a conflict took place in Borneo between the Madurese and the Dayak. JRS Indonesia helped the Madurese IDPs who were expelled from Borneo back to Madura island, by supporting local groups. However, we did not open an office there. In June 2001, JRS Indonesia started working in Aceh and Medan, in Sumatra.

When I started working as regional director in Bangkok in 2000, the system was already working very well. The only confusing thing was that the staff had concentrated only on the Thailand projects for a long time. The JRS Indonesia team had developed and I began to introduce the Indonesian work to the regional staff so that they could understand the situation. At that time, JRS Asia Pacific covered Cambodia, Thailand, Indonesia and Australia.

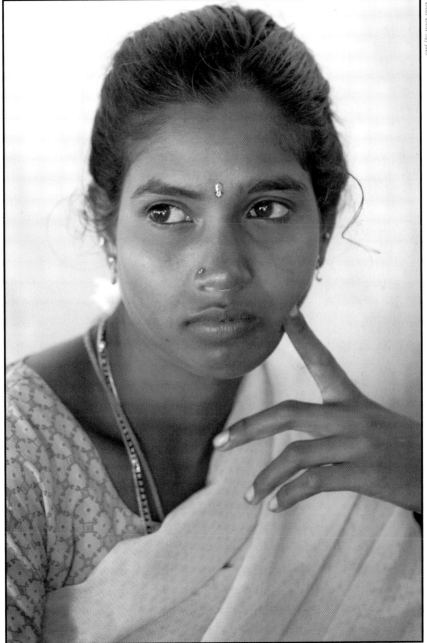

Longing to go back home

At the beginning of 2000, some lay Catholic people in Singapore wanted to support East Timor. They set up a group under the direction of Fr Colin Tan SJ and called themselves JRS Singapore. Later on they expanded their concern to all our works in the Asia-Pacific.

Now, when I am about to leave JRS (September 2005), JRS is present in Cambodia, Thailand, Indonesia, Australia, and Singapore. JRS tried to set up an office in Malaysia however the Archbishop of Kuala Lumpur did not permit Religious to work separately from the diocesan team. The Jesuit superior asked that the JRS name no longer be used in Kuala Lumpur. JRS also tried to open an office in Burma (Myanmar). When we were preparing the new work, the government changed and the new prime minister was not so friendly towards foreigners. We were not able to start this work because of these difficulties. JRS only supported a sister congregation working with displaced persons along the border with Thailand. After one year, the sisters stopped their work as the oppression from the military became too much.

I feel proud of Fr Arrupe's mission of serving forgotten refugees. The context of refugees might have changed, but JRS still responds to the real needs of the refugees. There is a need and we really come to help, especially in places where there are no NGOs. This is the case in Ranong, Thailand, where only two other NGOs are present. Of course we cannot only work in those remote places. In Aceh, Indonesia, JRS was there before the tsunami, when it was a remote area with few NGOs present. Now there are hundreds of NGOs. So I still think we are faithful to our mission of going where nobody goes and where there is a greater need.

I feel that the encounters with refugees and IDPs keep life going; every time I meet them I learn something. As regional director I think I am working still with refugees, although I spend so much time in the office and in airports. However, when I am speaking with the refugees, I am really moved. After the tsunami, I went to Aceh and on one occasion I served as a translator for an American woman. I sat down with a man who was 65 years old and I started to speak in a simple way with him, – 'How many children do you have?' – but he kept silent and cried. Everything had gone with the tsunami. I feel there is something beyond our power. When I meet people I know my work has meaning, even when I am in the office[10].

---

[10]Interview with Fr Sugijopranoto, Rome, May 2005.

Perhaps the end of this history of JRS Asia Pacific is the place to remember some of our workers who have died whilst serving with JRS. In November 1985, shortly after the office moved to Bangkok, Neil Callahan died. He had been unwell at Phanat Nikhom, was diagnosed as terminally ill when he returned to the United States, and eventually died after a prolonged and painful illness.

At the beginning of 1988, Surimart Chalernsook (Look Nut) died. She had given herself tirelessly in giving life to JRS workers during the time she worked in the office. She had then begun herself to find a rich life in the border camps. She was killed in a road accident on the Chonburi road. At the beginning of the next year Bill Yeomans also died after a short illness.

Ma Yee Yee Htun was not a JRS worker but a refugee who grew very close to the hearts of the JRS Bangkok team in 1989. Yee Yee fell ill at the Burmese border and was nursed at the JRS Office in Bangkok until her death, aged 29, in January 1990. In 1992 Sr Carmelita Hannan RSJ fell ill soon after arriving to work with JRS in Thailand. She died from cancer in Melbourne soon afterwards.

In 1996 Richie Fernando SJ was killed aged 26 years by a hand grenade released by a student in the Jesuit Service technical school for the handicapped near Phnom Penh. On 11th September 1999 the JRS East Timor Director, Fr Karl Albrecht was killed in Dili. Fr Dewanto a newly ordained priest was killed on September 6th in the massacre in Suai where he had been sent to help the Parish Priest to minister to thousands of people seeking refuge in the church.

These deaths were all griefs. But they also brought home sharply what is involved in refugee life. They were experienced as a call to share the life of refugees. They recalled the prolonged agony of life and the way in which so many refugees experience life as a slow process of dying. They recalled the precariousness of refugee life, where sickness, violence and war always threaten. They recalled finally the extraordinary courage by which many refugees contrive a generous life out of wholly inadequate materials.

Andrew Hamilton SJ, *History of JRS Asia Pacific*

Between 1980 and 1982, one million Guatemalans were displaced and 50,000 killed in a brutal war waged against the civilian population by the armed forces. It is estimated that 200,000 Guatemalans fled to Mexico.

Chapter Two

AMERICA

A s the Cold War ebbed, many of the liberation struggles in Latin America subsided, often without resolution of the fundamental problems that had given rise to them. For example, despite great loss of life during the 1980-91 civil war, the peace agreement in El Salvador addressed neither the land tenure issues nor the uneven distribution of power. Indigenous Guatemalans were given only shaky assurances to encourage them to return from Mexico. In Colombia new difficulties arose as a third force, the paramilitary, entered the conflict.

JRS' early experience in Latin America was among El Salvadorans dispersed throughout Central America. It also had an important program among Guatemalan refugees in Mexico, including a role in negotiations that enabled local settlement of some and the return of others. Today JRS is works with forcibly displaced people from Colombia and Haiti. The JRS programmes in Colombia show no sign of diminishing since the needs of people displaced within that country continue to grow. In neighbouring countries such as Venezuela, there are Colombian refugees, who call on the direct services of JRS on the ground and JRS intervention in policy formulation. Small JRS programmes have sprung up in other Latin American countries. In Dominican Republic, a sizeable program has been developed since the late 1990s due to the critical need of the Haitians who cross their joint border daily, driven by the harsh economic and political situation in their homeland.

The work of JRS in North America focuses on projects mainly related to detention of migrants, advocacy and the promotion of research and publication. It also supports JRS projects throughout the world through advocacy, fundraising efforts and the provision of personnel.

Throughout the Americas and the Caribbean there are massive migratory movements, generally northwards, motivated by poverty and the desire for a better life. These transmigrations are accompanied by violence and human suffering. In the Americas JRS has been caught between the demands of its mandate to serve the refugees and forcibly displaced, and the pastoral needs of migrants in general. The former, as one JRS worker has remarked, requires a 'bamboo' structure, while the latter demands a 'steel' structure. Fortunately the Jesuit Provincials of the two American continents, after careful study of the issue, have more recently decided on a common commitment to attend to the needs of migrant people.

This chapter offers an eye witness report of some of the major developments of JRS work throughout the American continent.

THE FIRST STEPS OF JRS IN CENTRAL AMERICA
Michael Campbell-Johnston SJ

As advisor for Social Justice to Fr Arrupe, Michael Campbell-Johnston was intimately involved in setting up JRS in 1980. He then went to Central America to set up JRS there in 1984, but was called to be Provincial of the British Jesuits from 1987 until 1993. He then returned to El Salvador in 1994 as Director of the Jesuit Development Service.

The first refugees from El Salvador began crossing the river Lempa into Honduras at the end of 1979. From the start the Honduran Government, which had not signed the Geneva Convention, merely "authorised" the presence of refugees on its soil, disclaiming any responsibility for them. They were thus placed under the direct protection of UNHCR.

The first regional JRS meeting for Central America and Mexico which I hosted in El Despertar, a parish house in El Salvador, took place in January 1986 and was attended by 17 Jesuits and a few lay volunteers. We spent two and a half days examining the refugee situation country by country, look- ing at some common problems (local church relations, volunteers, Jesuit training, communications, pastoral presence, etc.) and above all working out priorities for 1986.

The meeting was important for myself since it marked the end of what might be described as the experimental period of JRS Central America and Mexico and set out definite guidelines for the future. These were included in a general statement, not unlike the Chiang Mai one, that was signed by all present. They were then discussed by the Provincial and his consultors before being approved and set out in a definitive document entitled "Prioridades SJR: Centroamérica y México" which could be considered my job description and future agenda.

Five priorities were identified for the region with eight corresponding tasks:

"We saw that our work should be guided by the magis of the Spiritual Exercises: the same radical impulse of the Spirit which incarnated the Son among us when the Trinity contemplated our confused and suffering humanity. Consequently we say that our work in the camps of displaced and refugees should be profoundly involved and radically simple. But at the same time it should be capable of effectively changing structures, not only in the camp or area where we work, but also nationally and, if possible, beyond. Accordingly, it is not merely an involvement of simple presence and witness. However, given that our institutional apostolates tend to emphasize the structural work over and above the ministry of presence, 'we think it necessary to put special emphasis on being with' the refugees in order to better orient what we do for and with them. Otherwise efforts at structural change can become like 'clashing cymbals'."

The second regional meeting took place in January 1987, also in El Despertar. Jesuits and volunteers, representing six countries took part in the meeting. Dieter Scholz, then international director, from Rome, was unable to come due to last minute problems in the Sudan. The meeting followed much the same pattern as the year before, though no statement was issued and, instead of working out priorities, were more concerned with assessing how far we had fulfilled them. There was general optimism over the objective we had declared as our first priority for El Salvador: the setting up of a pastoral team with two Jesuits to work in one of the controlled zones of northern Chalatenango. After a frustrating year of discussions and delicate negotiations, it at last looked as if the Bishop had accepted the idea of sending Miguelito Vasquez and Jon Cortina to work in San José de las Flores and Arcatao. In view of changes in the Archdiocesan Social Secretariat, it was also decided to extend my own work with the displaced in El Salvador and put it on a more formal footing with the Archbishop.

There was much discussion too of the repatriation threat from the Salvadoran camps in Honduras; of our policy in relation to JRS volunteers in a situation where it was increasingly hard to get them in and, with the closure of the 'refugios', there are less opportunities for work; and finally of the need to develop more a spirituality of work among refugees and displaced people. All our deliberations were faithfully computerized by Chris Gjording and produced 50 pages of notes whose distribution, however, had to be severely limited for security reasons.

Let this life in you burst open

Seek first the reign of God, the realm of God,
The place where God resides, where God abides:
In the open places or in the field hidden,
The priceless jewel redeemed, the smallest seed
Sown, grown to great height. It spreads
Its sheltering branches upward to gladden
The hearts of all who seek its refuge. Good
Rises from root to branch to blossoming stem.
That fruitful tree seeded in you, seek first:
That space, that place, that realm, the soil of God
The holy ground within, wherein is come
Your God to dwell. Let this life in you burst
Open, let yourself become the very food
Of the feast you seek. Seek first the reign of God.

Sr Ann Manganaro

On June 6, 1993, Ann Manganaro, Sister of Loretto and paediatrician, passed away of cancer. She was 46. Ann lived in the community of Guarjila in El Salvador, a conflictive zone, during her five years of service with JRS. She was surrounded by but never surrendered to violence. When of her work of healing and training in El Salvador reached a natural conclusion, Ann volunteered to join the JRS team in Mozambique, but it was not to be[1].

---

[1] Taken from Ann Manganaro's journals, published on *Servir n.1*, November 1993.

JRS ACCOMPANIES THOSE RETURNING HOME[2]

When the Cold War era ended at the end of the 1980s, the Central American governments realized their common interest in ending the conflicts that affected El Salvador, Guatemala and Nicaragua and promoted regional peace negotiations. As a result, at various times and with the support of UNHCR, repatriation and reintegration operations took place so that refugees and displaced people could return to their homes, or in some cases, become integrated in the receiving society, as was the case for the Guatemalan refugees born in Mexico. JRS became Jesuit Development Service in El Salvador and is still present in Mexico, assisting the internally displaced from Chiapas.

The JRS work in El Salvador was divided into three types: a) Human presence with socio-pastoral and educational activities in the communities of Salvadorans who opted to return to their country from the camps in Honduras; b) Accompaniment of Salvadorans returning from Honduras; c) Emergency assistance in times of crisis, including protection, shelter and medical care for persons with gunshot injuries who would be arrested by the military if they went to a public hospital. Because of lack of safety for their personnel, the International Committee of the Red Cross suspended their services during the fighting and much of the work was carried out by the Archdiocese of San Salvador, Médicins Sans Frontières (MSF) and JRS.

From October 1987 to 1990, there were six massive repatriations of Salvadorans from Honduras. The refugees asked JRS both for accompaniment on their journey home and an ongoing presence in their communities upon returning to El Salvador. In 1990, this process continued with the return of other refugees from the Colomoncagua and San Antonio refugee camps.

JRS helped to design and directly support a coordinated social/pastoral plan by nine parishes in eastern El Salvador. The returned refugees arrived in this region, and most of the parishes had many displaced people living in them. The project was called COIDESAM (Inter-parish Coordination of the Diocese of San Miguel), and a JRS worker was the executive director. This pastoral work was always understood in a broad sense ("social/pas-

---

[2] Taken from JRS Central America/Mexico reports, 1990.

toral work" in the style of the Archdiocese of San Salvador), and included working in the fields of health, education, as well as the more directly "pastoral" activity of catechetical training, liturgy and music, and general support to the pastoral teams in the communities.

An extremely important service for displaced and returnee communities was the JRS centre "El Despertar", which was used to help shelter some of the thousands of people displaced by fighting, especially after the intense violence in the capital in November 1989. The demand for medical attention soared, so "El Despertar" was converted into a medical centre where people from the communities went and stayed while awaiting medical attention.

JRS was also directly involved in the preparations for the return of 1,200 Salvadoran refugees who had been in Panama for nine years.

JRS accepted the invitation of the refugees themselves to accompany the refugees back to their areas of origin from the refugee camps, and to work in some kind of pastoral capacity in the community. At the 1989 JRS meeting Segundo Montes SJ – killed later that year along with other seven persons on 16 November 1989 by the Salvadoran military – said "the future of this country is in organized communities such as these". The vast majority of people whom JRS tried to serve from 1987 to 1990 could not, technically speaking, be considered "refugees" in that they had returned to their homeland and were often in their own place of origin as well. El Salvador was always a priority in JRS work because of the ongoing war and great need involved, but also because of the political and religious space which the Church had carved out in its ministry to the displaced and refugees.

JRS Central America/Mexico,
Reflections by JRS volunteer workers, November 1990

97

The repatriation movement of Salvadoran refugees began five years before the peace accords were signed in January 1992

The repatriation of Salvadoran refugees from Honduras was largely completed before peace had returned to their homeland and despite the overt hostility of the authorities towards the returnees. For some observers the refugees' decision to return en masse to a country where they were not wanted was in fact a carefully calculated gesture of resistance to the incumbent regime. "They went home because they believed that the moment had come when, as organized communities in El Salvador, they could contribute to the political struggle against the government and military" (Weiss-Fagen and J.Eldrige, "Salvadoran repatriation from Honduras"). However, as Peter O'Driscoll the JRS Country Director at the time suggests, the reasons for return at this time may not have been so black and white: "It was also an acknowledgement that something had to give, that refugee camps were no place to raise children, and that sometimes even the risk of violence beats the slow despair of life in the camps... I think it is unfair to the people of those communities to suggest that their repatriation was just a political or logistical decision in the context of the civil conflict[3]."

[3] Peter O'Driscoll, July 2005.

98

Repatriation to El Salvador and the Peace Accords in 1992

Peter O'Driscoll

Peter O'Driscoll worked in El Salvador between 1987 and 1994. He replaced Dick Howard as Country Director there. The repatriation movement of Salvadorans began five years before the peace accords were signed in January 1992. In March 1994, JRS El Salvador handed over the programmes to the local Provincial of the Society and Jesuit Development Service.

I joined JRS El Salvador in 1987. Dick Howard SJ had just taken over from Michael Campbell Johnston SJ, who had founded JRS Salvador in 1984. For those first three years (1984-87) JRS had served a network of resettlement communities – places where internally displaced people (IDPs) who could not return to their areas of origin due to conflict had voluntarily resettled to get out of church-run refugee camps. JRS provided pastoral support and small community development grants, and supported a small group of volunteers in country and a few others scattered through UN-run Salvadoran refugee camps in Honduras. I arrived to join the team of 6 foreign volunteers living in the Calle Real refugee camp run by the Archdiocese of San Salvador. JRS was a free-wheeling, faith-driven group with a deep commitment to accompaniment and almost zero infrastructure for supporting volunteers. No formal orientation, no stipends or health insurance, just good committed friends!

JRS experience in El Salvador was based in two related but very different phenomena – attention to IDPs and service to returning refugees. When JRS officially began work in Salvador in 1984, the first waves of internally displaced people were being assisted by the Archdiocese to leave the churches and other makeshift camps many had occupied since being driven from their homes in 1980, to areas that were not their areas of origin, but were lands purchased by the church in non-conflictive areas to enable them to make a new start. JRS attention to these communities involved bi-weekly pastoral visits to about 10-15 such communities, and small-scale financial assistance at both individual and community level. This attention continued until 1992-93, but was increasingly questioned towards the end, especially with the end of the conflict in late 1991, on the grounds that such communities should be integrated into local parish and diocesan structures, rather than given special attention from an external entity. The challenges involved in integration often had to do with mutual distrust between internally displaced people and their new neighbours, usually rooted in the same passions, prejudices and ideologies that fuelled the war.

However, it should be noted that JRS' staff, budget and public profile grew dramatically in 1987 with the first repatriation of "refugees" who had crossed into Honduras in 1980-81 and began to return in 1987. The context was the signature of the "Esquipulas II Peace Plan" that year (which won a Nobel Peace Prize for Oscar Arias), which, among other things, recognized the right of refugees across Central America to return to their areas of origin, implicitly even if these areas were still conflictive. Refugees seized on this treaty, and began to return in organized groups within two months of its signature. Remembering the slaughter of civilians in these areas by the Salvadoran government's military in 1979-84, they specifically requested international accompaniment of the returns as a deterrent to human rights abuses. JRS was among a relatively small group of agencies willing to place volunteers in potentially hazardous, conflictive situations, and as a result, developed a core of 10-15 foreign volunteers from eight countries who lived and worked in these communities from 1987-91 (some stayed long after the war ended). While these volunteers were engaged in education, healthcare, pastoral work and small-scale development projects, their main purpose was faith-based accompaniment in defence of the civilian population's right to stay in their areas of origin, free from indiscriminate "scorched earth" depopulation campaigns and harassment from the military on the basis of their perceived support for the political and military opposition.

Our experience in Central America of *acompañamiento* gave new meaning to our mission "to accompany" the forcibly displaced. When North Americans volunteered to live with communities of refugees in El Salvador, local armies knew that if they used USA supplied M16s to kill American citizens, military aid and external political support for the dictatorship would dry up. Just by being there, one could protect human rights.

Mark Raper SJ, *To Build Peace and Bring Hope*, 2005

In thinking ahead to new repopulations, one must remember that the root causes of refugee flight – be they economic, political, ethnic, or natural disaster – have rarely disappeared when they return. In opting for faith-based accompaniment in recognition of the rights of refugees, JRS and others must be very careful to maintain appropriate distinctions between the causes of the displacement and the rights of the returnees. If JRS work is seen to be identified with political or ethnic projects, it is quickly delegitimised and can bring additional risks to the refugees themselves, as well as JRS staff.[4]

The major developments for JRS in my seven years there were:

a) The repatriation movement of Salvadorans. They came back in several waves beginning in September 1987 through mid-1991, and changed the profile of JRS by explicitly asking for foreign accompaniment as a deterrent to the human rights abuses that had driven them out of the country in the early 1980s. JRS responded by increasing recruitment of volunteers, developing more defined program areas for pastoral training, support for education and health care in the newly resettled communities, and increasing the budget of development project funding to respond to greater needs for income generation and infrastructure in communities that had been flattened by the conflict and were starting again from scratch.

b) The signing of the Salvadoran peace accords in January 1992. This fundamentally challenged the notion of JRS as a "refugee" service, given that we were now serving resettled Salvadorans and the focus was on democratic participation, integration of community services in health and education back into the national ministry system, conflict resolution etc – but no longer service to refugees. I took over as director of JRS Salvador the day the accords were signed, and very soon entered conversations with the local provincial to explore the possibility of "handing off" the JRS program to the Province as a local development NGO. We successfully completed this process in March 1994 with the legal incorporation of the "Servicio Jesuita para el Desarrollo", a program devoted to participatory community development programmes in two key regions of resettled refugees (Chalatenango and Usulutan), staffed by Salvadorans and Jesuit scholastics.

[4] Peter O'Driscoll, comments to *JRS experience in dealing with repatriation*, August 2000.

101

Despite the brutality of the war, hope came from the courage, conviction and spirit of the refugee communities we accompanied, and their determination to rebuild their communities in the face of intimidation and even death.

Responding to repatriation forced JRS to professionalize its attention to volunteers (contracts, stipends, insurance, orientation, volunteer coordinator position etc), and to formalize our program work into training and advocacy related to: education in resettled communities (approximately five volunteers in five communities, but with regional training focus); health care (three volunteers in three communities, but training promoters from around the region); formation of pastoral leaders (four volunteers working with resettled communities across the country); and project funding (two staff working with up to 20 communities). The focus was on empowerment of local people.

Michael Campbell-Johnston returned to Salvador in 1994 to take over Jesuit Development Service from me, and prospects looked good. I understand that the organisation continued to function for several years thereafter. The saddest development came when macroeconomic forces drove most young and able-bodied people from the resettled communities and sent them to work as undocumented migrants in the USA. Communities that were flourishing in 1994 were again almost deserted by 2004.

In 1992 JRS experienced a phase of consolidation, looking towards the end of 1993 as a time for closing down the JRS in El Salvador. A Jesuit Council, composed of members of the Jesuit Province of Central America, was formed to evaluate and make recommendations about what aspects of JRS' work the province would eventually choose to assimilate.

From February 1993, the Province of Central America assumed the whole responsibility of the activities of JRS, linking its implementation to the programmes developed by *Fe y Alegría*, a Jesuit organisation working in the field of education and development matters. There was a transitional period until February 1993, in which a Commission was formed so as to study the working planning, prepare the changes, inform about these changes to the counterparts and other tasks.

From the point of view of the personnel, the local personnel did not change after the new structure was settled. The expatriate volunteers stayed as personnel that JRS offered to the newly established entity and the JRS continued being responsible for the economic commitments, such as insurance matters.

A contact person was named by the Province so as to monitor and inform the JRS about the development of the events related to refugees and displaced in Central America. This function was independent from the new entity established in El Salvador.

Mark Raper SJ, *Servir n.1*, November 1993

AFTER THE REFUGEE CRISIS...
A TIME OF DEVELOPMENT IN CENTRAL AMERICA

Michael Campbell-Johnston SJ [5]

In 1992, JRS personnel supporting displaced Salvadorans faced an enviable dilemma. Once the Peace Accords were signed, suddenly there were no refugees. Salvadorans abroad, in Honduras and elsewhere, were free to return home. So were the internally displaced, many already on the road back to their places of origin.

So should JRS in Central America disband, or should a transition begin toward a new entity, one focusing on resettlement and human development? As founder of JRS in the region I had a special stake in the decision. Largely because of the excellent work of Peter O'Driscoll, the choice was made.

To determine the future of JRS in El Salvador, a special assessment committee was set up. Three Jesuits and the JRS director wrestled with the problems for six months and came up with three recommendations:
  • Our involvement with recently returned refugees and displaced persons should continue in health, education, socio-economic development, pastoral work and youth work.
  • The body succeeding JRS should be integrated into the Central American Jesuit Province as a regular apostolic work.
  • JRS should change its name in the region to the Jesuit Development Service (JDS).

The first round of changes was accepted and implemented.

But soon it became obvious that more decisions were needed. In the first place our personnel were too thinly spread to have much effect. More broadly, the end of the war saw flooding into the country numerous agencies and vast sums of money. Ambitious projects spawned everywhere. The majority of these arose from outside and from above, and paid little attention to the

---

[5] Taken from *Servir n.5*, August 1995.

real needs of the people. The newly arrived agencies scarcely involved the locals in any decision-making. In the event projects often collapsed, leaving bitterness and disillusionment. One contributing factor was widespread corruption. Another was the break-up of many communities once external pressures of war were removed.

As any agency knows, or should know, this was precisely the way not to promote development. Genuine development can only take place with the full participation of those concerned – from the outset and at every stage. Taking a cue from our confreres in Nicaragua, our fledgling JDS team decided to streamline itself and restructure its approach. Our aim was to try for development that is "integral, local and from the bottom-up". I became involved in putting together a document setting out this 'new' approach, explaining its objectives, methodology and immediate strategies.

The main innovation we proposed – one that required careful explanation and delicate negotiations with our funding agencies – was to abandon projects in favour of a long discernment process. The first step would be house-to-house visits and small meetings, to win the confidence of every member of the community and involve every member, not just the recognised or appointed leaders.

We proposed that several months later the process should end in an "Autodiagnostico Comunitario Participativo", a community self-analysis in which all could take part. Once the main needs and problems of the community had been expressed, all could genuinely own the process. Only then would it be time to talk of projects. And in these, too, the talking, planning and execution were to be the work of the people themselves in the light of their own diagnosis. Moreover, projects were to be financed by a rotating loans system, not by grants.

Our new approach meant phasing out the more dispersed work we had been doing in other parts of the country. Farewelling our transition team as they gradually bowed out was a painful experience. Many have had long records of service with JRS. They include two Americans, two Germans, two Spaniards, an Australian and a Guatemalan, along with our Salvadoran driver and Peter O'Driscoll himself.

Mark Raper SJ/JRS

Refugee from Guatemala in Mexico

THE GUATEMALAN EXILE AND REPATRIATION. JRS IN MEXICO BETWEEN 1991 AND 1997

Between 1980 and 1982, one million Guatemalans were displaced and 50,000 killed in a brutal war waged against the civilian population by the armed forces. It is estimated that 200,000 Guatemalans fled to Mexico, although only 46,000 lived in the camps under the protection of UNHCR. For ten years they lived on food donation or by farming small plots lent by the Mexican government.

JRS began its work in 1991 offering pastoral care for the 12,000 refugees in the camps in Campeche, Mexico. Programmes were initiated for the children and youth and for pastoral care in the broadest sense. The program of information and human rights covered all camps in Chiapas, Quintana Roo and Campeche.

The human rights team travelled hundreds of miles weekly giving workshops that helped refugees to know their rights according to international norms and social justice. Human Rights promoters were trained and peoples' associations were formed to continue this work on their return.[6]

JRS Activities in Mexico[7] focused on:
- Information: JRS Mexico informed refugees about the conditions of return to Guatemala in order to facilitate their decision-making in a freer and more conscious way. This was done through the drafting of a bimonthly bulletin.
- Promotion of human rights/Legal advice: This helped some groups of refugees to decide to return to Guatemala. JRS felt that the refugees needed information on Human Rights. Legal advice was also given so as to prevent refugees from abuses of the Mexican migration authorities, as well as to prevent illegal land trade.
- Workshops were held for groups of returnees on the situation in Guatemala, the peace process, the meaning of the peace accords and

---

[6] JRS Mexico, *Servir n.1*, November 1993.
[7] From 1997 JRS Mexico report and notes from Pedro Arriaga SJ, March 1998.

conditions of return. It also included workshops on the rights of women and the rights of the child, as well as pastoral workshops.

In 1995, the uncertainty of political life in Guatemala meant that the date for returns kept on being postponed. JRS teams feared that international attention for the refugee population in Mexico at risk was waning. They called international community to participate more fully in repatriation and solidarity to be extended until the last return.

The difficulties of return in 1997 were especially due to the Guatemalan government's objection to the massive return of refugees. The Guatemalan authorities blocked the organisation of these returns and from December 1997 only the so called "repatriations of isolated families" were authorised.

When massive returns were organised, JRS considered whether they respected the conditions of dignity, security and voluntariness. They were supported both by the governments of Mexico and Guatemala.

JRS Mexico ended its work with Guatemalan refugees in December 1997 but the office remained open until February 1998 in order to wind things up administratively. JRS Mexico had been officially designated by the bishop as the Catholic outreach to the refugee camps.

The Mexican government announced in November 1997 a push to move Guatemalan refugees from Chiapas to the camps in Campeche and Quintana Roo. This was because of security concerns in the sensitive and conflictive state of Chiapas.

First phase of the return process to Guatemala, 1997

Jennifer Bailey, seconded to JRS by Human Rights Watch, wrote the following in 1998: 'An agreement was signed on September 17, 1997 finalising the first stage of the return process for any refugees who wanted to return to Guatemala under the terms of the 1992 refugee accords. The deadline for registration was December 29, 1997. This agreement signified a new phase of resettlement and reintegration.

By 1998, about 30,000 Guatemalan refugees remained in Mexico. Those who decided to stay in Mexico would have their refugee status revoked and be allowed to register for immigrant visas, thereby opening the doors to land ownership, loans and credit programmes, public education, and temporary visits outside of Mexico. Thousands of refugees chose this option.

The biggest resettlement issues were, not surprisingly, land and credit. The September 1997 agreement included guarantees to continue to negotiate around issues of legal land security; several different returned communities alleged that they were given disparate treatment by the government in terms of credit plans and size and quality of land parcels. The September 1997 accord also reiterated the 1992 agreement that stipulated that the land each family was given should have been of a quality, productive capacity and location that permitted a dignified family life and the possibility of repaying the credits obtained[8].'

Return to Guatemala

Brad Reynolds

---

[8] *JRS Experience in dealing with Repatriation*, 1999.

THE COLOMBIAN CRISIS AND JRS RESPONSE

Carlos Esteban Mejía

Carlos Esteban helped to set up the JRS programmes in Colombia in the early nineties, where he worked until 1997. From 1995 he coordinated the Latin America region as well. In 2000, during the Kosovo crisis, he joined JRS teams in Albania and was later appointed Associate Regional Director in South East Europe. In 2003 he also served as Assistant to the International Director in Rome.

In 1993 Michael Campbell-Johnston SJ visited Colombia to assess the situation of displaced people there. In 1994, after this visit, Josep Sugrañes SJ came to Colombia to explore the humanitarian crisis in the country as a result of 40 long years of violence and poverty. These two visits involved many in-depth interviews with Jesuits, lay people involved in Jesuit social work and members of Colombian society and the church. Both of them dedicated time and reflection to understanding the complexity and scope of the conflict and its humanitarian effects. At that time, Josep was Associate Director of JRS, to then International Director Mark Raper.

In Latin America, JRS was already involved in assisting Guatemalan refugees in Campeche and Quintana Roo, Mexico. JRS work in El Salvador had been transformed into a development service to people in the aftermath of the war.

On 12 September 1994, the provincial of Colombia, Fr Jose Adolfo Gonzalez SJ organised a meeting with 35 Jesuits. Among them were the directors of CINEP, the Program for Peace, IMCA, the parishes of Tierralta-Cordoba and San Pablo-Bolivar, the Pastoral Delegation of San Pedro Claver of Barrancabermeja, the rector of the Javeriana University of Bogotá, and many others. I was also invited, given that I had accompanied Josep on many of his visits and Interviews. At this meeting, Josep gave a report to the provincial on how he saw the role of JRS in responding to the Colombian crisis.

Given the scale of that crisis and the suffering many men and women were facing, Josep recommended initiating a JRS presence, not as a new work, but as a presence of the Society of Jesus using the existing resources with the support of social and intellectual works of the Colombian province.

110

The provincial approved this proposal and he announced that I should be the one to develop a working strategy for JRS.

After this meeting, the provincial asked me to maintain a direct dialogue with his assistant in the pastoral and social area, Fr Horacio Arango SJ, who was always open to giving advice on how to shape an initial strategic plan.

For several months I focused on understanding the problem of displacement, visiting different areas of the country and meeting church people, government workers, NGOs and displaced communities. I got a clearer picture of the situation and drafted a text which was the basis for the next step of the work of JRS Colombia.

I then drafted the first proposal of action and shared it with 32 other Jesuits, among whom were Josep Sugrañes and the JRS contact person for Peru. It was decided that the next step should be to set up a presence in one of the regions affected by conflict and where the Province was already working. It was also agreed that a director and a Jesuit scholastic should be named, and together they should work on a plan of action for the province selected. The meeting established the kind of person needed and the provincial was the one to find him.

We decided to work in the province of Magdalena Medio because it was one of the regions most affected and also because there was a long-established Jesuit presence. It was agreed that the people chosen should live in the pastoral delegation of San Pedro Claver, a marginalised area of the city, with a strong component of political violence and the presence of displaced people from all over the Magdalena Medio region. I moved to the region and four months later Dionisio Rojas SJ arrived.

We first offered our help to support the work of the local church. Bishop Jaime Prieto welcomed us and gave us a space to work in coordination with his Justice and Peace team.

We took on the responsibility of working for the displaced people on behalf of the local church. We visited all the parishes in the diocese, spoke to all the parish priests and met grass roots organisations, displaced communities and international organisations. We sent a report to Fr Francisco De Roux SJ who was director of the Development and Peace programme in Magdalena Medio and was also shaping its involvement in the region.

At this time we responded to the plight of displaced people in different ways, such as organising camps to shelter and protect the population or by participating in inter-institutional commissions.

Dionisio finished his apostolic time and started his theology studies. He, in turn, was replaced by Cesar Casas SJ, who brought a fresh and dynamic energy. We opened a space and extended our house to receive volunteers. We both decided to expand the team and thus hired our first lay worker, Ledys Bohorquez, a woman from the region who gave much life to the work.

Mauricio Garcia SJ was chosen as the national director of JRS and from Bogotá he supported the regional team with administration and fund-raising activities. He had an important role in planning and helping us to deepen our analysis of a changing situation.

In 1995 we had our first JRS Latin America regional meeting in Campeche, Mexico, with the warm welcome of Vladimiro Valdes SJ and his amazing team of volunteers. I was chosen as the first coordinator for Latin America. My role, once again was to shape the vision and plan of action for the region. In 1997 the time came for me to leave JRS. At that time, Jorge Serrano SJ was coming back from Brazil. After a conversation with him and with his agreement, I proposed his name as my successor to the new provincial, Horacio Arango SJ, who accepted. We both went to Barrancabermeja. This period was a real gift for me.

Internally Displaced in Peru, 1993

Josep Sugrañes SJ/JRS

As Director of the Operation in Kosovo, Associate Regional Director in South East Europe, and Assistant to the International Director, I have had the opportunity to follow the inspiration of Ignatius and Arrupe in favor of the weakest of our history.

The principal cause of forced displacements in Colombia is the internal war which involves several armed factions: the Revolutionary Armed Forces of Colombia (FARC), the National Liberation Army (ELN), the Colombian self-defence units (AUC) and the National Army (EN). One of the factors that helps keep the conflict ignited is the illegal cultivation of cocaine and the national government's handling of the eradication of these illicit crops by means of fumigation. Conflicting interests converge in the struggle for control of rural areas where these illicit crops are a rich source of financial gain.

In this violent scenario, the implementation of "Plan Colombia", the Regional Andean Initiative and the subsequent militarization of the border zones respond to geopolitical and economic interests, mainly of the United States. On the one hand, the double war on drugs and terrorism become the crux of the United State's actions in Colombia, based on the premise that both are threats for national security. Besides material destruction, military operations cause fear in the population, and fear sparks the exodus of people who become displaced people.

On the other hand, some people are convinced that there are connections between forced displacement and economic expansion, between displaced people and so-called "mega projects" in Colombia. In a sense, displacement of persons is perceived not only as a consequence of the drug war, but war itself is seen as a means to displace people and open spaces for vast economic interests.

In the last decade, the armed conflict in Colombia has displaced, on average, between 300 and 350 thousand people per year.

JRS Latin America Strategy, 2005

JRS Colombia between 1997 and 2002. Setting up base at Barrancabermeja

Jorge Eduardo Serrano SJ

In 1997 Carlos Esteban Mejía moves on and is replaced by Jorge Serrano as director of JRS Colombia until 2002. In those years the conflict had already generated more than three million internally displaced people.

In June 1997, I left the parish of San Pablo where I was working and re-placed Carlos Esteban Mejía as JRS director in Colombia. At this time, the team in Barrancabermeja was formulating its first three-year plan 1998-2000. In 1997 Mauricio Garcia, national director, had received some funds for a 12-month plan.

In August 1996, the population of Cimitarra River, in Antioquia, had fled due to bombings by the Armed Forces and were displaced in Barrancaber-meja, living in shelters. JRS accompanied these people and also the dis-placed communities in Yondo.

The team was then formed by Carlos Mejía, Cesar Casas SJ and Ledis Bohorquez who had coordinated the communications office of the diocese. In Bogota, the work was supported by Dionisio Rojas SJ and Jorge Castro SJ.

The work developed by the humanitarian organisations in Colombia was emergency assistance (food, shelter, medical aid), return to their villages (reconstruction and first aid) and alert campaigns to evacuate people from the areas of high risk. This was deeply rooted in the methodology of work of emergency assistance and relief organizations, so even after law 387 was passed in 1997 (see below), the main partners with JRS were the local and national organizations which usually worked with victims of natural dis-asters.

JRS Colombia was welcomed. In 1997 as it was the only international or-ganisation in Barrancabermeja with experience of accompanying, serving and defending the rights of displaced people which offered a different meth-odology of work.

JRS chose Barrancabermeja because it was one of the areas with a large number of displaced populations, and it was identified as an area where the conflict would intensify. The Society of Jesus had an important presence through the delegation. So in 1997 the humanitarian aid team was established and during the first semester the JRS Colombia action guidelines were drafted. The methodology of "Plan de reconstrucción integral del proyecto de vida" (PRIPROVI) was adopted.

There were several events which I can highlight from my time in JRS Colombia between 1997 and 2002:

- Law 387 was drafted in 1997 to protect the life, dignity and property of internally displaced people.
- The exodus of some 10,000 "campesinos" towards Barrancabermeja between June and October 1998.
- The paramilitary attacks in the centre of Valle del Cauca, in 1999.
- The situation suffered by the communities of internally displaced people in the Tierralta, Cordoba region, abandoned after 1999.
- The lack of response of international and national organisations to the mid and long term problems of the displaced people. JRS believed that these populations were abandoned to the control of groups which managed the official government aid. This happened from 1998 until 2002.
- The massacre in one of the areas with the highest number of displaced people in May 1999.
- The paramilitary invasion of Barrancabermeja town in 2000.

In our work we often faced dilemmas, such as how to maintain our option to assist Internally Displaced People (IDPs) together with other institutions while at the same time being free to denounce the complicity of the government in displacement and lack of assistance to IDPs. Another dilemma was how to keep close to the people while being able to guarantee the security of JRS teams.

Not all were challenges, and we did experience signs of hope too. After some time, several of the people and communities we had accompanied since 1998 were able to get from the government what they needed (education, technical skills, financial help for a new house or to set up a small business). We also saw how the role of the diocesan church in Barrancabermeja and other dioceses grew in provision of services to displaced people, as well as several organisations of displaced communities which continued the process of rehabilitation.

Some creative initiatives were developed, such as a virtual legal counselling which JRS organised in 1999 together with the Javeriana University to assist internally displaced people. That same year, JRS drafted security guidelines for the staff. The prevention programme for children and youth was shaped so as to promote peace education among young populations at risk of armed recruitment.

In 2000 and 2001 new teams were set up in Tierralta, Buga and San Pablo. In 2002 the bishop decided not to renew the agreement with JRS Colombia so we moved out from the curia. The national office is still in Barrancabermeja and the team has grown and become more professional, with different people coming from different sectors such as psychologists, lawyers, journalists, social workers or agronomists. The work with internally displaced people continues at different levels.

Jenny Cafiso/JRS

Internally displaced girl in Colombia

Closure of projects

A question we had to discern many times was when does a refugee situation stop being a refugee situation and when can JRS go. The conflicts which caused the displacement of refugees we worked with continued to rage on for years, like in Sudan, Angola, Liberia, Burundi, Congo, Sri Lanka or Colombia. And even when peace agreements were signed, the conflicts were officially declared over and the government and the UN develop a timeline for the repatriation of the refugees, the options were never that clear or simple.

Most refugees long to go home, even if by our standards home does not have much to offer. Life of a refugee is hard not only because of the physical hardships, but also for the exclusion experienced and for the lack of future prospective. A community I visited in Colombia chose to return to their home which they had had to flee when they were bombed, despite the fact that it had been burned to the ground. The community was called La Felicidad – happiness – a name that seemed incongruous with the reality, but the people said that they were indeed happy to go back. Return is the preferred option, yet refugees are often reluctant to go back to their own country unless they are sure that it is safe to do so and that the basic requirements for living are there, such as land, a place to live, and school for the children.

Upon return JRS stays with the refugees for a period of time to help rebuild their lives, before leaving. This decision is made after much deliberation, thinking, discussion with many people and institutions and weighing of the options. While the refugees may be back home, it takes time to reestablish themselves. They go back to an already poor country, which has been further ravaged by war, with limited resources and support.

The decision to leave a refugee situation is made easier for JRS if the work will be continued by the local Jesuit province as was the case in Cambodia and El Salvador, or continued by the local Church, or by a local NGO.

Jenny Cafiso, former JRS Programmes Officer

Haitians in the Dominican Republic. The JRS response

José (Chepe) Núñez SJ

Chepe has been director of JRS Dominican Republic since the early 90's, working with Haitian refugees. In 2000 he was appointed Regional Director for Latin America and the Caribbean (LAC)

In 1992 following the *coup d'etat* led by Aristide in Haiti the number of Haitian refugees who fled to Dominican Republic rose enormously. Josep Sugrañes and Michael Campbell-Johnston visited the Dominican Republic and decided to set up JRS. The work with displaced Haitians began both in Santo Domingo and in the border.

Haiti has a situation of extreme poverty and strong political tensions. Since Jean Bertrand Aristide's government was installed in November, 2000, the opposition has constantly questioned the electoral process and accused the Haitian President of repeated human rights violations. As a result, the number of Haitian nationals arriving in the Dominican Republic seeking international protection has increased. Among these refugees, some has media connections and some were politicians with a certain status in their communities and could possibly run for municipal or congressional posts. Haitians who live in the Dominican Republic often suffer deportation to Haiti, even if they have documents that prove their Dominican citizenship. The police and the army periodically carry out raids, arresting Haitians regardless of having proper documentation or not. Each year, it is estimated that between 12,000 and 16,000 Haitians are deported from the Dominican Republic to Haiti.

JRS Latin America strategy, 2005

At that same time, the Society of Jesus had decided in its General Congregation 33 to work in favour of the Haitians. In those years I was studying in Paris, but my time there had almost finished so I was appointed to start JRS in Dominican Republic. I was familiar with the work since in the eighties I had been working with the sugar cane cutters in the *bateyes*.

In 2000 I was appointed regional director for Latin America. This was a difficult year for Colombia, since President Uribe's political decisions exacerbated the conflict. Forced displacement increased both inside Colombia but also towards neighbouring countries. Due to the new situation, JRS expanded its projects to Ecuador, Panama and Venezuela, and later on to Costa Rica and Brazil. Meanwhile, the projects in Chiapas, Mexico, continued to assist the indigenous displaced people.

In 2001, a long term strategy was drafted by JRS LAC, which would set the working priorities for the following 10 years. Unfortunately, JRS teams foresee that population movements will continue at least during these years due to the conflicts in Colombia and Haiti.

For me, the most touching part of Fr Arrupe's mission is to care for and welcome the refugee as an individual, not as a massive group of people. The JRS mission focuses on the individual, with his sufferings and joys. This vision will always be a valid one because it helps discovering the dignity of the human being, despite its fragility due to war and discrimination.

Another aspect I feel is very much specific to JRS is that we are not researchers but we accompany displaced people and it is actually from this presence that we are able to understand the causes of their situation. So by being close to people we understand the context where we work.

I always think of the way refugees look: their eyes carry the cross, with its bitterness, suffering and uprootedness. It is a nostalgic way of looking. But it also reflects hope and the desire to continue with their lives. Refugees do not choose to stay in the dark, they try hard to rebuild their lives. This reminds me that there is a gift hidden in the cross.

Background to the Chiapas conflict

Fighting began in early 1994 between the Mexican Federal Army and the Zapatista Army of National Liberation (ELZN). The succeeding counter-insurgent strategies implemented by the Federal Army, the police and paramilitaries have forced thousands of indigenous people to be displaced from their original communities.

Since the armed conflict in Chiapas began, the displaced population has suffered innumerable aggressions, food shortages and human rights violations ranging from death threats to massive assassinations, such as the one at Acteal in 1997.

Peace negotiations between the Mexican government and the EZLN have stagnated, so the population continues to suffer systematic human rights violations and deplorable living conditions, particularly in the autonomous municipalities under the control of the Zapatistas. They also find themselves under constant threat from the Federal Army that maintains military bases throughout the region and from paramilitary forces that still operate in some areas of the state.

While the low intensity war continues, JRS provides alternative health practices, spiritual support and agricultural training.

JRS Latin America and the Caribbean (LAC) strategy, 2005

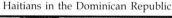

Haitians in the Dominican Republic

Jenny Cafiso/JRS

THE BEGINNINGS OF JRS USA, 1983

Frank Moan SJ

In 1983 Frank Moan was appointed JRS Country Director in the USA. In 1987 he moved on and in 1988 Si Smith, who was back from Africa, got involved with JRS USA.

I returned to my work at the Georgetown University Law Centre at the end of August 1982, after spending two months in Ban Vinai refugee camp, in Thailand.

During that school year I heard that the USA Jesuit Assistancy was going to open an office for JRS. I was very interested in that and wrote to my Provincial, Joseph Whelan SJ, and asked him to put in a good word for me with the president of the USA Jesuit Conference. He did so; I was interviewed by John O'Callaghan SJ, President of the Jesuit Conference, and offered the job of Director of JRS USA, beginning in early September, 1983.

So I was given an office at the USA Jesuit Conference in Washington DC. It was empty. I had to get the furniture and any other provisions I needed for the job.

The mandate of the office, as I understood it at the time, was to raise the awareness of Jesuits and Jesuit institutions in the USA to the plight of refugees, to enlist the volunteer services of Jesuits, other religious and lay people into the work of JRS worldwide, and to do whatever else I could to enlighten people in the USA about refugees. First I began a newsletter, *The Mustard Seed*, as a way of promoting contact with other Jesuits, Jesuit institutions, and friends. It was also a source of fund-raising.

The response of Jesuits and Jesuit institutions in the USA was very positive. A number of Jesuits, through my office, were assisted in finding positions in refugee camps; a number of Jesuit schools invited me to speak on their campuses or to provide them with information about refugees. I believe many have continued their interest.

The Director in Rome at that time was Dieter Scholz SJ. Over a period of time we worked out what our relationship was to one another and then to other Directors as JRS developed around the world. But at that time I believe there were only the office in Rome and the office in Washington DC. A year or two later, Michael Campbell-Johnston SJ, became the first director of JRS Central America.

In these initial years I attended some major meetings of JRS in Thailand and Manila.

I remained as Director of JRS USA for four years. I then founded another organisation, *Refugee Voices*, to continue the work of educating Americans about the plight of refugees. By the time I left JRS, it was well on its way to becoming the international organisation that it is today. I must admit that when I read *Dispatches*, I am amazed at the expansive growth of JRS and of the number of people who are involved in it.

DEFENDING THE RIGHTS OF REFUGEES IN CANADA
Jack Costello SJ

Jack Costello joined JRS in Thailand in 1981. In 1992, he again joined JRS in Canada. Since 1997 he has been the contact person for JRS in Toronto.

I ran into JRS for the first time during my tertianship in February 1981 when I came to Thailand in order to spend time working with Catholic Relief Services (USA) in Khao I Dang, a large refugee camp at Aranyaprathet near the Cambodian border. I immediately met Pierre Ceyrac SJ in Bangkok, and only at that moment did I realize Fr Arrupe had created JRS!

A lot of years passed for me in teaching and administration before I began to work with refugees again; it was 1992 and this time it was in Toronto. It was only in 1997 that I formally took on the role of contact person for JRS in our Province.

JRS in Canada has had much active service over the past 20 years – first in Montreal through André Lamothe SJ and Louis-Joseph Goulet SJ with Cambodian refugees and Vietnamese boat people. JRS work in Toronto has been situated for many years in our Jesuit Centre for Social Faith and Justice. Under the leadership of Colin MacAdam, Ezat Mossalanejad, and Ted Hyland in the 1980s and 90s, JRS in English-speaking Canada concentrated on solid research, gathered crucial documentation, and networked with other refugee-service agencies in areas of advocacy and influencing Canadian policy. They began a quarterly publication called *Refugee Update* which brought the latest data, analysis and reflection on international and Canadian refugee issues to people working in the trenches and to decision-makers. It continues to this day.

This group was joined for two years by Gordon Rixon SJ who focussed on spiritual support for refugee workers through weekend retreats and days of reflection on themes of migration. Richard Soo SJ became a lawyer, and as part of the JRS team concentrated on refugee and human rights in Latin America as well as settlement and doing individual cases for claimants.

In 1997 the Jesuit Centre closed for two years at a time of financial crisis. JRS stayed alive but had far more modest outreach. It always kept its ecumenical role vital in those years. The Jesuit Centre is alive again and the JRS work continues, but in somewhat different directions.

The current involvements of JRS in Toronto include active membership in the Canadian Council of Refugees and the Sanctuary Coalition, and related advocacy and action groups.

The tightening of borders is, of course, very familiar to JRS representatives in Australia, Europe, and the United States. Canada is riding on the coattails of this exclusionary trend. JRS Canada tries to be vigilant and responsive in the face of government and police appeals to *national security* that result in blatant abuse of refugee claimants.

The unaccountability in the public forum of national police services (especially since September 2001 events transformed *terrorism* into an alleged pandemic), is a dark fact in the western democracies at this time, and a JRS concern. The Canadian JRS shares the JRS International's concern about detention as a world-wide abuse. A less well known side-issue related to detention is interdiction. They form the book-ends of a growing policy of *exclusion*, the very opposite of the *welcoming of the stranger* that is at the heart of our faith and part of earlier practice in Canada.

Our Canadian collaboration with JRS Colombia in bringing members of their senior staff to Toronto to learn English has been a very rewarding activity over the past few years.

One of my main and happiest involvements as JRS contact person is with Romero House, a settlement community in Toronto where my work, from its beginnings 15 years ago, includes being a board member, chaplain for liturgies and companion, as well as coordinator of the week-long summer camp for our refugees – a success story that has just completed its 14th annual session this summer. Catholic in origin and identity, Romero House is inter-faith and totally undiscriminating in its outreach and welcome.

Romero House has been responsible for bringing a Canadian neighbourhood together in friendship and in shared service of our refugee newcomers. When we organized our nineteen-person pilgrimage to El Salvador for the 25th anniversary of Archbishop Romero's death this Spring, some six or seven people who were part of the journey were neighbourhood residents and friends and new staff members who had been caught up by the spiritual enthusiasm for honouring our patron and deepening our learning and our spirit. Romero House has been honoured by the Canadian Government by being called a *best practice* experiment in Canada for both receiving refugees and for creating neighbourhood community in which the refugees give as well as receive in their new country.

What shall the future of JRS in Canada bring? The decrease in claimants at our border with the US has resulted in an increase in the numbers of people in Canada being served with deportation dates. We see the intersection of issues of justice and of spirit here. Can the spirit of inclusion and of hospitality be resuscitated in Canada? Can suffering people be offered not suspicion but compassion and acceptance? Can we truly *accompany, serve and advocate* as current conditions require – and our modest capacities allow? These rather eternal questions are still very current ones. We want to be faithful to them. We also have Jenny Cafiso from the JRS international office back in Toronto and close at hand so we feel we won't be allowed to go very far off the true path!

Grupo Pueblo a Pueblo

Danse Marabou, a traditional Haitian dance group at a concert held to commemorate the International Day against Discrimination, Dominican Republic.

JRS USA BETWEEN 1991 AND 1997
Rob McChesney SJ

Rob McChesney joined JRS in 1991. He worked closely with the JRS teams in Central America and helped setting up the programmes with migrants in detention in the USA. In 1994 and 1995 collaboration between the national office, the lawyers project and Human Rights Watch (HRW) personnel grew. In 1997 Rob was appointed Director of the new JRS Detention Project in Los Angeles, where he worked for five years before returning to Province.

While serving as Director of Campus Ministry at St Joseph's University in Philadelphia in 1990 I became aware of a job posting for a new Secretary for International and Refugee Ministries at the US Jesuit Conference in Washington, DC. At the time this position included a part time role as national director of JRS USA. Though lacking significant missionary or refugee field experience, nevertheless I had useful graduate school training in international relations and American foreign policy.

More significantly, since the six Jesuits and two laywomen had been murdered on the campus of the University of Central America (UCA) in San Salvador a year previously, I was restless to work more closely with the economic underclass and to pursue a ministry more directly addressing issues of social justice and systemic change in which the United States played a major role. The fact that I had known Nacho Martin-Baro SJ, the Vice-Rector of the UCA, while we were fellow students in Chicago, made my interest in the position heartfelt.

It was the beginning of an eleven-year love affair with JRS, one which grounded and continues to animate me as person, priest and religious. Let me try to capture some key organisational developments from 1991-97, though others may well have different perspectives.

JRS USA was in radical need of mission and program definition in the spring of 1991 when I became the fourth National Director in five years. Since Founding Director Frank Moan had moved on (in 1987) the frequent turnover in leadership had taken a toll on organisational identity and profile in the USA, as well as the ability to constructively contribute within JRS circles internationally. The position was viewed at the Jesuit Conference as half time at best, and there was little profile among USA Jesuits and the Ignatian family. Lacking staff or mission definition, at the outset it was something of a re-imagining and rebuilding challenge.

Though JRS USA in 1991 lacked organisational integrity, the potential was evident. The JRS USA National Director answered directly to the President of the Jesuit Conference, Fr Pat Burns SJ. It was a matter of working with Fr Burns and the ten USA Jesuit Provincials to identify a coherent, constructive mission, and then to hire and develop staff to support that mission. The generous support given by Fr Burns, and later his successor Greg Lucey SJ, quickly made possible some exciting initiatives and very positive organisational steps forward.

Three particular challenges from this period stand out in my memory. One was to immediately address regionally with JRS in Central America and Mexico the violence and human rights violations which were creating large numbers of refugees and displaced people in that region. Much of the problem was the result of USA foreign policy during the 1980's, driven by the Cold War. The bullets which killed the eight people on the UCA campus were made in the USA, while Washington resolutely opposed any negotiated solution to the war in El Salvador. Such USA policies in turn were driving mass human displacement in Central America.

Ironically, historians now suggest that the notorious UCA murders were the most important single variable which led to the signing of the Salvadoran Peace Accord in 1992, precisely the negotiated outcome for which the deceased Jesuits had been working. For USA-based non-governmental organisations, for the Society of Jesus and for JRS regionally and internationally, lessons learned in El Salvador during this period were formative and decisive.

At this fascinating historic juncture I was asked to serve as a point person between the USA Jesuit Conference and the Central American Jesuit Province, which had jointly retained the Lawyers Committee for Human Rights in New York to represent the Society of Jesus in the legal proceedings taking place in San Salvador in the early 1990s. I was back and forth between Washington and El Salvador with some frequency in this period. Working with Central American Provincial Chema Tojeira SJ, as well as with Dick Howard and later Peter O'Driscoll of JRS/Central America, all based in San Salvador, we collaborated on various solidarity and advocacy efforts, designed to change USA policy in support of negotiations for peace. I believe that our efforts, in solidarity with broader ecclesial and civil society efforts, met with some success.

What was our orientation? When in 1991 I asked a forcibly displaced person in Chalatenango, a conflictive zone of northern El Salvador, how JRS USA could help, she said I should go home to Washington and tell the President to stop sending so many weapons to her country. Naïve and dangerously simplistic? Not necessarily. JRS advocacy efforts sought to find legitimate and intelligent faith-based modalities so as to let this woman's plea be heard. Through good friends of the Society of Jesus on Capitol Hill, like Congressman Joe Moakley of Massachusetts, it was clear that such voices were welcome.

In similar fashion during the early 1990s JRS USA began to work closely with JRS/Mexico, particularly National Director Vladimiro Valdes SJ. Refugees fleeing the repression in Guatemala were streaming into southern Mexico. JRS/Mexico had been appointed by the Bishop of Campeche to take responsibility for the many refugee camps in that Yucatan Diocese, and the personnel and program resources deployed were extensive.

The authoritarian Guatemalan government was strongly supported by the USA government, and lessons learned from El Salvador proved valuable. Vladi and I were in regular communication, visited each other and planned regionally, including a variety of advocacy efforts. Vladi was a very effective spokesperson in Washington, whether at the USA Conference of Catholic Bishops, with Congressional aides, the Catholic press or Washington-based solidarity and human rights non governmental organisations.

In turn I was frequently in Mexico City or Campeche, visiting the U.S. volunteers in the refugee camps, meeting with Jesuit and ecclesial leaders and identifying individuals and initiatives worthy of solidarity and advocacy support from the north. At one point during this period, death threats on colourful posters appeared immediately outside several Jesuit communities, featuring a large dagger thrust through a map of Mexico and proclaiming "Death to Jesuits in Mexico". Among other ridiculous charges was that Zapatista Comandante Marcos of the EZLN was a Mexican Jesuit. In such cases I was quickly alerted by colleagues in Mexico, and able to arrange a meeting with the Mexican Ambassador in Washington the following week to ask for an explanation. If silly, the threats were nonetheless dangerous.

Vladi and I were convinced of the importance and efficacy of advocacy within JRS' organisational vision and methodology, and regularly shared our experience and observations with the JRS Directors gathered at the General Curia in Rome for the annual meetings during this period. I believe this JRS regional experience in North and Central America played a significant role in shaping JRS' organisational methodology to include organically the place of advocacy grounded in the field.

A second challenge of this period was to adequately support the dozen or so USA citizens, mostly lay men and women, serving on the ground around the world through JRS. The largest number was in El Salvador and later Mexico, but there were others in East Africa, Thailand, Malaysia and Hong Kong. JRS USA often handled the health insurance for the lay volunteers, corresponded with them and tried to visit on an annual basis. Their dedication to the refugees and displaced invariably touched us deeply. Such visits to the field also enabled JRS USA to have direct contact with the refugees themselves. For this we learned there is no substitute.

By 1994 we included Ms Laurie O'Bryon, our Asia specialist, Mike Linden SJ, who focused on Africa, and Ms Marcia Timmel who held it all together in the office back in Washington as administrative assistant. We viewed this aspect of our mission as accompaniment of the accompaniers, and through the latter to meet those displaced directly and listen to their stories.

When the field volunteers (lay, Jesuit and religious women) returned to the USA, we made every effort to bring them to Washington for celebration and debriefing. Both were important. This enabled national staff to maintain a fresh perspective, and was a vehicle for introducing such volunteers from abroad to policy makers, press, and church and NGO leaders in Washington. If our first responsibility was to support the JRS volunteers abroad, it became clear how important it was as well to view the reentry phase, its possibilities and requirements, as organically important as well. Many of the returning volunteers had experienced some degree of shock, burnout or even trauma.

The final organisational challenge of this period that stands out in my mind was to ground JRS USA in direct, face-to-face accompaniment and service, which we understood must be central for an integral methodology. JRS USA had never developed a coherent operational program in service of those forcibly displaced. Of course, the unique circumstances of the USA will always circumscribe what might be accomplished here.

Nevertheless, we did have the benefit of some direct legal experience with asylum-seekers, gained in the early 1990s by placing a few lay and Jesuit attorneys in Miami to provide pro-bono legal assistance to Haitians fleeing repression and poverty back home. Additionally, JRS USA had sponsored two volunteer attorneys to work in Hong Kong doing pro-bono legal work with the Vietnamese asylum-seekers. This experiment proved valuable and significant organisationally to JRS USA.

After a fair amount of staff and organisational-wide murmuratio, in 1996 I decided to convene a weekend of discernment at the Leonard Neale House Jesuit Community in Washington. It included about 25 friends of JRS, including former National Directors Frank Moan and Si Smith. Mark Raper came from Rome, and the meeting was ably facilitated by Rick Ryscavage. Many former JRS field workers joined us, such as JRS/Mexico veteran Tim Lambert. The USCCB's Catholic Legal Immigration Network, Inc. (CLINIC), was represented by Director Don Kerwin. The purpose of the gathering was to decide whether it was time for JRS USA to conceive and develop a formal domestic operational program in direct service to the forcibly displaced, which didn't duplicate services already available.

Over the course of the weekend a remarkable convergence of heartfelt opinion emerged that it was essential for JRS USA to move more vigorously in this direction, as the next step towards embrace of the full JRS vision and methodology. I believe this was an important, graced moment for JRS in the USA. Now, some years later, as migrants and asylum seekers are increasingly conflated in the public discourse (not to mention in the detention centres) with *terrorists*, I believe the wisdom of this discernment is evident. That is not to say that needs, opportunities and limitations will not change.

The question quickly became, 'what then are we actually to do, given our national context?' Our own former volunteer attorneys from Miami and Hong Kong, as well as CLINIC Director Kerwin, were among those noting the increasingly xenophobic attitudes of Americans and USA policy in the wake of the first World Trade Centre bombing in 1993. Now, in 1996, a Republican Congress and Democratic President were supporting bi-partisan legislation which was about to legally mandate the detention of an unprecedented number of asylum seekers, migrants and others who had problems with the federal Immigration and Naturalization Service. The clear recommendation from the Neale House discernment was to focus on this growing system of *immigration detention* in whatever direct services were found to be needed within the scope of JRS.

In a subsequent national assessment JRS USA concluded that the needs were religious/pastoral as well as legal. The USA Jesuit Conference approved and generously funded the initiation of services at several detention centres, including Elizabeth, New Jersey (near New York City), El Paso, Texas and Los Angeles. JRS would provide religious and pastoral care (and related services), while in an imaginative partnership CLINIC would provide expanded legal services. We are still too close to this experience to fully assess it, and circumstances change, but in my estimation this was the crucial decision of this era for JRS USA.

By 1997 I was enormously pleased with the organisational development, which could never have happened without the support of the US Jesuit Conference, including the ten Jesuit provincials. The interest of Jesuit leadership in the organisation was phenomenal. So too I was regularly touched by the enthusiasm of the broader Ignatian family of friends of USA Jesuits. The quality of JRS leadership in the other regions and from Rome was also remarkable. For me it remains the formative apostolic experience of my life.

One is always tempted to gild the lily, but I recall that by 1997 JRS USA had developed a coherent national vision and mission with staff to support it. We had just initiated the first program on the ground. Our advocacy efforts and lines of communication and solidarity regionally and internationally were strong. We had amplified the profile of JRS USA enormously, leaving much good will to build on. We had identified Rick Ryscavage SJ, a bright, experienced church and refugee veteran, to assume the role of Country Director. Since so much remained undone, in this we were fortunate.

I was so excited by the incipient new JRS USA immigration detention program, and the opportunity to work more directly with displaced people, that I volunteered for one of the new sites. The Provincial was very positive, and after sabbatical in Mexico I was missioned in late 1997 to be the Director of the new JRS Detention Project in Los Angeles. I worked very happily there for five years before returning to Province. The experience confirmed for me the organisational coherence and strength of the JRS methodology, from direct accompaniment to advocacy for structural change. But that's a story for another day.

Building coalition with others
Rick Ryscavage SJ

In 1997 Rick Ryscavage moved from being the JRS Pedro Arrupe Tutor in Oxford to being JRS USA Director instead of Rob McChesney. The JRS Immigration Detention project begun, in support to people who were held awaiting civil action on their immigration status. In 2003, Ken Gavin SJ took over from him as JRS USA Country Director.

I arrived at JRS USA after having spent a few years as the first JRS Arrupe Tutor at University of Oxford UK, between 1995 and 1997. At that time JRS in Washington was rather submerged under the USA Jesuit Conference office. I eventually held three jobs simultaneously: the director of JRS USA; the President of Jesuit Missions Inc.; and the National Secretary for domestic Social and International Ministry. It was often difficult to balance these three positions. I reported to the ten provincials of the USA Jesuit Assistancy.

JRS USA had been incorporated separately from the USA Jesuit Conference but, in fact, its budget and personnel were often intermingled. JRS was largely an office of advocacy. It published the "Mustard Seed" which carried both analytic and reflection articles on forced migration. JRS USA also handled the processing of candidates for volunteer positions with JRS world wide.

I was personally very active in policy circles in Washington and in my JRS role took an increasing leadership position in INTERACTION, the largest American coalition of non-governmental humanitarian agencies. It became apparent to me, however, that because of the immigration reform legislation in the USA during the 1990s, there were some serious migration problems within our own borders for asylum seekers and others. So we began the long process of providing religious and some social services to asylum seekers and immigrants inside the detention jails. We also formed a strategic partnership with the USA Bishops Conference's legal aid organisation (CLINIC) to provide lawyers for work in the detention sites.

We also recognized that JRS USA needed to develop its own structural identity separate from the Jesuit Conference. The Provincials asked me to create a board of directors to help guide the organisation and to establish both an endowment as well as a clear operational budget.

Mark Raper SJ/JRS

Haitian woman in the Dominican Republic

By the time I left Washington, the provincials had agreed to establish JRS director as a full time position. The Jesuit Conference national secretary became an entirely separate job. We had created a board of directors and the provincials had set up a special endowment for JRS USA. The religious coordinators at the detention jails had were becoming more accepted by the federal government and funding was more secure. The program services of JRS had become a very central part of our work while the policy and advocacy initiatives continued in Washington.

Sudanese refugees studying in Rhino camp, Adjumani, Northern Uganda, 1992

Chapter Three

AFRICA

In Africa, poverty and the kinds of instability that produce it are invariably at the root of the social difficulties that lead to forced migration. Poverty itself has complex causes. At the end of the Cold War, artificial and ideologically motivated economic subsidies and arms contributions were suddenly withdrawn from political leaders who had otherwise fragile social or electoral bases. Frequently a power vacuum resulted. Often, as in Ethiopia, Mozambique and Somalia, countries were left awash with small arms provided during the Cold War period in the name of 'maintaining stability'.

While African people have many reasons to be proud of their countries and their achievements in institution-building, almost every African country has been touched by conflict at one point or another in the post-colonial period. The unresolved legacies of colonialism, bad governance, weak state structures and lack of leadership, the criminalisation and militarisation of economies and the contest for control of scarce resources, migratory pressures, are all factors that now make conflict more likely. Interstate and intra-state disputes are fought out as conflicts in terms of territory, culture and identity, religious difference and nationalism. All armed disputes invariably create refugees. Poverty in turn contributes to further instability, to brain drain, to an exodus from the rural areas and to the exploitation of women and children.

The roles played by the African Church in general, and the strategic placement of JRS teams among the people displaced by conflicts, are ways in which essential social services can be continued, formation and education opportunities can be provided, vulnerable groups such as women and children protected, and human rights become better respected. Where JRS was present both in the camps and in the countries of origin, its teams could facilitate speedier and safer return and reintegration of refugees.

In 1982, Jesuits began the work of JRS in Ethiopia for those displaced by the Ethiopia-Somalia war and later by the Wallega famine of 1984-85. Seeing clearly the endemic nature of conflict in the region, and the prospect of enduring displacement of large populations, JRS accepted that its work there would not be accomplished quickly. In the mid-1990s, JRS arranged the purchase of property in Nairobi in the name of the Eastern Africa Jesuits, in order to provide a management base. It undertook deeper formation of JRS members serving there and saw the need for more in-depth studies.

The length of this chapter reflects the breadth of JRS presence and the number of forcibly displaced people. JRS works in many different scenarios throughout Africa: from large refugee camps in Tanzania to urban settings in Johannesburg, with the internally displaced people in Burundi or with former child soldiers in Liberia, to name but a few. JRS personnel, past and present, have contributed their own personal accounts of that work in this chapter.

Taona

Taona was born in Mozambique, fourteen years ago, when the Renamo insurrection had already ravaged much of the country. By the time he was ten, he knew more about death than life. Then his father was blown up by a land mine. And a few days later their village was burnt down. That was when his mother decided they had to run for their lives. They fled to Zimbabwe.

The next three years Taona stayed at the Mazowe River Bridge camp, one among thirty thousand other refugees, behind a barbed wire fence. The things he remembered from home were fire, guns, hunger and death.

Then Taona fell sick and came to our Hospital. He had cancer. When I first met him, the growth in his belly was so big and he had already lost so much weight that he could no longer walk on is own. But he insisted on sitting outside on the veranda to watch the nurses and other patients.

Taona was brave. I never saw him cry. But when the spasm of pain set in, his expression changed and his face suddenly seemed that of an old man. Each time I visited him he asked if I could find a medicine to take the growth out of his belly. Each time I had to tell him that I had failed.

One day I asked Taona if there was something else I could do for him. He hesitated and then, in a voice even lower than usual, he enquired if he could have a bar of soap. He added that never in his whole life he had had his own bar of soap – not at home in Mozambique, nor at the camp, nor here at the Hospital. The other visitor who had come with me was already at the door of the intensive care ward when Taona made a sign to call me back. Could he make a second wish, he asked. Could he also have a towel? He had never had his own towel either.

When Taona had his bar of soap and towel, he decided they were too precious for everyday use. He kept the bright red and yellow towel neatly folded beside his pillow and underneath the towel, the bar of soap.

After each pain-killing injection and before falling asleep for a few hours, he would pull the bar of soap out from underneath the towel, hold it to his nose, draw in the smell with his eyes closed and then place it back under the towel.

Late one Saturday evening, I was called to the Hospital. Taona's end was near. His face was peaceful now and for the first time since I had met him he looked like the fourteen year old boy he was. The towel lay neatly folded by his pillow.

The following morning we buried Taona at the small cemetery behind the hospital. His grave had been dug in a corner at the far end, reserved for refugees from Mozambique who died at the Hospital, without relatives. Government officials told us to keep their bodies separate. One day, the Mozambican authorities might wish to claim them. Taona was covered by a clean white bedsheet and wrapped in a new reed mat, which was tied at the feet, the waist and the neck. When Taona was lowered into the grave, an old woman stepped forward, knelt down and carefully placed the towel and bar of soap by his head. The soap was still in its original wrapping.

Dieter B. Scholz SJ, JRS International Director, 1984-1990

Recollections on the birth of JRS in Africa
Angelo D'Agostino SJ

In 1981, soon after the foundation of JRS by Fr Arrupe in 1980, Angelo D'Agostino was appointed to take responsibility for refugee concerns in Africa.

In August of 1979 while I was finishing my stint in Thailand with Catholic Relief Services, Fr Arrupe happened to stop off en route to Rome with his associate Fr Bob Rush after a meeting in the Philippines. After concelebrating the Eucharist for the Feast of the Transfiguration, during which he delivered his annual homily on the evils of atomic warfare – it being the anniversary of the atomic bombing of Hiroshima, where he was living at the time – we all had dinner. During the meal he confided that he was considering setting up the JRS in Africa and asked if I would like to go. I remonstrated saying that I had a contract and had to return to my teaching and professional obligations in Washington but he responded by saying that it would only take a few months... That was 25 years ago and I have been here all but 3 years of that time. Nonetheless, I acquiesced and postponed my commitments. Sadly, however, when Fr Arrupe got off the plane the next morning in Rome, he suffered a stroke which left him with an expressive aphasia which meant that although he could read, see and understand everything still he could not express anything orally or by writing. It was as though he was in a glass prison.

After a short stay in USA I returned to Rome where Fr Michael Campbell-Johnston was heading JRS and Dieter Scholz was his assistant. I spent a month at the Curia under their tutelage and then headed for Africa for the first time in my life. Landing unannounced in Mogadishu, I was the beneficiary of the saintly and later martyred Bishop Colambo who headed the Franciscan contingent, the only priests allowed in the country. After reconnoitering the tragedy of the Ogaden at the time with thousands dying of starvation and being displaced, it soon became evident that the area was swamped with a myriad of NGOs providing a wide spectrum of relief and anything I could provide would be hardly effective.

Moving to Nairobi I set up office with the East Africa Region Jesuits, with Fr Polycarp Toppo as the Regional Supervisor. With his moral support and that of a welcoming group of mainly Canadian Jesuits with whom I lived in Nairobi, I began exploring the needs and possibilities. Briefly, over the next two years this is what was established:

In Southern Sudan from Torit to Yei some 12 schools were set up for Ugandan refugees by an Indian Jesuit, Fr Victor Mathias who has since died. But he was so well appreciated that UNHCR hired him directly later on.

Probably the most intrepid apostle for the refugees is Fr Salvador Ferrao, a native of Goa, India who has spent his whole life as a priest with refugees in many parts of Africa and also Asia. During 1981 and 1982 he worked most effectively to establish a multi-sectoral mission with the Burundi refugees in a newly established camp called Mishamo in Western Tanzania.

In Zaire, Erman de Weerdt, a Belgian Jesuit of long experience in Zaire, set up work with Ugandan refugees in several camps. He worked closely and diligently with a veteran Comboni missionary and the Canossian Sisters.

Another programme for internally displaced persons was developed in Ethiopia. Together with the Franciscan Missionaries of Mary from USA and India and a JRS volunteer nurse, a Belgian Jesuit Father and Brother, a mission was pioneered in southern Ethiopia below Awasa among the Gugi tribe.

From those humble beginnings, an extensive programme was forecast and thanks to the insight and encouragement of Fr Arrupe, JRS Africa has brought relief, compassion and hope to millions of voiceless and hopeless refugees.

ETHIOPIA: VIOLENCE AND DRAUGHT IN THE 1980S

Roland Turenne SJ

> *In 1982, Jesuits began the work of JRS in Ethiopia for those dis-placed by the Ethiopia-Somalia war and later by the Wallega famine of 1984-85. It was an internal displacement, and most controversial, since the Derg removed the social base of its opponents, the Tigrayans. JRS helped to move them, but ultimately many people went back to their homeland. Fr Turenne SJ was the JRS Country Director in Ethiopia[1].*

JRS started operations in Ethiopia as far back as 1982. JRS Ethiopia developed itself into a different direction from the beginning because of the way the need presented itself.

A mobile medical team was set up to assist the victims and displaced people of the Somali-Ethiopian war in the beginning of the 80's. At considerable personal expense, a double team of Jesuits and Franciscan Missionaries of Mary sisters was at work to minimalise the damage done to human lives.

When a couple of years later an unprecedent drought situation occurred in the country, JRS set up a base camp of tents in the Weleita area and assisted the drought victims, together with many other organisations.

When the Mengistu regime started forcefully resettling people from the drought stricken northern parts of the country to the more fertile and lush parts of the South and South-West, JRS developed a programme to assist the Relief and Rehabilitation Commission (RRC) putting the people on their own feet and enabling them to get going again in their lives and that of their dependants. JRS involvement in the region was terminated abruptly by the overthrow of the Mengistu regime and the base camp was totally looted. Fortunately both the Kisha and Argoba projects had by that time been completed and handed over to the respective peasants' associations by the new country director Joe Rodrigues SJ.

---

[1] Taken from notes written in the early 90's by Fr Turenne and shared with us for this book.

Plans were developed to engage in educational work in Fugnido refugee camp, South of Gambela. Expatriate experts had been nominated already when the plans to start a Teacher Training Institute among the Sudanese refugees had to be abandoned. The refugees had suddenly fled en masse into Sudan when EPDRF forces (opposed to SPLA presence) were taking control over the country.

The prolonged Eritrean and Tigrean war being over, a whole new situation was created: Thousands of war victims, internally displaced and returnees had to be cared for. JRS assisted the RRC and the Ministry of Agriculture (MoA) in developing a rehabilitation programme for the population in and around the town of Hawzen, between Mekele and Adigrat in Tigray. This town was bombed at various occasions and practically destroyed during an air raid in 1988, where 2500 people lost their lives.

Considerable time was spent on working out the details of the different programmes – education, agriculture, water development, animal husbandry and income generating activities – so as to help the people in their effort to rehabilitate. A tri-partite project agreement between RRC, MoA and JRS was signed at the end of June 1993. JRS had started beforehand with several programmes, namely water development and education. The Ethiopian Government has always had firm control of agencies. JRS' agreements had to be vetted and precise contracts signed.

At the same time, JRS started supporting the Catholic bishop of Adigrat, Mgr Kidane Mariam, in his efforts to assist and rehabilitate the people in his diocese. JRS set up a mechanical workshop and engaged in teaching automechanics to students who could take over the workshop at a later stage.

During the years of war it was agreed that a mobile medical team would be operational to assist the victims. When the war was over it was decided that the members of the team would be spread over the existing clinics. In 1994, JRS had three Australian Mercy Sisters working in Daughters of Charity run clinics in and around Mekele to assist in catering for the many returnees and displaced in the area.

Michael Coyne/JRS

Ethiopia, 1994

JRS IN AFRICA BETWEEN 1984 AND 1986
Simon Smith SJ

Si Smith took up the concern for refugees in Africa between 1984 and 1986 and encouraged work in northern Sudan, after which a team was formed in Port Sudan. He was replaced by Michael Schultheis SJ.

In 1983, after nine years working as Executive Secretary of Jesuit Missions for USA and Canada, I was ripe for change. So grace came along in the person of Fr Dieter Scholz, the head of JRS. He was a guest speaker at a meeting of the board of Jesuit Missions. He eloquently shared with the board members the genesis, current engagements and worldwide challenges of JRS, still in its infancy at that time: South East Asia, where JRS had formally been born a few years earlier, plus Central America and the tremendous, daunting needs in Africa. During that meeting, he heard me tell the board that I was not offering my name for reelection for a fourth term; and so he asked me to take on JRS in East Africa. I accepted eagerly though I had nagging doubts about my own fitness for the task. My predecessor of a couple of years in JRS Africa was Fr Angelo D'Agostino.

In 1983 we went together to visit the projects already underway in Ethiopia, Sudan, Tanzania, Zaire and Kenya. That Christmas we celebrated midnight mass in a camp of 35,000 Hutu refugees from Burundi who had been there in Tanzania for ten years waiting to go home. An open mud hut, a thatch roof, rough logs for benches, a choir of tremendous force and joy and a Mass as down-to-earth as ever I had known. No more nagging doubts! I was captured by God.

In southern Sudan Fr Victor Mathias, an Indian, was supervising for UNHCR 28 primary and secondary schools among Ugandan refugees. He had just inaugurated a process of turning them into *self-help* schools. JRS and the UN supplied textbooks, slates, chalk, pencils, encouragement and support.

Further south in Sudan, along the Ugandan border, Fr Pio Ciampa was working in several refugee settlements, forming catechists, setting up parish councils, teaching and even running open-air cinemas for the youth.

Not far south of Fr Ciampa, across the border in Zaire, Fr Erman de Weerdt, a Belgian of long experience in Zaire, was also working with Ugandans who had fled Idi Amin or Milton Obote, just as had the other Ugandans in Sudan. His ministry, too, was primarily pastoral. We lived with him in a mud hut, accompanied him on visits to sick people and crossed back into Uganda with him to see where these refugees had come from.

Down in Tanzania, where we had celebrated Christmas with the Hutus, Fr Sal Ferrao, from Goa, was chaplain in the huge Mishamo Camp. His sense of humor got us through some awkward moments with officials in the camp and his rootlessness taught us something about what it means in the Jesuits to be *available*.

In Nairobi we dealt with dozens of needy refugees from Angola, Uganda, Burundi, Ethiopia, Somalia and from even as far away as Namibia. There were endless requests for food, money, school fees, for every imaginable need. We served as scribes, notaries, advisors, advocates... As happens so often in countries flooded with refugees, the host country cannot or does not give residence permits or work permits. So the refugees float on a sea of need, grabbing at every bit of help they can touch.

Once Angelo D'Agostino left, I sat down to draw up priorities. Though my first duty was obviously to the refugees and the JRS staff serving them, I also knew we'd need to raise money and get the word out about the horrendous situations around this continent. So I started *Africans on the Move*, a little newsletter which I sent to everyone I knew worldwide, and I never mentioned a syllable about money. But money came. All I did was tell stories of refugees.

One new project among Eritrean refugees in Port Sudan was initiated. Advice and consultation was given to IMBISA (Southern African Bishops' coalition), among others. Public relations, publication, fund-raising and administration occupied huge chunks of time and energy.

Shortly thereafter I got word that Frank Moan SJ, who was the new director of JRS USA – which the Jesuit Missions board had created at that earlier meeting with Fr Dieter Scholz-, was coming to visit JRS Africa sites. So we planned to visit a couple of projects.

Frank and I then headed to Rome for a meeting of JRS Directors with Fr General Kolvenbach. He was wonderfully affirmative of our work with all its problems and we parted with confident assurance that we had his backing for all of our endeavors.

While there at the Curia, Frank Moan and I dropped into the Infirmary to visit Fr Arrupe. It was heartbreaking to see him so impeded by the effects of his stroke. Our visit was very brief and poignant. The next day we were surprised to be summoned to revisit him. It seems he hadn't been aware that we were from JRS and he wanted to see us again to present us with a gift. He gave us each a copy of his latest book and autographed each with great difficulty. What a treasure!

Running back and forth from site to site for crisis interventions and even out-side Africa for meetings was taking its toll on my physical and psychological well-being. After talking it over with the Rome staff and with Fr Kolvenbach, who were all wonderfully fraternal and supportive, I called a meeting of the JRS Africa staff, Fr Provincial and Fr Scholz in Nairobi. We de-centralized the whole operation so that none of the projects would suffer and I came home to Boston.

I thank God that JRS Africa continues with greater vigor than I could have imagined in 1986. And I pray God that its activity can continue to be seen for what it actually is: the presence of the living Lord Jesus in today's world.

In 1983, civil war broke out in Sudan for the second time since independence (1956), leading to the displacement and the death of millions of people. Some of the people displaced by war sought refuge in neighbouring countries, such as Ethiopia (in the photo, 1990) while many more remained internally displaced.

Mark Raper SJ/JRS

Rebuilding the bridges and clearing the footpaths: A parable of the JRS

Michael J. Schultheis SJ

In 1988, Michael Schultheis, then Assistant to the first International Director Dieter Scholtz SJ, was appointed JRS Director for Africa. He set up an office in Nairobi and developed the networking on refugees concerns. In 1992 he moved on to take up a particular concern for the Mozambican refugees in Malawi.

The following story, almost a parable, expresses for me much of the spirit of JRS. It involves the Mother of Fr Cirili Mateus SJ, then the Regional Superior of the Jesuits in Mozambique (Fr Cirilo was killed in a car accident near Tete, Mozambique, in 2002). In 1986, Fr Cirilo's mother had crossed into Malawi as a refugee and spent the next seven years in an open camp there. When Fr Cirilo came to meet with the JRS teams in Malawi, he always would have time to be with his mother and other refugees, many of whom were personal friends and relatives. I once asked him to inquire of his mother and her friends about their concerns for the time when they returned to their home to Mozambique. When next we met, he related that his mother had stated as her principal concern: 'Who will help me rebuild the bridge and restore the footpath so that I can visit my neighbors when I return home.'

Those of us who have been involved at various stages with JRS have seen its growth as it accompanies refugees and refugee communities in their time of flight and need, and yes, helps them rebuild the bridges and restore the footpaths of their lives on their return to their home areas, if and when that becomes a possibility.

JRS is not a response to statistics and numbers but its mission is to accompany persons and communities in need. JRS is not defined by functions but by the faces and features of persons whom we come to identify as part of our family and community. This leads to the importance of analysis and advocacy, but to be effective, these are based on a deep understanding that is obtained from personal presence and shared experiences. Presence is the central feature of the JRS: To be with displaced and refugee communities in the traumatic experience of flight and search for survival.

Each of us has our own story of involvement with JRS. In some respects my involvement with refugees pre-dates Fr Arrupe's vision and JRS. I was in Uganda between 1970 and 1973, teaching at Makerere University (Kampala) and doing research studies in South West Uganda. Three refugee moments from those years: Idi Amin's forced expulsion of the Asian community, some of them still personal friends; Sudanese refugees, fleeing the first Anana war in southern Sudan, selling baskets and fish along the shores of Lake Victoria; the refugees and displaced from Burundi (Hutus) and from Rwanda (Tutsis), struggling to survive in Uganda. Later I was at the University of Dar es Salaam (1976-81) and minimally involved in refugee issues in Eastern Africa. Tanzania under President Nyerere was the prime example of stability and good governance in all of Eastern Africa and provided a welcome to large numbers of Hutu refugees from Burundi.

In 1980 I returned to the USA to work as staff member of the Center of Concern. At that time the JRS was being established as a separate Secretariat at the Curia in Rome, with Fr Dieter Scholz as the first Director. As he began to strengthen its organisation and outreach, he needed someone to assist him in the International Secretariat. His search somehow turned up my name, perhaps because of my previous work in Africa.

Early in 1985 I joined him at the Curia, together supporting the JRS initiatives and presence in Southeast Asia and Central America, but increasingly with Africa as the focus of concern. Fr Angelo D'Agostino and then Fr Si Smith had by then established a JRS presence in Africa, with a base in Nairobi and programmes in Sudan and Tanzania. In late 1985, Fr Smith left the African office because of health reasons. From Rome, Fr Scholz and I continued the JRS work in Africa, while encouraging the African provincials and regional superiors to name a Regional Director for Africa. Given their commitments and limited personnel, they found it difficult to release someone for this purpose. Consequently, in June 1988 I returned to Africa to revive and coordinate JRS there. The obvious location was Nairobi; for one year I resided at Hekima College, in part to involve young Jesuits in studies there.

The Nairobi office was first of all an administrative office, but with the flows of refugees into Nairobi – Sudanese, Ethiopians, Somalis, Ugandans – gradually it seemed impossible not to respond directly to the pressing needs of refugee communities in urban areas. Out of this grew a repatriation programme for undocumented Ugandans; a parish outreach programme where JRS supported local parishes and encouraged their social concern commit-

147

tees to respond to refugee families living in their midst; and a health programme which referred sick refugees to parish health centres for treatment
and care. JRS also became the clearing house for educational and family
support programmes, assisted by the UNHCR and Caritas funds and directed by Sr Louise Radlemaier. At the request of Bishop Paride Taban, JRS
became involved in helping Sudanese refugees in Kenya. Hekima College
opened its doors and chapel to serve as the parish centre for Sudanese in
Nairobi – once a month Catholic families gathered for Mass and for family
events – baptisms, confirmations, weddings – guided by the Apostles of
Jesus, a Sudanese congregation of priests and brothers. Br Michael Bennett
SJ provided strong support for the regional office one year. Sr Frederika
Jacob helped with publicity and with an outreach to the Sudanese community – with her guidance, JRS with other Church groups in Nairobi brought
together two southern Sudanese factions (John Garang and Lam Achol) for
peace and reconciliation talks – ambitious but it did not hold. Later Fr Gene
Birrer coordinated a UNHCR-JRS programme that screened new asylum
seekers in Nairobi. He also promoted small income generating programmes
for refugees. JRS was a leading voice in the formation of a local NGO, 'People for Peace in Africa.' The JRS Regional Office for Eastern Africa continues
to support and nourish several of these initiatives.

From Nairobi the JRS Africa Office was also developing refugee support
programmes in other areas. One of these was Mozambique. In 1988 two
Jesuit priests were killed near their parish residence in Angonia District
(Tete Province, Mozambique). That was followed by a major exodus of
Mozambicans across the border into Malawi and the closure of the Jesuit
missions in that area. JRS sought to place a pastoral team in Malawi to care
for these communities. Eventually this consisted of Fr Isaac Mlauzi, Fr Richard Guerrera, Fr Luis Goncalves and Fr Salvador Ferrao. This team worked
with refugee communities along the border for nearly three years. When
these communities began to return home in 1993, Fr Goncalves accompanied them and JRS assisted them to rebuild the missions. Sal Ferrao went to
Zambia to be with Angola refugees in Meheba Refugee Camp. Fr Guerrera
shifted to Lichinga Diocese to work with refugees returning to their homes
in Northeastern Mozambique.

In 1989 JRS Africa began discussions with UNHCR about establishing a
secondary school programme for Mozambican refugees in Malawi. This led
to discussions with the Ministries of Education in Maputo and in Lilongwe.
In 1991, JRS initiated what became known as the MOLU education project

(Mozambican Open Learning Unit). Jose and Angela Cunya, a Portuguese-Italian couple who had worked in Mozambique, helped to set the programme in place in the first two years, assisted by Sr Lolin Menendez. Patterned somewhat on the *Fe y Alegría* schools that the Jesuits had set up in Latin America, MOLU followed the Mozambican school curricula and examination schedules, with the idea that students eventually would return to their home areas and be able to continue their education.

MOLU began as a single refugee camp school in southern Malawi. A central team coordinated the school programmes and directed a teaching staff of refugee teachers. Few of them were qualified teachers, but with the guidance and direction of the central team, a teaching-learning programme was established. Ambrosio Tsamanea, an experienced teacher who was himself a refugee, was a key person in dealing with the teachers and students. JRS appealed to the Jesuits in Portugal for teachers. Out of this grew the Portuguese Jesuit Volunteers Corps, which continues to place young women and men in Angola and Mozambique. Two Jesuit scholastics, Charles Chilinda (Zambia) and Jose Ignacio García (Spain) also worked with the MOLU programme and taught in the schools.

When Fr Michael Evans arrived in Nairobi in 1992 as JRS Coordinator for Eastern Africa, I relocated to Malawi, to support the expanding JRS presence among Mozambican refugee communities. Later that year, Fr Franz Chanterie SJ, an experienced secondary school teacher from Belgium, arrived to give direction to the academic aspects of the MOLU Programme. The following year, Sr Delvina Pasquale, a Sister of Divine Providence from Brazil, also joined the MOLU team.

With the Peace accord in October 1992, refugee communities cautiously began to return to their home areas and JRS began a programme to support their repatriation. Jim Rebbechi, an Australian builder with work experience in Mozambique with the Australian Volunteer Corps, joined the JRS team in Malawi in 1993. During the next two years, he supervised the restoration and construction of several schools, parish residences, health centres and churches in Mozambique. At one time, JRS had about 100 men involved in this reconstruction work.

At the same time, JRS continued to expand the MOLU programme and began to shift schools into Mozambique. In one instance, refugee families waited to return to their homes until after JRS had transferred the MOLU school and students across the border to Mozambique. By the end of 1994, when JRS transferred the MOLU programme to Mozambique, the ten MOLU schools had an enrolment of nearly 1,000 students, about one quarter the size of the public secondary school system in Mozambique. By early 1995, the transfer was completed. MOLU schools in Lichinga Diocese were under the joint sponsorship of the Diocese and the Province Office of Education and those in Tete Province and Angonia District were under the direction of the Jesuits. The Jesuits continued these for two years and then brought them within the parish school system or passed them to the District Education Office.

In November 1995, I left the JRS programmes in Malawi-Mozambique and Africa.

Mozambique, 1994. With the peace accord in October 1992, refugee communities cautiously began to return to their home areas and JRS began a programme to support their repatriation.

Michael Coyne/JRS

A SPIRITUAL GIFT
Salvador Ferrao SJ

Fr Ferrao worked with refugees in Asia and Africa during the 70's, before JRS was set up. In the early 80's he started JRS works in Mishamo refugee camp, Tanzania and later in Sudan. He was kidnapped by southern Sudanese rebels in 1987, together with other two Jesuits. During the 90's he worked in Mozambique and Zambia. In 1999 he joined JRS teams in East Timor and returned to Sudan in 2001.

During the Indo-Pakistani war, sometime in 1971, I was still a student of Theology. Fr Rector Ugarte SJ told us that all those who had good muscles should do their theology not in a classroom but in the refugee camps up North of India, where there were ten millions of refugees from Bangladesh.

In 1972, I went to Tanzania. There was a war in Burundi and many Hutus had fled to West Tanzania. Still a student of Theology, I was sent to help out. Some 180.000 refugees were living in three big settlements. The Missionaries of Charity and I would meet the refugees at the Tabora railway station. Those sick would be taken to Kitete government hospital and the hungry ones would get a few biscuits. Those without clothes would be provided with a covering somehow or other.

When JRS was set up, Jesuits who had had experience with the refugee phenomenon were called to join in. So I went to Mishamo camp, Tanzania, a very large settlement without any transport, not even a bicycle. The Bishop of Sumbawanga left me there with some food and cooking pots and told me that now I was married to this camp! I did not see him again for a year. I walked many miles and was a regular victim of malaria.

The time to see the refugees on their best form was on market days. Each week, on Wednesdays and Sundays, people put on their best dresses and clothes, met in the market area, bought, sold, drank beer and visited friends. Burundians are hard workers and tireless walkers.

African wars are fought between brothers. They are generally civil wars, many of ethnic origin. But ethnic groups do not normally have the resources

AFRICA

to fund wars, so these are funded by those who have economic interests. Take the war in Angola: it was not an ethnic war, but a war of diamonds. I can say this because I lived among members of the UNITA rebel group and also with members of the military. They both fought for the diamond-controlled area. But who had a real interest in those diamonds? Surely not the Angolans, but foreign groups in USA and South Africa. The consequence is that the ones who are affected by these foreign interests are the poor, who have nothing to do with this war[2].

The hardship of the camps did not mean much to me for what we were searching for together was the presence of Christ among the sick, the thirsty, the naked, the hungry, the prisoners and the strangers, who had become unwanted in their own homes by their own people. Together we searched for a lost hope and we shared their fate in a new and human environment.

---

[2] Interview with Fr Ferrao in *Belo Horizonte*, page 10, 26 September 1999.

With the internally displaced in Sudan
Edward Brady SJ

In the mid 80's, JRS worked in an UNHCR education programme for Ugandan refugees in southern Sudan. Ed Brady SJ, who had worked with Indochinese refugees in Thailand (see Asia chapter), was part of this programme. After the Ugandan repatriation, he moved to work with the huge number of displaced Sudanese and Eritrean refugees in and around Khartoum. He worked with JRS until 1999.

My direct involvement with refugees first in Thailand and then later in Sudan spans the years 1981 through 1999. For myself it has been a privileged form of Jesuit ministry. I will share some experiences which stand out as highlighting for me JRS essentials, namely JRS is a Jesuit ministry that accompanies and empowers refugees and internally displaced persons (IDPs) and advocates for their rights with and for them.

Accompaniment

In Sudan, after the Ugandan refugees had begun returning home in large numbers I moved to the north of the country and was based in a parish in Khartoum in order to minister to refugees from Eritrea and Ethiopia, as well as to internally displaced Sudanese forced north by the civil war. Getting an entry permit for new JRS personnel to do refugee ministry in the north of Sudan was a lengthly process with success not guaranteed as the initial efforts to staff our JRS project in Port Sudan had shown. However, in the parish in Khartoum I found myself part of a team of pastoral workers made up of Sisters of the Sacred Heart, a local Sudanese congregation, plus a number of talented refugees and IDPs who had sought refuge in the north and lived in the parish.

The parish itself was situated on the southern edge of the city where both bus and train lines from the south terminated with the result that many of the hundreds of new arrivals fleeing the civil war in the south first landed in our parish. We did not always have sufficient food or other essentials to share with the many who came daily to the parish. It was the elderly Sudanese Sister who was always available to the refugees and IDPs whether we had material assistance available or not. She continually pointed out that the needy required and deserved more that material assistance. By her constant word and example she taught us all the value of a compassionate presence which does not regard the needy person merely as a problem or statistic, but affirms their self worth and dignity particularly by listening to their problems with sympathy and kindness.

Empowerment

In the refugee camps in Thailand and in Sudan, typical NGO activities were aimed at providing the means for the refugees to prepare for a more productive future through a variety of educational and self help programmes. However, since the internally displaced arriving in Khartoum during the long years of the recently ended civil war did not benefit from the UNHCR mandate of protection and assistance, there were no such UN or government programmes or even the planning for such.

Shortly after the civil war in Sudan forced the transfer of the Major Seminary from the regional capital of Juba in the south to Khartoum, I found myself along with my JRS ministry also agreeing to be the interim Spiritual Coordinator of the Major Seminary, awaiting the arrival of a fellow Jesuit who had volunteered for the post but whose visa was not being readily granted – a common situation at the time.

In the early 90's government authorities opened the IDP camp of Jebel Aulia where displaced families were forcibly sent after local officials in the name of 'urban slum clearance' destroyed their simple mud and thatch dwellings. The camp, some 40 kilometers south of the city, was in desert surroundings and had initially no provision for shelter, water or other vital necessities, so life there was especially harsh.

Some months after the Jebel Aulia camp was opened a shelter programme was started to assist the elderly, disabled and sick. Funds initially provided through JRS International from Caritas Netherlands enabled the purchase of rough poles for roof support and grass thatch for roofing. With the seminarians organizing the youth to do volunteer labour making mud bricks and doing the simple construction work, the shelter programme had a successful beginning and was later able to include any family in need, as selected by the parish committee. This model proved workable and as more funds became available the programme was extended to the outskirts of town where many of the IDPs had settled and where the local authorities sometimes destroyed their dwellings but only moved them some distance away.

Since the Archbishop had set up the Vicariate for the Displaced to attend to the specific needs of the IDPs who by then numbered over one million, the shelter programme was able to be administered within that structure as one more programme to assist the IDPs, along with food assistance, primary education, etc. In addition to seeking and accounting for the needed finances through JRS, my contributions were mainly occasional field visits as well as visits to the various centres to assist with the accounting and recording procedures.

This shelter programme served me as an example of how the IDPs were ready to help themselves, if given the means, and I was particularly happy to cite it whenever a visitor with little experience of the IDP situation, would speak of the fear of our assistance to refugees and IDPs fostering among them a 'dependency syndrome' – an attitude of not wanting to help themselves.

Advocacy

My limited experiences with advocacy have come mainly in the form of making the refugees' immediate humanitarian needs known through JRS and a network of fellow Jesuits and friends in order to find required support. However, some years ago in Khartoum I found myself advocating for an understanding of the IDP situation in northern Sudan that was in direct opposition to the government authorities' statements, namely that Sudan had all the means for self reliance and no longer needed humanitarian aid from the international community. Since some representatives of the international donor community along with some Church personnel not known for their presence among the IDP community took up the same theme, I was happy as occasion offered to invite them to become more familiar with the actual IDP situation on the ground rather than read 'official reports'.

I have always dreamed of helping the refugees and IDPs to advocate for their own needs and rights, much like the much admired refugee involvement with the JRS advocacy initiative against landmines. However, there were tight security arrangements in northern Sudan. Sudanese who were thought to oppose government policies, including several fellow Sudanese priests, were imprisoned or worse. Such experiences indicated that any advocacy initiatives regarding refugees and IDPs had best take more indirect means than public opposition to the status quo.

Refugee girl in Nimule camp for displaced people, South Sudan

JRS in Africa from 1987
Stephen Power SJ

*Stephen Power worked in Sudan between 1987 and 1993. In 1997 he
was appointed Regional Director in East Africa, until 2001. In 2002
he worked in JRS Ethiopia, until 2004 when he joined the JRS international office.*

In 1987, when I joined, the JRS world was developing fast! In Africa, Si
Smith SJ had just finished assessing and proposing projects mostly in Eastern Africa. He had investigated work in Sudan for the Eritrean and Ethiopian refugees. Ed Brady SJ, who moved up from Juba in southern Sudan,
where he had been working for UNHCR, could not get the permits to join the
new JRS Port Sudan work for Eritreans and so the project was started by Sr
Fidelma Mahon OSF. For logistical support, the project relied both directly
on Rome – the International Director was then Dieter Scholtz, working with
Hilda Serrano – and it was also assisted by the presence of Fr Brady in
Khartoum. I was to be involved with the Port Sudan project from 1987 until
1993. We had many excellent lay volunteers, from Ireland, United States,
England, Egypt and Australia. The work was enabled to by very good collaboration with the Comboni Congregation and with the Archdiocese. From
the beginning of my time in JRS this collaboration with other people, clerical
and lay, has been one of the most inspiring apostolic opportunities.

Ed Brady was fully involved with the Archdiocese of Khartoum but he also
fostered the work for refugees in Khartoum, developing a night school for
refugees and displaced in the parish of St. Peter and Paul, Amarat, and later
setting-up a shelter fund for those displaced whose house were broken up
and who were forcibly relocated to the outskirts of Khartoum. The programme
of the Sudan Open Learning Unit (SOLU) developed for refugees also benefited from Ed's assistance. A Regional Office did not exist in Africa at that
time. The organisational structure of JRS was still in need of clarification.

Si Smith had to leave the work as JRS Director for Africa, exhausted by the
size of the task. In 1988, Mike Schultheis SJ, then Assistant International
Director in Rome, was sent by Dieter Scholtz SJ to replace Si Smith. Apart
from a concern for Sudanese and Eritreans, Mike got involved with the
Rwanda and Burundi exodus and later the vast movement of Mozambicans

into Malawi. Mike left Nairobi to take up full-time direction for the distance education programme in Malawi/Mozambique, when the first Regional Director in East Africa was appointed, Mike Evans SJ in 1990. Some confusion in the appointment highlighted the fact that JRS was a new style of organism within the Society, with its direction (for the regions of greater urgency) from a Rome office and not through the various Jesuit Provinces.

The time from 1990 to 1996 saw a big expansion in the work of JRS not just in Eastern Africa but also in the Grand Lacs area, which became a JRS region in the years following the 1994 Rwanda genocide. The Southern Africa region was formed at that time too. In Eastern Africa, a major development was the work with Sudanese refugees in Adjumani, North Uganda in 1992. This presence continues till today. An excellent assessment by the long-time JRS consultant Virginia Hasson RSM, ensured that JRS work in education in North Uganda (Adjumani, Ikafe, Rhino Camp and also in Koboko reception centre) became very noteworthy. The work was not without difficulty and staff had to be evacuated more than once due to rebel activity. Around the same time in 1991, the split in the southern Sudanese rebel movement, the SPLA, caused flight of the lost boys and others from Sudan into northern Kenya. Kakuma camp was formed and JRS became involved, seconding staff through Radda Barnen and later Lutheran World Federation (LWF). With the fall of the Mengistu regime in Ethiopia, refugees from that country joined many Somali refugees in Kenya. Somalis have fled to Kenya ever since the Siad Barre regime collapsed in 1991 and the country became ungovernable. JRS projects in Kenya and Ethiopia involved many Somali refugees after this time.

The way JRS has had to deal with expanding itself has led to growing pains especially in managing this change. Just as important has been the need to consider how long JRS should stay in a project and how it can better empower the people with whom it works so projects can be handed on. To retain its mandate, JRS cannot afford to become more of a development agency.

Another big expansion of work in Eastern Africa was in 1994, in trying to respond to the huge needs of the Rwandan refugees in the vast camps of West Tanzania. The area around Ngara, Karagwe and further North and South, also hosted many refugees from Burundi who had fled after the 1993 coup. Work in Tanzania was so overwhelming that the International Director, Mark Raper SJ, had to help organise an overstretched Regional Director,

Mike Evans SJ at the time. One of the innovative projects set up in 1995-after an assessment by the Programmes Officer for Africa, Tom Fitzpatrick SJ[3] – was a radio station: Radio *Kwizera* ('Hope' in Kinyarwandan[4]). JRS has certain specialisations like pastoral work and education but all the time each context needs a new approach and assessment as to how to respond. The Radio has been one of the most successful.

In 1995 in Kigali, the first *In-Service Training* was organised for JRS workers worldwide. These seminars continued until they were stopped with a view to being done regionally. Training nowadays is a priority to ensure that JRS projects are works of competence and quality.

In 1996, JRS did the 'Communications Audit'. This evaluation, ostensibly of JRS communications capabilities around the world, led to a review of how JRS organised itself. This work was done by Rick Ryscavage SJ, who was to become the first Pedro Arrupe tutor in Oxford, an innovative position continued by Sr Maryanne Loughry RSM. This position was a development of one of the original themes in the setting up of JRS: to research the world of refugees and the causes of refugee movements. Research is an area constantly in need of development in JRS. Meanwhile, the world of communications was developing fast and email via satellite phones became the most effective means of contact between JRS workers.

JRS staff is our most valuable resource. When I started as Regional Director in Eastern Africa in 1997, it was apparent that the expansion of work and subsequently the number of personnel employed led to the need to manage these people effectively. So in 1999, I appointed a Personnel Director, Bernadette Mangan LSA. This was a big help in addressing the human resource needs in JRS work. With her full and varied experience in Ethiopia, she has done much to provide effective support to personnel.

Meetings of Africa Regional Directors started with the need to discuss common policy over the Cordaid Block Grant[5] in 1997. Cordaid started a process of funding Africa projects by giving a block grant, worth several million dollars over the years. This relationship was considered of mutual admin-

---

[3] Tom Fitzpatrick SJ passed away on 27 August 2005, while this book was being compiled.
[4] See contributions by Katie Erisman MM and Fratern Masawe SJ, in this chapter.
[5] Most of the funding for JRS Africa had come from Caritas Netherlands and then Bilance; the two Catholic agencies which merged with Memisa to become Cordaid.

istrative advantage given the number of projects already funded by Cordaid. Tom Fitzpatrick SJ was appointed Programmes Officer for Africa to manage this grant. For the first time, and partly with the demands of this block grant, it became policy that all JRS projects, at least in Africa and Asia, should be audited. This started a process of financial review. In Eastern Africa, after Mark Harrington joined the staff, a system was designed for project use which was gradually adopted Africa-wide.

The need to improve financial reporting also led to a review of our reporting system. The International Office led a gradual introduction of a more or-dered form of project-cycle management, which led to the formation of JRS programme officers.

In 1998, an important meeting in Harare was that of JRS pastoral workers from around the world. The report of this meeting is still the most authorita-tive guideline for JRS pastoral teams. 'The Pastoral Dimension of JRS', as it is entitled, is a reminder of how the pastoral approach is the spirit behind all our work. For me one of the most important principles is that, whatever the wider context is that we have to aware of, political, economic or social, we are known by God and we know other people in a personal, individual way. As I have come to love individual refugees and others with whom I have worked, I have become more aware of how much more God loves them and each one of us.

The work of Virginia Hasson, mentioned above, is a reminder of the impor-tance of the JRS work in education. In Africa, this was highlighted by the establishment of the Resource Base for Refugee Education (RBRE) in Nai-robi in 1999, directed first by Sr Lolin Menendez RSCJ, a first in the world of refugee education.

Work with Human Rights Watch (HRW) was developed under the direc-tion of Mark Raper SJ. It became one of the main planks for making advo-cacy effective in JRS, whereby JRS could help human rights organisations to pinpoint and report on issues.

The setting up of regional offices in Africa – first in 1990-was followed by the creation of country offices. But the development of the JRS structure only became fully clarified when the JRS Charter and Guidelines were agreed and published in 2000 by Mark Raper SJ in consultation with his council and the regional directors.

The work in Ethiopia was quite particular though. Soon after its inception in 1982, it involved humanitarian work on a broader basis, not just with refugees. It covered those affected by the famine of 1983-5, and highlights the difficulty of defining what exactly is JRS' mandate. Ethiopia had, in effect, run its own country office since the beginning of its work. But this was because the local Jesuits, led by Roland Turenne SJ, had taken responsibility for it and run it without any regional office.

My work in Europe between 1994 and 1996, was a time of setting up the JRS UK office, working with Bernard Elliot SJ, a long-time refugee worker. I also helped Eddy Jadot SJ developing the JRS Europe region. A challenge for JRS is to connect its work in the affluent countries with its presence in Africa, Asia and Latin America. A considerable help to reminding me of these interconnections is the presence in the UK office of the Cambodian, Ms Souhuoy Lam. Her story is another marvel of refugee survival.

Near the end of this time in JRS UK, I was fortunate to work a few months in Nepal with the Bhutanese refugees. It was striking for me to witness the similarities in the refugee situations. Around the world, those forcibly displaced have to struggle for their basic human rights and for the possibility to live in freedom.

JRS medical programme in Gulu, North Uganda

Don Doll SJ/JRS

JRS and Mercy Refugee Service Cooperation in Africa

Mercy Sisters and other Mercy Refugee Service (MRS) members, worked with JRS in East Africa, mainly with Sudanese women and children in northern Uganda, but also in Kenya, Ethiopia and Angola.

In the Adjumani camp in North Uganda, MRS was largely involved in education and pastoral care, with a focus on teacher training, nursery, and formal education for over 27,800 children. Mercy Sisters worked particularly in gathering women for weekly support groups and providing pastoral care. The education program that Maureen Lohrey, Virginia Hasson and many others helped to build, has flourished, notably Maureen's special interest, the education of the girl child.

One of the most shocking challenges faced by JRS/MRS workers in Adjumani was that of child soldiering. The camps were under a constant threat from rebel attacks and the kidnapping of refugee children to be trained into a life of violence.

'One memory that stays with me is how the rebels took a group of children and one boy kept falling over and not keeping up. They sat the children in a circle and had his brother kill him', recalls Catherine Corbett RSM.

From 1995 onwards, some Mercy Sisters worked in establishing teacher-training programmes for nursery school teachers in Kakuma camp, northern Kenya. Working with a mix of 22,000 Somali, Sudanese, Ugandan, Ethiopian and Congolese refugees, this nursery school training had particularly widespread potential in that it gave an education opportunity to girls who in many African cultures were given little education. Life in Kakuma was precarious and totally dependant on the patronage of NGOs. This often impacted negatively with the result of food riots.

MRS was also involved in educational and medical work in Ethiopia, namely in Latchi clinic, under the direction of Michael Evans SJ, Joseph Payeur SJ and from 1997 onwards of Stephen Power SJ. War swept across the Eritrea-Ethiopia border and through eastern Moxico Province of Angola, two places where Lizzie Finnerty had given her heart.

Don Doll SJ/JRS

Refugee women in Rhino camp, Northern Uganda

The JRS/MRS commitment in Africa brought forth new challenges for both organizations: The increased risk of violence from hostile rebel groups, the danger posed particularly to women and children by rebels groups and the precarious nature of camp life owing to limited food aid. MRS was able to contribute with its particular spiritual commitment to the education of women.

I would like to say that some of us benefited a lot from your knowledge. We Sudanese women can now talk openly and with voice in our community. We can hold responsibilities and our girls are learning. In the future I hope there will not be any violence against women in Sudan. So thank you very much.

(A Letter from a Sudanese Refugee to Catherine Corbett)

163

Speak passionately
Virginia Hasson RSM

Virginia Hasson worked as JRS consultant in various parts of Africa and Asia (see chapter on Asia) and set up the education programme in Adjumani, Uganda, where she worked for some years. The major activities of JRS in Uganda were in the education and pastoral programmes for Sudanese in northern Uganda and southern Sudan.

My first experience in Africa happened in 1987 while I was still working in Asia. I was invited to a small 'think tank' meeting in Nairobi. This was a gathering of five JRS educators and we were looking at the question of how JRS could best serve the refugees in the field of education. We had animated conversation and dreamed dreams. Only slowly did some of these dreams come to fruition. An example is the Education Resource Centre that JRS opened in Nairobi some years later. What does this say about how JRS works? Dream about how best to serve refugees and, in time, let those dreams that have real possibility evolve into actions.

In the early 1990's I moved to Africa. One of my first responsibilities was to visit JRS programmes already in existence. Time and space does not permit me to revisit each of those experiences but, in general, I did learn the way JRS functioned: Allow the flexibility for field personnel to utilize their own personal gifts in service of the refugees rather than providing a strict formula of how programmes should be organized.

One situation I visited lives on in my memory. The refugees in Khartoum were actually living in the desert needing to walk distances in extreme heat even to get water. JRS was working with various groups to try to alleviate the suffering of these people as well as support various educational endeavors showing that: Collaboration is often the key to helping the refugees survive and better their lives.

JRS was working in a collaborative project in Port Sudan. Three times I went to the Khartoum Airport to try to fly to Port Sudan and three times the flight was cancelled. Finally, my visa expired and I left Sudan without getting to Port Sudan but realizing that JRS understood that: While refugees are often found in difficult to reach and remote areas, means must be found to connect with them.

Speaking of remote places reminds me of a two-day journey that a group of us took across Ethiopia to Gambella on the Sudan border. There we found a large group of Sudanese refugees who had almost no services and were living in very bleak conditions. We talked to the leadership about the possibility of JRS being of assistance to them. The Sudanese responded enthusiastically and were particularly interested in having help in training teachers and setting up schools. We made preliminary plans and promised to return. Unfortunately, not many weeks later, Gambella was bombed and the refugees were scattered. We were feeling very sad because JRS tries to work out of the premise: Only promise what you can reasonably expect to accomplish.

However, this story had an unexpected turn to it. Two years later I was helping to organize some teacher training for Sudanese refugees in West Nile in Uganda. A man approached me and said: 'You said you would come back and you have.' Imagine my surprise and delight when I realized that this was one of the refugees I had met many, many miles away in Gambella.

JRS had asked me to find an underserved refugee population in Africa. Since at that time only one agency was working consistently with the thousands of Sudanese refugees in the Adjumani Area of northern Uganda, I went there to speak with the refugee leadership. At first they were a bit skeptical because other agencies had made initial visits but never returned. They became more hopeful when I told them that JRS believed: Go to those situations where no one else has chosen to go. JRS did go to Adjumani and remains a strong presence there even now.

In the years that I served in Adjumani I learned much. One important lesson was: Working in a refugee situation is the most fruitful for all when there is a spirit of mutuality. I felt this spirit of mutuality very strongly at the time of the genocide in Rwanda. As my vehicle approached one of the Sudanese camp schools late one afternoon, the principal and some of the teachers ran up to me and started offering condolences at the death of my friends. At first, I was startled but then they told me that they had heard on the radio about the killing of the Jesuits at Centre Christus in Kigali and they were saddened for our team. That afternoon, as I sat on a rock with the teachers, listening to the radio commentator describe the horrific details of what was happening in Rwanda, I felt a true sense of solidarity. The team's relationship with the refugee teachers had reached that point where they responded with great care when they thought the team was experiencing pain. We were all a people working and caring for each other.

Of the myriad of stories swirling in my memory, I will tell just one final story. In 2000, I was facilitating a seminar for JRS educators working in Africa. One of the educators, a refugee himself, spoke very passionately about a comment in an article he had read in an international news magazine. It seems that someone was trying to explain away the great disparity between the funds being allocated to the Bosnian refugees compared to the amount being allocated to refugees throughout Africa. The explanation was that 'Africans are used to being hungry.' The response of the JRS member was 'No one ever gets used to being hungry.' So we are reminded: *Speak passionately to dispel the myth that any human being can get used to not having basic needs met.*

Internally displaced students in Nimule Primary School, South Sudan

Don Doll SJ/JRS

The 'new' JRS project at Rhino Camp was not exactly new, as thousands of refugees had already settled there when the JRS staff arrived in September 1994. In order to decongest the camps in the neighboring district of Adjumani, UNHCR transported refugees, first by barge and then by lorries, to the newly opened settlement on the other side of the Nile.

On our arrival, we found six primary schools already operating under trees and in makeshift shelters, with little assistance from outside sources. But it was only after six months did the first trained teacher arrived in the settlement with his documents.

The refugee community had put in place the primary schools, selected teachers, put up structures, created Parent Teacher Associations. Although the efforts of the refugee community were commendable, further assistance was needed, especially the provision of learning, teaching, and building materials. JRS personnel immediately identified the basic and on-going training of teachers as the most pressing need. This became the focus of the JRS education project in Rhino Camp. Not all of the training took the form of workshops or in-service sessions. Much of it was shaped by walking with the refugees, accompanying, discussing, questioning, planning and listening as teachers and parents became more confident in taking charge of the education of their children.

A year and a half later, there were 11 schools, each with a trained teacher as Headmaster. Later on, as Education Resource Person, I visited Rhino Camp in 1997 and in 2002. So much had changed, but so many teachers, pupils and parents with whom I had worked were still there. I was proud to see how the schools have flourished, and how many refugees have completed their training as teachers or upgraded their qualifications. My real joy came from still being called by name and being asked for news of other JRS members, still remembered and appreciated. These two visits have been special moments, for it is not often that one can return and delight to see others reap the seeds that we once planted together.

Lolín Menéndez RSCJ,
Education Resource Person for Africa, 1997-2003

Expansion of JRS East Africa between 1990 and 1996

Michael Evans SJ

The East Africa Region was formed in 1990. Michael Evans was the first Regional Director there, between 1990 and 1996. At this time there were two major events affecting the region: The huge refugee flows from Sudan into Adjumani, North Uganda in 1992, and the sad events and exodus in Burundi and Rwanda in 1993 and 1994 respectively.

My time as Regional Director for JRS East Africa coincided with three main directions:

First, the division of JRS Africa into more manageable units. Before, there were directors for all of Africa. East Africa became the first region, comprising Tanzania, Uganda, Sudan, Ethiopia and Eritrea, to be followed by Southern, Central and Western Africa.

Second, a virtual explosion in numbers of refugees in the region due to the disintegration in 1991 of Somalia as a nation-state; the collapse of the regime in Ethiopia in 1991; an intensification of civil war in Sudan in 1991-92; the many internally displaced from tribal clashes in Kenya between 1991 and 92; the genocides in Burundi in 1993 and in Rwanda in 1994; and the disintegration of Zaire as a nation state between 1994 and 1996.

Third, a conscious decision to move away from a JRS model that was a 'think-tank' involved in publications and peace talks promotion to an 'NGO-styled' model that actively promoted projects working with refugees, both in camps and urban settings, in every country of the region. By the time I left, that was the case.

My goal was to have Jesuits and co-workers responding to refugees and their various needs either in our own JRS projects if possible, or seconded to other UN, NGO's or church groups if that was not possible.

Depending on the country or situation, projects were extremely diverse: pastoral care; formal and informal education; teacher training; income generation; formal registration of refugees; health care and training of health care workers; media and creation of an FM radio station; reforestation, water and agricultural development; promotion of refugee handicrafts; and working with urban refugees.

All of these projects and their rapid expansion cost money and needed volunteers. The time that I was Regional Director was marked by solid and deep relationships with donor agencies, the negotiation of long-term Block Grant Funding, and the strategic partnerships with key religious congregations, most notably, the Sisters of Mercy, Loreto Sisters, Missionary Sisters of our Lady of Africa, Vincentian Sisters and Fathers, Maryknoll Sisters and the Religious of the Sacred Heart, to name a few.

Finally another goal that was only met with limited success was to get the local Jesuit Province to commit local Jesuits to work and to train others for future work. After some disagreements between JRS International, JRS East Africa and the Jesuit Province, a new Regional Director was appointed in 1996.

Letters from Liberia

Miriam Therese O'Brien SSL

The war in Liberia started in 1990, displacing over one million people within the country and some 700,000 as refugees in neighbouring countries. JRS started working in Liberia in 1992, with Sr Miriam O' Brien, a sister of St. Louis, as Country Director. In 1999, when the war was over, JRS handed over the work to a local organisation. In 2001 JRS re-launched activities in the region due to renewed wars in Guinea, Liberia and Ivory Coast. The following are some extracts from Sr Miriam's letters[6]:

September 1, 1993

...As yet no relief supplies have reached Gbarnga – and the cease fire is over one month old. It looks very like food is once again being used as a weapon. – I feel so angry and helpless when I look at the children with swollen feet, hair discoloured and falling out, big staring eyes and whose every bone I can count. The plight of the women too, tears me asunder – they've walked for miles, been displaced two or three times, have literally nothing, do not know anything of the men in their lives and more often than not have children in addition to their own to care for.

September 17, 1993

What we need desperately is the lifting of the embargo. Food is sitting in Côte d'Ivoire but the UN forbid its movement. It is a catastrophe – a sort of madness has taken over. MSF tell us that a whole generation of children has been wiped out; those who survive are permanently damaged...

September 23, 1993

It is important that the outside world does not forget Liberia. The ceasefire is holding, but only just, and another armed faction has emerged.

---

[6] Taken from *Servir n.1*, November 1993.

JRS in Southern Africa: Five crucial years
Peter Balleis SJ

Two major events affected the refugee movements in Southern Africa, and thus the work of JRS, during the nineties: The Angola crisis and the war in DR Congo. Peter Balleis joined JRS in 1994. In 1995 he set up the regional office for Southern Africa in Harare, and was the Regional Director there until 1999. He is now member of the Council of the JRS International Director.

1994 – The Rwandan refugee crisis

On 7th of April 1994, as usual my clock radio woke me up with the BBC news. The main news was Rwanda, the shooting down of the presidential plane and the killings. Somehow this bad news among others touched me more directly, because I was preparing for my Jesuit assignment with JRS in Southern Africa. Some days before I had visited Mozambique and Malawi to see an end to a conflict, the return of refugees and the help given by JRS in the phase of repatriation. It was a happy event, which followed the peace accord of 1992 in Mozambique. The same year 1994 saw for Angola too, a peace protocol signed in Lusaka, Zambia and the hope for a lasting peace.

In June 1994 I attended one of the first international meetings of JRS in Rome. The clearest role of responsibility within JRS was the regional director for East Asia and for East Africa, but JRS had not yet adequate global structures. Sudan, Ethiopia and Mozambique had been the first involvements of JRS in Africa, until the Rwanda genocide exploded. This event forced JRS to move faster, to put adequate structures in place and to respond to the enormous needs of the refugees. ·

The early beginnings were hard and showed the inadequacy of JRS in Africa to face a major crisis like Rwanda. There we were in December 1994, Margaret Burchell IBVM, Mary Gitau IBVM and myself on the hill of Chabalisa, North West Tanzania. At our feet were the camps Chabalisa One and Two with 120,000 Rwandan refugees. We were the start-up team for JRS to prepare the work. The national director Fratern Masawe SJ was the country director but at the same time the logistics man. The need for stronger structures was obvious.

171

Mateo Aguirre SJ was appointed Regional Director for the Great Lakes in February 1995, and set up an office in Bukavu, Zaire. I took office as Regional Director for Southern Africa, based in Harare, in April 1995. Mike Evans SJ was already in place as Regional Director for Eastern Africa and Tom Fitzpatrick SJ helped us with the 'block grant' funding from Cordaid.

The structure of JRS in Africa was nominally in place, but it took some years to develop it in each region and on a continental level.

1995 – The successful repatriation of Mozambican refugees

I moved with my laptop to Malawi in May 1995, where we organised the hand-over and partial closure of JRS operations in Malawi and Mozambique. Mike Schultheis SJ was directing the school and rehabilitation programmes in the camps of Southern Malawi and in Mozambique. By the end of 1995 the school programmes were ready to be handed over to the Diocese of Lichinga and the Jesuits in Tete. Until today the MOLU distance education programme is successfully running in the Diocese of Lichinga, Northeast of Mozambique.

Later in 1995 the focus shifted to the major refugee crisis of Angola. A JRS team, led by Sal Ferrao SJ, had moved from Malawi to Meheba refugee camp, in Zambia, to assist Angolan refugees. The peace accord of Lusaka encouraged us to prepare for the repatriation. It was clear that JRS would follow the Mozambique model, helping refugees in the first stage of rebuilding their lives. The former mission of Cazombo, in East Angola, became the base for the JRS team.

1996 – With the Internally Displaced Persons in Angola

In August 1995, just after our first African regional directors meeting in Kigali, I flew to Luanda, Angola. It took less than a year and a number of visits to Angola until JRS could get teams in place in Luanda, Luena and Negage. The year 1996 was marked by the set up of JRS in Angola.

The 1.3 million internally displaced people and the activities in Luena, Negage and Luanda opened a new field of work. During his visit to Angola in September 1996, Mark Raper SJ decided that the mandate of JRS should be extended to the IDPs. I still remember visiting, together with Mark, a group of people living in a school in Luena in terrible conditions. Still today

I see the faces of the people, the face of Augusto, a man with his little child, who had lost his leg due to a landmine. He featured often on JRS posters. In the meantime the little son also lost a leg due to a landmine. The Campaign to Ban Landmines in collaboration with JRS Cambodia became an important part of our mission in Angola.

1997 – Refugees in urban areas in Zambia and South Africa

The Rwanda crisis and the forced repatriation of Rwandans from Tanzania and Zaire in late 1996, led many Rwandans and Burundians to flee further down from the Grands Lacs region. Southern Africa was by then the most stable region in Africa. So refugees from the Grands Lacs Region, and even from Sudan and Somalia made their way to Southern Africa with the ultimate goal of reaching South Africa, always a magnet for Africans. But many refugees got stuck in the newly erected Dzaleka refugee camp in Malawi or in Meheba camp, Zambia, and in urban areas such as Lusaka, Harare, Johannesburg or Pretoria.

So projects for refugees in urban settings started in Lusaka, Johannesburg and Pretoria in 1997. In Harare a small pastoral project had started right from the setting up of the regional office there. In Malawi, the work with non-Mozambican refugees in Dzaleka camp and in Lilongwe was taking place since the closure of JRS in Blantyre.

1998 – The new war in Angola and the African War in DR Congo

In mid-1998 it became obvious that both warring factions in Angola had used the cease-fire to regroup and rearm under the eyes of the UN. JRS tried to hold out in Cazombo after UNHCR and LWF felt forced to leave due to security reasons. But after heavy bombing by government planes against UNITA strongholds, JRS decided to pull out from Cazombo on 17 November. Two weeks later, on 3rd December, a full scale war started again between UNITA and the MPLA (Angolan government). It lasted until the death of Jonas Savimbi, leader of UNITA, in February 2002.

Refugee flows to Meheba increased to over 50,000, so new camps were opened in Nangweshi. The number of IDPs in Angola doubled to over 3 million. The situation got worse than ever before.

Meanwhile, in August 1998, the events in DR Congo developed dramatically.

173

Zimbabwean and Angolan troops were flown into Kinshasa to rescue President Kabila and his government from the rebels and Rwandan intervention in the East. The country broke up. Zimbabwe, Angola and Namibia were fighting on the side of the government and Uganda and Rwanda on the side of the rebels. The country was exploited by all sides, with three million dead in a conflict which has dragged on until today.

1999 – Southern Africa's full scale refugee and IDP crisis

At the time of the handover as regional director to Joe Hampson SJ, the situation had developed into a full scale displacement crisis in Southern Africa. My hope was for a lasting peace in Angola and the repatriation of refugees there. But the reality in Angola and in the Great Lakes region presented new challenges to JRS in Southern Africa. In view of these developments, the task of JRS was to respond to the needs of the refugees by developing an adequate regional structure, with country offices and project sites in the countries. All the projects in Angola, Malawi, Zambia, Zimbabwe and South Africa were kept and new ones started in Namibia and Zambia. After five years, JRS in Southern Africa was better equipped to respond to the new and greater challenges than it had been in 1994. The organisational structure, the procedures and the teams were in place.

Un corps pour l'esprit, 1995

This organizational development also applies to the continental and international levels. The Kigali meeting of 1995 was followed by regular meetings. A strong cooperation between the three Africa-based regions grew. The size and magnitude of the refugee and IDP crisis in Africa and the growing volume of JRS works made Africa the major focus of JRS during the nineties and shaped its broad development.

From 1996 onwards, participants in the annual international meetings included all the regional directors, the International Director and the staff of the International Office. In 2000 the JRS Charter and Guidelines and other essential documents were drafted. These were signs that JRS had grown into a fully fledged organisation, internationally recognized and highly appreciated by the refugees.

I refer back to an article where I reflected on the beginning of my time as regional director. By 1995, we were all full of JRS' spirit: The pastoral mandate to accompany, serve and plead the cause of refugees was our clear mission. But we felt the lack of adequate structures to give this spirit the necessary body in order to translate it into concrete services. In 2000 we managed to shape the spirit of JRS with the necessary body.

Un esprit pour le corps, 2005

Ten years later, in 2005, I may write out of my nostalgia for the pioneering nineties in Africa, when things were at times chaotic but the spirit of volunteers and their hard work was driving JRS. I remember young enthusiastic volunteers like Andrea, Francis, Jackie, Umberto, Francis, Johan and senior Joe and Maria, and senior sisters like Cass, Nora, Lizzie, Joan, Virginia, Dalila, Sandra and Jesuits like Luis-Maria, Joao, Arturo, Herbert, Francois and many others who gave themselves to the service of refugees.

Institutionalization and organizational structures are very important, but they should always be at the service of the spirit. Fr Pedro Arrupe was asked by the World Bank President if the Jesuits could work in the camps. The reason was that the many organizations were busy providing services so no one had the time to say hello to the refugees and ask them about their hopes and anxieties. JRS was created to spend time with refugees and to become their friends. Surely the original inspiration of Fr Arrupe still holds inestimable value. I wish JRS to be filled with this spirit, the spirit of Christ which sends us to the poor.

Don Doll SJ/JRS

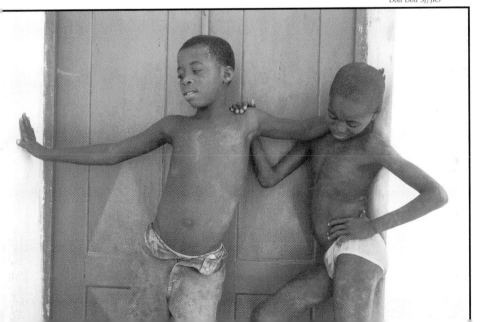

WITH THE ANGOLAN REFUGEES IN ZAMBIA
Francis Leong

In the early 90's a JRS team moved from Malawi to Meheba Refugee Camp in the Northwest of Zambia. Francis worked with Angolan refugees there between 1992 and 2000.

Having spent seven years with JRS in Zambia, I experienced the whole gamut. Periods of tremendous hope and consolation at being in close relationship with refugees were frequently interspersed with times of chaos and uncertainty, disappointment, failure and helplessness, soul-searching get-togethers where we constantly asked ourselves who we were and where we were heading.

Two personal stories vividly colour my experience during this time. In a way they define my sense of the evolving charism and distinct nature of the JRS presence.

The first was our expulsion as a JRS team from Meheba refugee settlement in Zambia's north-western province and our subsequent return after months of uncertainty and up-rootedness. At the time, the three of us, Fr Salvador Ferrao SJ, Br Herbert Liebl SJ and I had been living and working in this settlement for less than a year. It started with para-military police arriving at 'the Mission', our place of residence in the settlement, on Good Friday. They issued us with a 24-hour expulsion order. Allegations had been made that we were involved in instigating the food riots in the settlement the week before, that we were a subversive element in the settlement, and an illegal presence. These allegations were never substantiated, but we stood accused and condemned.

Months of frustrating and fruitless negotiations followed. Appeals by us and the Zambian Bishop's Conference to higher authorities in government and UN circles were made, but we remained expelled. This limbo continued until the intervention of 'Sr Dragica', an elderly Croatian lay missionary who had spent nearly 30 years working with lepers in the local area. She had come to hear of our plight.

After praying and fasting for three days, Sr Dragica found the courage and conviction to approach the Government minister responsible for the district and the refugee community there. She asked him for just five minutes of his time. She tells him that when God finally asks her what she did for his people, she can give a good account of her work with the lepers. She then asks the minister how would he respond when God asks a similar question of him. After a minute's silence she asks the minister to do something for the refugee community he is responsible for. 'Minister', she says, 'Do God's will as I have done and give the refugees back their Shepherd.' Within five minutes an order from the minister rescinding our expulsion was signed and sealed. Within the next few days we returned to the community of refugees we had grown to love more deeply through our expulsion.

Celebration of our return reverberated throughout the settlement for the next two weeks. Everywhere we went, every village we visited, people broke into spontaneous dance and applause. Our return was seen as their victory. Sr Dragica received a Papal commendation for her act of grace which resulted in the shepherd being returned to the flock.

The second story happened a few years later. As the JRS team, people always referred to us as from *the Mission*. In those early days when we had no corporate identity, even UNHCR and the plethora of NGO implementing partners working for them referred to us as *the Mission*. There were no gates, no perimeter fences that defined the Mission. It was as much a concept as it was a roughly defined area separate from the surrounding villages. People were free to come and go as they pleased. There were many *regulars* that *camped* outside our bedroom doors each day. One such *happy camper* was Roger. He was Angolan and had been a refugee in Meheba for nearly 20 years. Every day he would be at our door steps, demanding this, demanding that. On many occasions he would be drunk and abusive. He was a feature of our daily life and work whether we liked it or not.

One balmy night around midnight a lone gunman strolled into the Mission area and open fired with his AK47. He made a beeline for my room, kicked open the door and continued firing randomly inside. The acrid smell of cordite still fills my nostrils as I recall this. He asked me to get out of bed and hand over the money. I reached for the drawers near my bed and handed him what spare cash I could get my hands on. He then fired two more shots straight at me, one hitting me in the upper thigh. As I lay sprawled on the floor, I heard from a distance Roger screaming at the top of his voice, "Don't shoot 'Brother' Francis, shoot me..." I heard stones being thrown hitting the roof of the house... but nothing more. The gunman had left. Minutes later

Roger came into my room. He helped me to my feet. He helped me out of the room and across to the Sister's convent. He got one of the Sisters to come out and helped me into her car. I sat, holding on to Roger by my side in the back seat as Sr Alice drove to the nearest health clinic some 15 kms away. Numb with pain from my throbbing leg I looked at Roger and asked; "Why did you do such a stupid thing screaming at the gunman? You could have been shot too...!" He looked at me and said; "I was frightened for you and wanted to help because the Mission always helps me." I retorted; "But many people help you in the settlement, we're not the only ones, we're not so special to risk your life for us the way you did tonight." I sensed a twinkle in his blood-shot eyes as he looked at me with a wry smile spreading across his craggy face and said; "Ah... Brother Francis, but it is special, it is different, because I know you love me..."

It took a while for his words to sink in, but when it did, I certainly felt the tears well up in my eyes. I wondered how he could know something that I didn't fully realise myself. I saw the truth of his words and the shallowness of mine. I wondered how this young man, living on the fringes of his own

Asked if the Braille lessons and literacy groups for adults helped them and how, a refugee answered: *Now we are prepared to do some work; our families will not look at us like a heavy stone to carry.* Another one said: *When we are an amputee, a blind person or have any other physical problem, 'Normal people' separate us. I don't know if it is for fear or sadness. When you get some training, you can work and be useful. The same 'Normal people' respect us and treat us like normal human beings.* And yet a third one explained *If you are handicapped and you have nothing to do or you don't know what to do, you become a 'double amputee'. Your life is absolutely dark.*

Claudia Garzón
JRS Zambia

community, broken by his own demons and daily alcohol abuse, could so fully understand and appreciate the real purpose of our presence amongst the people there.

My tears were a mixture of shame at my own arrogance and the joy of something really special being revealed to me. I wondered whether I would have put my own life on the line for him as her did for me. Roger's insight helped me realise that I probably would. He put Christ back into my work. He revealed to me my own brokenness which was far deeper, and would probably take longer to heal, than any bullet wound. I returned to the settlement and spent a peaceful night in my room at 'the Mission' two days later. I then spent a month recuperating at the Jesuit infirmary in Lusaka. I returned to Meheba more humble and in many ways more loving.

In my last years with JRS, the administration and personnel management of ever expanding projects and programmes became an all-consuming preoccupation. I remember the countless project proposals that had to be written up for the numerous donors. 'Performance indicators' was the buzz word. I remember wracking my brain for the appropriate, well-meaning, technical jargon when in my heart all I wanted to write was '... being loved and loving back..." I have a very strong hunch that Pedro Arrupe would have approved the projects on this basis alone.

Don Doll SJ/JRS

Landmine survivors in Luena, Angola, 1997

LANDMINE SURVIVORS IN ANGOLA AND JRS: TEN YEARS TOGETHER

Andrea Lari

In 1995 the focus shifted to the major refugee crisis of Angola. It took less than a year before JRS could get teams in place in Luanda, Luena and Negage. 1996 was marked by the setup of JRS in Angola. The Campaign to Ban Landmines in collaboration with JRS Cambodia became part of JRS mission in Angola. Andrea worked for five years in Angola, setting up a programme for landmine survivors displaced by conflict, and then as JRS Country Director.

JRS involvement with Angolan landmine accident survivors started 10 years ago with the first visit of Peter Balleis SJ, JRS Regional Director in Southern Africa, to the isolated province of Moxico, in the eastern part of Angola bordering with Zambia. JRS plan was to establish a presence in the country on the eve of a possible imminent return of thousands of refugees who had been living in Zambia and helped for years by JRS. Once visiting Luena, the provincial capital of Moxico, the Regional Director was shocked to see so many amputees in the streets of the city or in the local market. He called for an assessment which took place in July 1996 when two JRS workers came all the way from Cambodia to provide expertise for the Angola team and devise an appropriate set of projects to be implemented with the amputees.

Luena was a new frontier for JRS. The overall focus of the operation was to help the internally displaced that had fled the conflict since the failure of the 1992 elections and gathered in the city searching for sanctuary. In 1994, the Government of Angola and the UNITA rebel group had signed the Lusaka Peace Accord which had stimulated hopes for peace and a possible return home for hundreds of thousands of displaced. JRS saw clearly the need to side with the displaced, help them to prepare for the imminent return and accompany them to their areas of origin. Among the IDPs, JRS chose to help the most vulnerable groups, such as women, children and the amputees.

Although the principles of serving and accompanying that guide JRS intervention were clear, the team had to know the amputees better and understand the social and economic context in which they were living at that

181

moment. To avoid the risk of creating tensions between displaced groups and residents, amputees living permanently in Luena had to be included as beneficiaries of JRS projects. It took a good nine months of preparation before the first concrete activity started in September 1997. I believe that those months were the most important period that guaranteed sustainability and success of the projects for the years to come.

The most impressive result of those months of hard work and frequent challenges was the regained dignity of the amputees and their families. They slowly moved away from dependence, becoming more in control of their lives. They managed to create new ideas for the future, based on the desire to improve living conditions and to support their children going to school again. And slowly these ideas started to materialize. Paulo who attended a 12-month long carpentry course started his own business, moved out of the IDP camp and started to build a proper house in town. Nelito's kids successfully graduated after two years of intense courses at the JRS special school and reentered the local school system, which had been abandoned due to displacement. Luisa is now sitting by the local market with her sewing machine and produces school uniforms at competitive prices, managing to support her family. In these and many other cases, human dignity was restored and hope continues to shape people's lives.

April 7th 1994
Death of Patrick Gahizi SJ, Rwanda

At our Jesuit retreat house, Centre Christus, I found the blood-soaked room where just months before, on April 7, a group of people had been murdered. Among them were three Jesuits, Innocent Rutagambwa, Chrysologue Mahame and Patrick Gahizi. Patrick was the superior of the Jesuits in Rwanda and director of the local JRS programme, helping refugees who had fled Burundi after the assassination of its president the previous October. Patrick was the superior of the Jesuits in Rwanda and director of the local JRS programme, helping refugees who had fled Burundi after the assassination of its president the previous October.

Mark Raper SJ, on a visit to Rwanda soon after the 1994 genocide

JRS Tanzania between 1994 and 2002
Katie Erisman MM

*In 1994 in the aftermath of the genocide of approximately 800,000
Tutsis and moderate Hutus in Rwanda, fear of vengeance caused a
human exodus of two million people. They fled to surrounding countries, in particular into Tanzania and Zaire. Sr Katie was the JRS
Country Director in Tanzania between 1994 and 2001. These are
some extracts taken from Sr Katie's memories, written in June 2003.*

1994

The genocide in Rwanda, which began in April 1994, horrified the world. Over
500,000 refugees fled into Tanzania and settled in camps in Karagwe and
Ngara districts in northwestern Tanzania. JRS had not been active in Tanzania up to this time but felt that it must respond in some way to this tragedy.

Therefore, in July and August of 1994 a planning mission under the direction of Tom Fitzpatrick SJ came to Tanzania. After visiting and consulting
with Bishop Christopher Mwoleka, UNHCR, several NGOs and refugees, a
report was made, suggesting three possible projects for JRS: Pastoral services in both districts, Ngara and Karagwe based on the pastoral plan of
Rulenge Diocese; A Refugee Information Network (RIN) including an FM
radio station; A secondary school project in Karagwe District.

Fratern Masawe SJ postponed his studies for one year and was named the
first Country Director. By the end of the year Fratern was very busy negoti-
ating to get the radio station licensed and the Constitutions approved so
that it would be registered as a Society and a Trust.

1995

The preparatory work in setting up JRS Tanzania continued as the new
year began. After much work and many trips to Dar es Salaam the Constitutions were approved and JRS Tanzania was registered both as a Society and
a Trust. The Mwanza guesthouse was set up, recruitment of personnel continued, and the three projects were planned.

1996

Pablo Alonso SJ was appointed Director, Elias Omondi SJ and Elias Lopez SJ came to join the project and several Tanzanians were recruited and trained. There was much programme development. The radio was appreciated for its value in dispelling rumours, giving accurate news, and for its special programmes on reconciliation, health, and environment. At this time the refugees were from Rwanda so besides French, English and Kiswahili programmes were presented in Kinyaranda.

Two learning centres were in operation in 1996. The libraries had an impressive number of books, almost 5000 in Chabalisa II and 2000 in Omukariro.

December 1996

The sudden, unexpected announcement came that 'there is now peace in Rwanda, therefore you are no longer refugees. You must return home by the end of December.' This forced repatriation was a great shock to the refugees and NGO workers who were totally unprepared. All of the camps in Karagwe District and the Rwandan camps in Ngara District were emptied. Materials were given away, property of UNHCR was returned, and the JRS team terminated their contracts. The effect on Radio Kwizera was equally traumatic. UNHCR's funding would now terminate, and the position of the radio was very unclear. Pastoral workers could still enter the two Burundian camps of Kitali Hills and Lukole. JRS workers joined the other NGOs in aiding in any small way they could as the Rwandans began their trek back home on foot.

1997

Naturally this year began with discouragement and great uncertainty. The pastoral work continued but only in the two Burundian camps in Ngara District, while the work of Radio Kwizera was greatly curtailed. The first half of this year saw JRS on a holding pattern, recovering from the traumatic experience of repatriation and not certain of the future.

In April an assessment team went to Kigoma to dialogue with Bishop Ruzoka on the possibility of JRS being of service in some of the many camps in Kigoma Diocese. JRS was offered a furnished house on the compound of Kakonko Parish, Kibondo District. JRS provided pastoral services to Mtendeli camp and later an outreach to Nduta camp. This work included pastoral ministry, a psycho-social programme, seminars on conflict resolution and peace building.

1998

This was a year of change with a new project and continued development of the previous projects. Tanzania did not escape *El Niño* and the road conditions were dreadful. This affected all travel and food supply into the camps as the main railway was washed out. The security situation in and around the camps deteriorated. Relations became strained between the Minister of Home Affairs and UNHCR and it was now necessary to get permission from Dar es Salaam to enter the camps. Peace talks in Arusha gave some hope but little progress. UNHCR went from *encouraging* voluntary repatriation to a position of *facilitation*.

Hugues Deletraz SJ arrived at the end of the year to become the next Radio Kwizera Director. Louise Reeves became the Pastoral Coordinator, the last JRS person to hold this position. A pastoral plan was formulated with emphasis on developing Small Christian Communities and leadership roles.

1999

The Grands Lacs area was very unstable and volatile. As the number of refugees increased due to political upheaval, voluntary repatriation was suspended by UNHCR. There was increased insecurity with many armed attacks. The death of Julius Nyerere, the mediator for the Burundi Peace talks, increased fear among the refugees that there would be a forced repatriation. Tension grew between Tanzania and Burundi. Despite this the JRS projects continued to develop, although we no longer had anyone doing full-time pastoral work in the Ngara camps.

The objectives of the pastoral team that year were to consolidate the small Christian communities, support family life within the camp, work with youth, trauma and bereavement counseling and peace education. This was a busy year for the radio. An evaluation was done with a staff organisation chart.

After a long four-month delay, the pre-school project was able to continue with 240 six year olds. By the end of 1999 two more schools were functioning, in Lukole A and B, with the total enrolment of 950. Parent participation continued high and the refugee builders were becoming skilled.

2000

With Nelson Mandela as the new mediator speeding up the process, the Arusha peace talks continued and on 28 August a Peace Accord was signed. However there was no negotiated cease-fire, the rebel groups who had not been involved in the negotiations were not supportive and others had little commitment. There was not much hope for change.

Due to reduction in the food distribution this was a year of real hunger and security problems, as the number of robberies increased. The Pastoral and Social teams continued to build and reinforce the small Christian communities, emphasize peace education and the formation of leaders.

2001

This was a year of political unrest in Tanzania between two political parties on Zanzibar, causing religious tension. In addition the anti-refugee feeling increased, fueled by the media, local officials and insecurity. Tanza-

Tanzania, Jubilee Cross carried by refugees in Mtendeli Camp during Ash Wednesday

John Kleiderer/JRS

nia suggested that safe camps be established in Burundi, under an international peace-keeping force. Burundi accused Tanzania of aiding bases for rebel activities.

On 1 November a Transitional Government took power in Burundi with the power-sharing agreed to in the Peace Accord. President Buyoya, a Tutsi, became President for eighteen months.

Despite the continued instability there was increased emphasis on repatriation as plans were drawn up. Official refugee numbers decreased by 10% this year totaling roughly 480,000.

A Tri-Partite Commission was formed composed of the governments of Burundi and Tanzania and UNHCR, to coordinate repatriation plans. Cross-border groups were formed on education, protection, health, communication... Many meetings were held in both Tanzania and Burundi in which JRS members participated. The pastoral work continued with more increased emphasis on conflict transformation and advocacy.

With five pre-schools now operating and since repatriation was surely in the future, an important objective was to prepare the teachers to develop their own pre-schools back home when they return to Burundi. Good cooperation continued with the partner agencies, UNHCR and parents.

Programmes on Aids, Peace and Reconciliation and the Arusha Peace Accord were emphasized. The radio played an important role in helping the refugees know what was happening in their own country, after the Peace Accord and plans for Power-Sharing with the Transitional government.

2002

I officially finished my service to JRS in February, but continued unofficially and part-time, filling in, until May. This first part of this year saw increased communication between JRS Tanzania and JRS Burundi, with continued talk and worry of repatriation. However it was clear that insecurity made this an impossibility.

I know that JRS Tanzania will continue to accompany and be of service to the refugees in Tanzania until that day for which we all pray when they can end their exile and return in peace to their homes.

KWIZERA: A RADIO STATION TO GIVE HOPE

Fratern Masawe SJ

Fratern Masawe worked in JRS Tanzania right after the Rwandan genocide took place in April 1994. In 1995, he helped to set up the first radio station project in JRS history. Radio Kwizera continues to be a voice of the refugees and of the local community, aiming to provide balanced information.

Significant memories do not fade away, at least not easily. In 1994, I joined JRS in Tanzania. Ten years earlier the last Jesuit moved out of Mishamo refugee camp. At that time some thought the worst was over and we would soon forget about it. The Grands Lacs States were coming of age. We consoled ourselves. In 1993 trouble broke out again in Burundi and over 100,000 refugees walked over to Tanzania. Most of them were sheltered in Lukole Camp in Rulenge Diocese. Many of us thought it was a temporary measure until the panicky home situation settled and once they found a suitable person willing to sit in the hot seat after the mourning of the assassinated president. Surely the refugees would soon return home, we hoped.

In less than 12 months, the worst happened: The abominable genocide of Rwanda. Over half a million people crossed the Kagera river to Tanzania at one time. The world was left dumb-struck, JRS included.

Within weeks JRS began to act. Internationally organised then, with a JRS Regional Office in Nairobi, Kenya, with an already good reputation of a humanitarian as well as a pastoral presence among refugees, JRS saw the need to go back to Tanzania. With the invitation of the Tanzania Episcopal Conference (TEC) and the government of Tanzania, we soon saw the birth of JRS Tanzania. Mark Raper SJ, at that time International Director, and Mike Evans SJ, Regional Director, were very supportive of the move. Celso Romanin SJ, Country Director of JRS Uganda, became my colleague as he had worked in similar conditions. He helped us with information regarding, for example, how to register JRS with the national government and how to work in refugee camps. He also assisted our collaboration with many humanitarian NGOs and a partnership with UNHCR.

The JRS International and Regional offices dealt with international staff and finances, which provided the structures necessary so that JRS Tanzania did not need to worry. It was clear for us; ours was a frontline action with the refugees in the camps. Before the end of 1994, a decision was made that we were going to be based in Ngara and in Chabalisa. From these two places, we would have access to the many camps around – Benaco, Lukole, Lumasi, Kitale and Chabalisa. The JRS Tanzania international staff included: Katie Erisman MM, Marc Van Nouwenhove SJ, Peter Balleis SJ, Margaret Burchell IBVM, Mary Gitau IBVM, Jesuit novices and scholastics who volunteered their time to be at the service of the refugees. Among them were Jacob Okumu, Deo Mutayoba and Gilbert Mardai. The Arusha Novitiate staff did not want to be left behind. They kept the interest going through regular visits, from Leo Amani, Groum Tesfaye, Joe Shubitowski and David Rowan from South Africa.

Three initiatives developed simultaneously in the same year of operation: The Refugee Information Network (RIN); informal schools and libraries; and pastoral work.

With the RIN, JRS became an implementing partner of UNHCR. We were able to get direct access to the refugee camps. We were to provide the refugees with all the important information, such as days of food distribution, meetings, news through notices on bill-boards and public address systems. Marc Van Nouwenhove was at the heart of these services. Soon we realised that a radio would be most efficient in the implementation of this task. The idea of Radio Kwizera was imminent and most appropriate for a refugee community used to listening to the radio. Moreover, with a radio we could have educational programmes including those for peace and reconciliation, as well as entertainment programmes.

The Informal Schools: Three Mary Ward Superior Generals from Italy, Germany and USA visited the camps. They decided to send in a team of sisters to work with refugees in different capacities. One such place was Chabalisa, where informal schools developed into learning centres and libraries. As secondary schools were not allowed in the refugee camps, the informal centres also helped the refugees with some games that provided avenues for coping with traumatising experiences. Srs Noelle Coscarden, Lwanga Katana, Ann Manuel, Judy Illig IBVM were among the first team members to initiate the schools.

The Pastoral work: Christopher Mwoleka, the then Bishop of Rulenge, wanted JRS to co-ordinate the pastoral teams in the different camps, the

189

work which brought JRS there in the first place. The White Fathers were already with the refugees and had the necessary languages. They concentrated their efforts in Benaco, Lumasi and Lukole. They worked hand-in-hand with the Srs of St Bernadette of Rulenge. The Society of the Missionaries of Africa (SMA) worked in Kitale Camp along with the Diocesan Clergy. The Holy Ghost Fathers, Jesuits and Maryknollers, OFMCap, the Sisters of Unlimited Love took pastoral work in the northern camps in Chabalisa and beyond. Sr Colette Msola became the head of the pastoral teams.

The word went round like a bush fire. The spirit was high. Everyone was ready to go the extra mile. The desire to be with our brothers and sisters in need was electric. Like in many human endeavours, there were challenges. Some members of the JRS team were not well prepared to work in hardship conditions with the bare minimum of supplies. Communication difficulties and adapting to the work was not always easy. It was learning on the job, so to speak.

I left JRS Tanzania in August 1995, soon after the inauguration of Radio Kwizera in Ngara with a possibility of booster station in Omurushaka, near Chabalisa. Tom Fitzpatrick SJ, John Dardis SJ and Otieno Ndong'a SJ worked tirelessly to get the radio broadcasting on the 12th of August in four languages, Kinyarwanda, Kirundi, Kiswahili and in French, to over a million people, the majority of whom were "our guests" in Western Tanzania.

JRS Tanzania had two field offices by then, in Ngara and Chabalisa, and a country office in Mwanza staffed by Sr Katie Erisman. The Jesuit Community in Dar Es Salaam (including the late Frs Louis Plamondon and Thomas J. Broadley) was our contact office with the government and the branch offices of UNHCR. The new JRS Country Director, Noelle Coscarden IBVM, was to begin her work with immediate effect. For me great bonds of friendship developed with the teams, men and women from all walks of life. Indeed a fond memory of JRS which does not fade away.

Burundian refugee working in Radio Kwizera, Tanzania

1996: A FORCED REPATRIATION TO RWANDA

Noelle Corscaden IBVM

*Noelle was the Country Director in Tanzania. The forced repatria-
tion of Rwandan refugees from Tanzania and Zaire in 1996 was a
dramatic experience for JRS workers[7].*

At the end of November 1996 the Government of Tanzania made a very
strong statement that all Rwandan refugees would have to return home and
repatriation would begin on December 31st.

All economic activities would be suspended on December 10th and refugees
would not be allowed to travel or to work. Individual refugees could apply for
asylum. Plans were made for a *comfortable*, if fast, repatriation. But events
changed and repatriation was accelerated, and all the plans of UNHCR and
the NGOs were discarded. Repatriation was to be a military manoeuvre.

The reaction of the refugees was frantic. Given the events in Zaire in October
1996 they feared for their lives. Young men and women in particular feared
what their future would be in a society where the leaders were their enemies.
They were determined not to return. Many left early to go to other destinations. There were reports of some being caught and driven directly to the
Rwandan border. Others paid their way to government officials to help them
out. Their destinations varied from Malawi to Kenya, to Cameroon and for a
lot they left just to go to anywhere that was not Rwanda. In those early weeks
many of our friends came to say goodbye or just disappeared overnight.

On December 8th we witnessed the first mass movement of refugees from the
camps to the bush. We were in the midst of a meeting, when reports came
that over 8,000 refugees had left Kagenyi camp. We learned that thousands
of the refugees from Kagenyi and Rubwera had got up en masse that morning and moved. Initially, rather naïvely officials thought they were heading
to Rwanda but that was not so. They simply walked into the bush, they said
they would go in any direction that was not Rwanda. They spent over one
week there: Women with children, some heavily pregnant, men young and

---

[7] Comments from Noelle Corscaden to *JRS experience in dealing with repatriation*, JRS, 1999.

old. It was the rainy season and their health was a major worry. Later in the week thousands of refugees from Musuhura camp in the Ngara district and from Chabalisa moved out of their camps en masse, and headed as well into the bush. People thought it was a protest, but we heard rumours that it was probably their way of helping to remove the arms and the militia from the camp safely. The people caused a distraction allowing the militia to leave unnoticed, and it is believed that they eventually made their way to other countries or places to re-group. When these militia were safely out of danger, the others returned.

On December 10th the Tanzanian army moved to Ngara and took over the operation of repatriation. It proceeded as a forced repatriation. NGOs were not allowed to help. The army had taken control. All were to walk to the border. No trucks were provided, except for the very sick or vulnerable, but most people were afraid to avail of this as they feared separation from their families. They would have to walk, in fact they were herded like animals. Between December 10th and 18th all the camps in Tanzania were cleared. The refugees from Kagenyi and Rubwera were the last to move and they started their walk home on December 18th. They crossed the border on December 29th.

Since their return some wrote describing the walk home as calvary and their situation there not much better. Constantly people confided in us their great fears and distrust. There had been no time to prepare them for the journey, for their return and so fear and panic was widespread. Their protectors were powerless and their leaders had been scattered. They complied silently and against their wills to the dictates of the military.

On the morning of December 20th the army was to move in to Chabalisa to start the repatriation. We drove to the camp that morning. People were quiet, but busy packing up, selling their belongings to the Tanzanians who had come along to salvage what they could. We could not stay within the confines of the camp so we sat on the hillside overlooking the camp and at 11 am as the army drove in, the people all stood up and walked in silence. It was their first steps in a journey which would take over two weeks, to their homeland. Within a few hours the camp was empty and like a ghost town.

Some days later the people from Kagenyi and Rubwera passed through Chabalisa on their way to the border. They were exhausted, they had the longest walk of all. On Christmas Eve I requested that the people could at least stop and rest. But we were told that even though it was Christmas

Day it would be as an ordinary day and they would have to walk. There seemed to be an urgency about getting them across the border.

Although the roads between Ngara and Karagwe were closed we managed to go to Omukariro on December 22nd. We witnessed the soldiers beating the people. On our return a group of angry refugees surrounded the car. Initially I was afraid but then realised that these were our friends and so we got out of the car to talk to them. They were upset and angry. The soldiers had beaten them and stolen their food. They begged us to do something. I went to the Home Affairs Officer and complained. He said he would do what he could to investigate the matter.

Each day after the last of the refugees had passed through Chabalisa, we awoke knowing that they were still walking. Each morning it was as if our heartbeat was an echo of their footsteps. Day after day they were still walking. And ten days later as the last of them crossed the border into Rwanda it was still not over, they still had more miles to walk, for it would take them many more days to reach to their own villages. For some the journey was a walk of over 400 kilometres. On their way they received a high protein biscuit every so many kilometres and some water. There was no time to provide any form of sanitation.

This was hailed by officials and politicians, as a very *successful and peaceful* repatriation.

The Grands Lacs region, which for JRS comprises Burundi, Rwanda and DR Congo, has suffered war and exile for decades. In the early sixties, violent attacks prior to the independence of Rwanda provoked the exile of hundreds of thousand of Tutsis, mainly towards Uganda and Zaire (now DR Congo). In the 70's, due to other waves of violence in Rwanda many others fled to the region of Kivu (Zaire), particularly to the area of Bukavu.

Violence attained unimaginable proportions with the assassinations of President Ndadaye in Burundi in 1993, which led the country to a civil war still going on today, and that of President Habyarimana of Rwanda on 6 April 1994. The latter confirmed the failure of the transition towards a multiparty system, as foreseen in the Arusha accords, signed by the armed opposition FPR

(Front Patriotique Rwandais), the non-armed opposition and the government of the old party. It was the beginning of the genocide. We will never know the exact number of victims who died in those three months of violence, but the numbers given range between 500,000 and one million.

The speed of victory of the FPR on the military front led to one of the quickest massive population movements in the history. Between April and May 1994, some 600,000 Rwandans crossed the Tanzanian border. Despite its fragile security situation, Burundi hosted tens of thousands of Rwandan refugees in July 1994.

But the most dramatic exodus took place in mid 1994, when the defeat of the Rwandan Armed Forces (FAR) was clear. In only a few days, an avalanche close to one million people fled to Goma, former Zaire (now DR Congo), leading to a humanitarian crisis without precedent. An estimated 70,000 people died of cholera.

In August, in Goma a minority of refugees went back to Rwanda, leaving behind 700,000 fellow countrymen in immense camps, refugees continued to arrive to Bukavu until the end of August 1995. The total number of refugees in the Bukavu region was around 300,000.

In this context, JRS, conscious of the deep uprootedness people suffered in the region, identified four objectives:

- Accompany and serve people who had survived the genocide and suffered exile, regardless of their ethnic origin. Some weeks after their arrival, JRS had set up operational projects in Burundi, Congo and Rwanda.
- Special attention was given to children, who were the main victims of the "non-sense" of the adults. JRS offered new possibilities for the future by coordinating schools and centres for orphans through some ten teams in the three countries.
- Contribute to reconciliation and social rehabilitation, providing traumatised people with appropriate psychological services.
- Keep alive the light of faith with pastoral programmes in the camps and give support to religious congregations deeply traumatised by the events.

Mateo Aguirre SJ, July 2005
Regional Director in West Africa (former Regional Director in the Grands Lacs)

A FAITHFULNESS WHICH BEARS FRUIT
Mateo Aguirre SJ

Mateo was the first Regional Director in the Grands Lacs region, between 1995 and 2000. In the aftermath of the 1994 Rwandan genocide he set up a team in Bukavu, Eastern Zaire. JRS Grands Lacs region expanded soon after these events to Burundi, Rwanda, Republic of Congo and other parts of Zaire (then DR Congo). From 2001 he is the Regional Director in West Africa, based in Abidjan.

JRS Grands Lacs took shape after the shocking genocide in Rwanda, in 1994. But before this, some activities were already being developed by the Jesuits in Rwanda. In 1993, Patrick Gahizi SJ had been assisting Rwandan returnees with first aid. Patrick felt proud of being part of JRS and mentioned the importance of its mission during a meeting in Kinshasa. He was killed on 7th April 1994 together with a group of people at Centre Christus, the Jesuit retreat centre in Kigali. In Burundi, Jesuits, such as Yves Brasseur and Alberto Guerrero were working with returnees together with the Franciscan Missionaries of Mary, like Sr Dina.

My memories go back to Bukavu, formerly Zaire, where we started working after the exile of one million refugees. I arrived there on 26 December 1994 from Kisangani, (now DR Congo). I had been in Congo for the last twenty years, first in Lubumbashi and then in a Kisangani University parish.

The JRS international office had a radical reaction towards helping the refugees who had fled from Rwanda in massive numbers. JRS was deeply touched by this crisis. We experienced on one side very positive feelings of wanting to be there but also the awareness of our poverty. We wanted to help but the needs were beyond our imagination. When I arrived in Bukavu, Quim Pons SJ, a Jesuit from the Catalunya province, was already there.

This was my first experience in a refugee camp, my first contact with a particular and massive population – uprooted and in extreme suffering. In the lives of all the volunteers who worked there, the time in Bukavu drew a line which determined their vision of life. There was a *before and after* the refugee experience of Bukavu, because the injustice and suffering we saw overwhelmed us and at the same time stimulated us to further commitment in the future.

It was a phase of welcoming people who came to work with the same motivation; to facilitate their stay and together work towards possible responses to the needs of the refugees. It was a very stimulating experience for me to receive nine volunteers who were sensitive to injustice and ready to live and work in difficult conditions. I felt great solidarity and commitment and I witnessed something that I experience even now: how refugees act as catalysts among people from totally different backgrounds. To me it was like a cocktail of solidarity. Life in the JRS teams was very rich because of the diversity; there were men and women, religious and lay, black and white, of different nationalities, with one vision and one motivation. This has been a wonderful experience in every country I have worked during my time in JRS.

It was also a time of awareness of the historical background of the refugees, to understand what it means to be a refugee and to realise the ambiguity of their situation. They fled the genocide in which some of them had participated. They were at the same time victims and perpetrators. This brought us to discover that same ambiguity in our presence too. But we were clear in our mission; we desired to help the most vulnerable, those who should not be abandoned. We thought that widows, orphans and the handicapped should not be left aside even though we knew that among their neighbors there were perpetrators of the genocide. There were innocent people who deserved our service. So in a context of inhumanity and cruelty, JRS opted to give a testimony of humanity. We took the side of the people in need, regardless of their ethnic origin. Our priority was the individual in need.

Although we were actually there in December 1994, the work did not start seriously until August 1995. Needs assessments took place. We also had to win the trust of refugees, who were hurt in their confidence towards NGOs, so the teams spent some time just visiting people and talking to them.

JRS Bukavu was faithful to Fr Arrupe's vision because the priority for the team was to spend time with the refugees and to listen to them. From that accompaniment, technical programmes started, such as a pedagogical programme to assist the victims of trauma, which JRS organised together with IFHIM (Montreal Integrated Human Training Institute), but the priority was not the programme per se, but our presence with the refugees, who were extremely traumatised. This response was not pre-meditated, it was very spontaneous. I remember seeing the members of the team leaving at 8 am and coming back at 6 pm. This was very much appreciated by the refugees. They understood we were really with them.

197

A style of work in Panzi camp

In many cases, our education work consisted in confronting refugees and questioning their status as 'eternally innocent victims'. We tried to shake their minds towards a wider horizon of reality. Even if this sounds paradoxical, we felt that part of our service to refugees was to question them. In the camps there was an atmosphere where the ideas and their interpretations were easily manipulated. Only someone who had won the trust of refugees could offer some objectivity.

We were conscious that there was some moral ambiguity in the camps. By realizing this context, a worker could manage to serve refugees' interests and avoid being manipulated by the interests of politicians or the military.

It was important for us to feel that we were loved by those whom we served but not because of what we offered them in terms of goods or the money. It was very easy for the relationship to turn false. It was this that the JRS team in Bukavu tried to avoid from the beginning. But it required time.

In the end, this was a gratifying experience. After some time we witnessed how much refugees appreciated our way of proceeding. Froduald Mugemanyi, one of our refugee collegues, said that he was grateful for the low profile and the constant way of working of JRS. It was the way of *doing* and *being with* them which refugees really appreciated: 'You are in the camp in a different way'.

Joaquim Pons SJ, JRS Bukavu[8]

---

[8] *The Bukavu experience*, written by a group of six JRS workers, 1999.

Mark Raper SJ/JRS

Joaquim Pons SJ with Rwandan refugee children in Panzi camp, Bukavu, 1995.
In 1994 in the aftermath of the Rwandan genocide, fear of vengeance caused
a human exodus of two million people. They fled to surrounding countries,
in particular into Tanzania and Zaire. In eastern Zaire, the two main border
cities of Goma and Bukavu quickly became a focal point for fleeing refugees.

Projects continued on the other side of the border too. In Rwanda, Francois Xavier Ngarambe and the Benebikira sisters helped the orphans who had survived the genocide. JRS also worked with the Emmanuelle community in Kigali with the 'rescapés' of the genocide. It was a global response, regardless of the ethnic background of the people.

The war and evacuation in Bukavu started in September 1996 and went on throughout October. During these months the service was incompatible with such great insecurity. Refugees fled the attacks, some further inside Congo and many others were killed. We experienced destruction of all our efforts and energy, and the death of many of our colleagues, such as four Marist brothers.

After this catastrophe, we felt that we should continue to be faithful to the suffering of the people. JRS stayed in Bukavu until June 1997, at the service of the local church, collaborating with the local Caritas helping it to restructure. The group experience was strong even if there was fear.

In July 1997 the regional office in Bujumbura was organised. Activities in Rwanda and Burundi continued. We started assisting the Congolese of Rwandan extraction who had first fled to Goma and later on, due to *Interhamwe* attacks, to Rwanda. We established our presence in Byumba and Kibuye, where JRS is still present.

Cinema and Olympic games in Bukavu

The Xaverian fathers had a rich video library which they offered for use. Among the favorite films, The Chap, starring Charlie Chaplin, was a great success: his sense of humor and the way he laughed at himself are of universal value. I think refugees saw themselves reflected in this poor Charlot, who showed a type of solidarity and spontaneous generosity which we actually found in the houses of refugee families. In fact, many of them were hosting children who were lost during the great exodus of 1994.

Was all this effort worthwhile? I think it was, even if only for something simple: to laugh! It was surely one of the most efficient therapies against the distress suffered by many refugees in the camps.

This laughing brought together all the people who were present for the cinema sessions: the nine year old boy together with the Zairean military, who for a moment forgot his kalashnikov and came to enjoy this atmosphere. The magic of the screen allowed refugees to feel free from the roles they had been assigned in the camp. Surely these cinema sessions did not change the tragic fate that awaited the Rwandan refugee camps. But I have the feeling that those moments were not useless. They gave joy of deep humanity, through curiosity, laughing and emotional expression. A humanity which a refugee camp tends to kill.

The artistic festival we organised at the end of the school year and the sports competitions were also very strong moments. I still don't know if the risks we took to transport all these young people from one camp to the other were reasonable, or if the energy wasted in discussion with the teachers on the need to save money in these competitions were worth it. But I am sure that the joy refugees felt when their team won or the resignation felt when the adversary was impossible to defeat, were also signs of celebration of our common humanity.

During those days, I walked with a tape recorder in my hand. I felt very touched when I witnessed the enthusiasm refugees expressed while organising and participating in the Olympic Games. They had been living in the camp for two years, in miserable conditions with their future full of fear rather than hope. The images of the children of Nyakavogo, wearing a a skirt of banana leaves, celebrating the victory of their team, singing and dancing to the rhythm of drums, remains registered not only in a cassette player, but also in my heart.

Christophe Renders SJ, JRS Bukavu[9]

---

[9] *The Bukavu experience*, JRS, 1999.

My experience in this so-called second phase was that since the suffering of the people continued, our presence also had to continue. It was like an obsession to be faithful to them. If the suffering in Bukavu had ended, our work would have ended too, but unfortunately this was not the case. I witnessed how this faithfulness bore fruit. After two or three years, the JRS Grands Lacs region took shape and grew in quality service to refugees and professional personnel. I also felt the joy of being able to restart what had already been done and to witness the response of many new volunteers.

Once again, JRS had the joy of being the catalyst which made possible the consoling encounter between the suffering of many and the solidarity of many, both volunteers and donors.

Projects started in different parts of Burundi, like Bubanza and Munanira, two remote areas in great need. In Rwanda the service to the Congolese refugees continued and expanded with the help of local congregations. In DR Congo we started projects in Lubumbashi and Kinshasa with the internally displaced, and services were offered to the displaced people of Congo Brazzaville.

In 2000, when the Grands Lacs region was organized, I was replaced by Joaquín Ciervide SJ. The international office in Rome identified a great need for our presence in West Africa, a region where JRS had worked in the past, but which had again experienced severe turmoil due to the conflicts in Liberia, Sierra Leone, Guinea and later in Ivory Coast. I witnessed the vision of the international office in the face of situations which demanded a response, as well as the availability of JRS to accept challenges. The Rome office was like a lighthouse which can see the world globally and identify the greatest needs. I understood JRS to be truly universal, not focused on a specific area. So I was invited by the International Director, Lluís Magriñà SJ, to assess the needs and give structure to a JRS presence in West Africa.

Our first response was in Guinea, where JRS could not have worked without the support of the local church, which provided unforgettable staff like the sisters Gertrude Lama and Marie Agnes Soropogui, from a local congregation called Servants of Mary Virgin and Mother. I arrived there in July 2001, together with Gonzalo Sánchez Terán, a Spanish volunteer who was a priceless worker. The projects did not start until December 2001. I remember we were very keen to start the first food distribution of rice and palm oil so that refugees could have food on Christmas day.

I realise how the fact of being in the field and close to suffering people gives us capacity to respond. From our presence in Guinea, JRS gave response to other needs in other parts of the country and outside Guinea.

After a first evaluation by Josep Sugrañes SJ and Gonzalo Sánchez Terán, a modest JRS presence started in Liberia. Bishop Michael Francis of Monrovia greatly facilitated our work.

Congolese refugee in Byumba camp, Rwanda

Mark Raper SJ/JRS

The project in Ivory Coast was an experience of great collaboration with the local church. It was extremely rewarding to discover the richness of religious communities who were ready to run to help the weakest people. In April 2003 the Association of Major Superiors requested JRS for some possible apostolates with internally displaced people. JRS offered its knowledge to this group and the work started in September 2003 with the involvement of six religious from different congregations: Teresians of Osso, Ursulines, Providence de la Pommerais and Annunciation.

My experience of closure of projects has also been a good one. It means that peace is finally there and people can go back to their homes and re-assume their own responsibilities. Of course it is hard to say good-bye to people we have accompanied, but it also means the satisfaction of a job well done. I recall the closure of the reconstruction project in Guekedou, Guinea. That day Lluís Magriñà was there, as was Gonzalo, and the JRS teams. Many people came from different backgrounds to thank JRS. We felt this to be deep gratitude, coming from the local authorities, Muslims, Animists, Christians, everyone had the same grateful feeling. It was very moving because I witnessed the virtue of refugees thankfully acknowledging our work.

Let me finish by offering an image of the faithfulness of JRS to Fr Arrupe's mission in Laine refugee camp, Guinea. This camp was meant for 6,000 people but, due to insecurity in Liberia, the population grew to 30,000. JRS has been working as an implementing partner with UNHCR for non-formal education since 2003. The lesson we have learnt is that the refugees themselves have told us what they want to learn. The project was discerned by the refugees, not by JRS. Sr Covadonga Orejas of the Vedruna Carmelites was chiefly responsible for making these desires possible. The refugees asked for activities which would give them self reliance in the camp and on return to Liberia. They told us that they wanted to learn how to make soap, since there is a lot of palm oil in the area. They also learn how to dye clothes, a typical activity in the region. All these were and still are clear signs of the dignity of hope.

The original charism of Fr Arrupe is still alive after 25 years. Our work is confirmed when we see so many people coming from different parts of the world, ready to continue to accompany, serve and plead the cause of refugees, and taking seriously the dignity of the human being[10].

---

[10]Interview with Mateo Aguirre, Rome, May 2005.

Ken Gavin SJ/JRS

School children in Salala camp for internally displaced people, Liberia

Expansion of JRS Grands Lacs from 2000
Joaquín Ciervide SJ

Joaquín Ciervide replaced Mateo Aguirre as Regional Director in Grands Lacs in 2000. Due to the volatile situation in the region, especially DR Congo, JRS maintained the existing projects and started new ones, expanding its presence among the many forcibly displaced.

In August 2000 Mateo Aguirre SJ ended his six years as Regional Director of the Grands Lacs region, and I replaced him. At that time the region covered Burundi, Rwanda and DR Congo. Due to the civil war in Congo Brazzaville in 1997, JRS also developed some reintegration projects there over a short period of time.

When I started working in Bujumbura, the finances of the regional office were managed by Javi Marticorena, and Oihana Irigaray had just been appointed as information officer.

The years 2000, 2001 and 2002 were a period of expansion, especially due to the conflict in DR Congo and the new projects which we started there. In 2002, Oihana and Javi got married, Javi was replaced by Mateusz Tuniewicz and Oihana by Nicolas Dorronsoro. In 2002, Louis Falcy was appointed as policy officer. Elisabet Montserrat joined the team in September 2003 and has helped greatly in responding to the requests of the funding agencies, which require more and more technical skills. In 2004, Nicolas was named country director, after Vincent de Marcillac SJ had finished his five year term in Burundi. Steve Hege came to work as information and policy officer. 2005 was the year of strategic planning for the following three years.

JRS in Burundi

The civil war in Burundi started in 1993 and caused population movements towards Bujumbura, where people found more security than in the rural areas. From 1997, JRS worked with UNHCR in the construction of Kiyange, a settlement for people coming from the Cibitoke and Bubanza provinces. Once the houses and communal latrines were built, JRS started a cooperative with the help of Alberto Plaza SJ, so that displaced people could start income generating activities. In 2000 this cooperative was made up of a bakery, a tailoring and basket production workshops, carpentry, a deposit for drinks and a mill. Other activities were developed that year, including a restaurant in downtown Bujumbura. At the end of 2000, Pascal Martin, a Belgian volunteer who was the JRS Kiyange director, moved to Bukavu and was replaced by Adolf Fabregas until mid 2002. Samuel Gyger SJ and Marcos Ibanez would then be in charge of the Kiyange project.

In Buterere, near Kiyange, there were displaced people who were offered vocational training programmes by JRS. Sr Teresa Florensa, Sr Macon Lopez and Encarna de Mendoza were subsequently in charge of the programme during all these years. Other projects in Burundi included a dispensary in Munanira, Muramvya province, and a hospital in Bubanza, under the management of Sylvie Clement and Meg Hicks. Insecurity in both areas forced JRS to withdraw. A project of HIV/Aids awareness under the direction of Sr Chantal Gerard started in 2000 raising awareness through 14 parishes to an already widespread problem in the country.

On the 3rd of October 2000, Br Antoine Bargiggia was coming back from Mutoi to Bujumbura, accompanied by a young man from his area in Buterere. At the top of Kibimba, in Gitega province, two men stopped his van and started arguing. Suddenly one of them fired at him, pulled his body out of the vehicle and stretched it out on the road. The young man with him managed to escape and the two attackers got away with the vehicle. A few minutes later, a second vehicle found Br Antoine already dead.

Brother Antoine was a member of the *Friends of the Poor*, a recently founded congregation from the Diocese of Milan. For 20 years he lived in Burundi, first in Mutoi and afterwards, for his last nine years, in an area of Buterere, north of Bujumbura. Living according to the charism of his congregation he shared the life of the poorest people. For the last three years Br Antoine had been Project Director in Buterere for JRS Burundi, a project intended to help the most vulnerable, especially HIV/AIDS patients and displaced people. He used to visit the Rumonge prison regularly and also the wounded in the Bujumbura military hospital.

Joaquín Ciervide SJ
Regional Director in the Grands Lacs

In 2001 the government decided to re-install around one hundred Batwa families close to Buterere. This group of nomadic traditions was a minority group (1%) in Burundi and had also fled the fighting. JRS expanded its programmes integrating this population into an agriculture project.

During the night of 24 February 2001, the rebel group FNL attacked the Kinama area, in northern Bujumbura. For some weeks there were violent attacks and many people moved to Buterere. JRS, together with WFP, Care, CRS and IRC, responded to this population through a medical programme. In March, FNL turned back to the hills of rural Bujumbura. More than 200 people lay dead in the streets of Kinama. Slowly the displaced people made their way back to their homes. The Health Centre in the Catholic parish was completely looted, and even the electric installation had been stolen. JRS, thanks to Sr Chantal Gerard, rebuilt the centre which is now operating normally.

Vincent de Marcillac SJ, country director in Burundi and present in the country since 1999, attended to the plight of Congolese refugees living in urban areas in Bujumbura, as an implementing partner of UNCHR for education. In 2004, Fr Vincent left the country due to threats against him after five years of service to the forcibly displaced people. Nicolas Dorronsoro replaced him. A sad event that shocked the team was the assassination of the Apostolic Nuncio in Bujumbura, Mgr Michael Courtney, on 29 December 2003. He was a dear friend of JRS and one committed to building peace. The circumstances of his death are still uncertain. JRS Burundi engaged with different networks working in this country: with the civil and military authorities, with NGOs and the UN, and with the Catholic Church. It aimed at finding paths towards peace, despite the risks. In an ambiguous world, JRS always was available to all peace mediation initiatives.

Rwanda

In Byumba and Kibuye camps, JRS assists Congolese refugees of Rwandan extraction, who fled the areas of Masisi and Rutsuru in 1996. This has been the most stable project in the area, and JRS works as a UNHCR implementing partner for formal and non-formal education. The Congolese priest, Desiré Seruhungo started the Byumba project back in 1997, staying with it until 2004, when he was sent to Goma. Fr Védaste Mugimbaho manages both camps, together with religious from different congregations, especially the sisters of St Marie de Namur.

Republic of Congo

Between May and October 1997, this country suffered a war, bringing Denis Sassou Nguesso to victory and power. In 2000 the return of refugees was almost in its final stage. JRS worked with the reintegration process of the refugees, both in Kibouende and Nkayi, rebuilding houses and offering mobile health aid. Fr Patrice Batantou SJ worked in Kibouende, and Sr Antoinette Loulendo, together with Christelle Noirault took care of the mobile clinic.

Democratic Republic of Congo (DRC)

In 2000, JRS was present in Lubumbashi with the internally displaced by a violent war which involved many African countries, still causing mass movements of people.

During the following five years, six projects were developed in different areas of the country: JRS Lubumbashi itself continued in very difficult conditions to offer education and health with the help of Sr Justine Kahungu; in Kinshasa, JRS started offering vocational training and education in different settlements to the displaced people who fled their homes in 1998 and 1999. Many of these displaced are slowly returning home, despite the war. About one third of them will stay in Kinshasa because they have a stable job. In Bukavu, Pascal Martin and Maria Grazia Massaro developed a primary school project, rebuilding twelve schools and training teachers. When the Nyiragongo volcano exploded in Goma in January 2002, the education project expanded to this area, offering help in restructuring the education system.

In mid 2002, the International Committee of the Red Cross (ICRC) published research on the isolation of two million people, who were trapped with no possibility of access to health. So JRS responded to the call of the Bishop of Basankusu, opening a health project in Baringa, in the Equateur province, and rebuilding an old hospital. Médecins Sans Frontières provided the medicines. Despite the logistical difficulties and harsh living conditions, the project developed thanks to the efforts of Adolf Fabregas, Sr Chantal, May Martinez Pacheco and Juliette Maquart. The project is now under way and the situation has more international attention, so JRS plans its withdrawal at the end of 2005, since other NGOs are in charge of the nutrition and health situation.

In Kongolo (Katanga province) and Kisangani, JRS has been present through education programmes since 2003 and 2004 respectively. In the latter, two Congolese jesuits have initiated projects in five primary schools in the outskirts of the city. As in other cities of Congo, the challenge is the great number of children who have to abandon school because their parents cannot afford to pay school fees. In Kisangani, JRS offers special lessons to drop out children.

In 2001, a national office for JRS Congo was created. Victor Wilondja has been in charge since then, and JRS has been officially recognised by the Home Affairs ministry.

While the situation in the region remains very unstable, JRS continues to accompany and serve forcibly displaced people, with the hope one day they will return back home.

Amaya Valcárcel/JRS   Camp for displaced people in Bujumbura area, Burundi, 1999

Millions uprooted from their homes: the DR Congo conflict

Victor Wilondja

In August 1998, the situation in DR Congo developed dramatically. The country broke up. Zimbabwe, Angola and Namibia fought on the side of the Government and Uganda and Rwanda on the side of the rebels. DR Congo was exploited by all sides, with three million dead in a conflict which lasts until today. Victor Wilondja is Country Director in DR Congo since 2001.

The beginning of the story of JRS in Democratic Republic of Congo is closely linked to the daily life of a parish, Kindele, on the outskirts of Kinshasa, in 1995. Back then, the parish priest, Joaquín Ciervide SJ, was worried about recurrent land erosion in his neighbourhood, so he resolved to raise awareness about the anti-erosion struggle among youths in the parish.

In the Democratic Republic of Congo, life is extremely precarious for those who have been forced to leave their native region. Displaced people and former town-dwellers find it very difficult to integrate into their new environment. There is a severe lack of adequate shelter and facilities to cater for basic needs. Though there are some NGOs working within the country, the number is woefully inadequate to deal with such pressing needs. It was against this background that JRS first became involved in DR Congo in 1998. With the aid of the local church, JRS began working with IDPs in Lubumbashi, supporting an education programme, and later expanded to other areas of the country.

When Joaquín Ciervide was appointed regional director of JRS Grands Lacs in May 2000, he successfully appealed to those with whom he had defied nature. So a JRS project started in Kinshasa. Three people – a doctor, a jurist and an engineer – were designated to coordinate JRS activities in three sites, which are former factories or old garages. Around 4,000 people were regrouped there; those displaced by war, widows and orphans of military servicemen of the old regime.

There were huge needs and we did not have a great deal to give them. But we had time and availability to offer, so we quickly got in with the crowd.

211

Refresher courses were organized in sites where we planned to get a teaching corps going. The two JRS coordinators devoted themselves to preparing stew for malnourished children. Despite administrative jobs which kept us in town, we spent most of our time at the sites, listening to people, their problems and their desires. And together, we found solutions.

Other projects were set up in similar settings elsewhere. In 2005, four projects closed in DRC. My thoughts are with families at the sites as they prepared to return to the provinces they fled. They unanimously expressed their gratitude to JRS, saying '*we will never forget you*'.

We were not the only organisation among them, nor were we the most powerful. What was special in what we did, other than our constant presence and closeness to our brothers and sisters? I understood that the experience I had searched for so much in my service to refugees was above all to be with them.

As in Kindele parish, I realised that the involvement of the entire refugee community is vital to take up the challenge to serve, accompany and defend their rights. The worth of their contribution makes them protagonists in this service just as much as we JRS workers are.

THE AFRICA EDUCATION PROJECT
Lolín Menéndez RSCJ

Lolín first met JRS in Rome in 1988, and spent some time as a volunteer in Centro Astalli. In 1991 she went to Malawi and was involved in a distance education programme. In 1994 she was Education Coordinator and Project Director in Rhino camp, Uganda, until 1996. She has been the Education Resource Person for Africa, based in Nairobi, between 1997 and 2003.

The premises of the Resource Base for Refugee Education were formally opened in 1998. The initial impulse came from a meeting held in the late 80's, but it was not until JRS Directors met in Kigali in 1995 that the Africa Education project began to take shape.

A first consultation held in Nairobi in December 1996 brought together experienced JRS personnel in order to discuss the concept of the Africa Education project and suggest concrete steps for its implementation. Colleagues from UNESCO and UNICEF joined the group for part of the discussion, and welcomed the initiative as an instance of collaboration that would ultimately benefit the refugees whom all the organizations present sought to serve.

JRS personnel were aware of the valuable experience accumulated through years of involvement in the education of refugees throughout the African continent. However, the fact is that JRS field staff often work in difficult and isolated circumstances. What is needed in order to make the most of the considerable experience and the collective wisdom of JRS so that precious time would not wasted 'reinventing the wheel' each time a new education project begins?

Thus began the Africa Education, with its twofold purpose: to gather the *institutional memory* of the experience of JRS in education, and to serve a practical resource to JRS projects. The aim was to facilitating the task of field workers by providing resources and expertise, so that the quality of education and professional formation given to refugee teachers and children would be enhanced.

The Project has made available both a place and a person at the service of field personnel.

213

A place: The Resource Base

The beginning of the Resource Base was small and original. In May 1997 the resources were housed in the JRS premises in Nairobi, in a room whose main attraction was a large closet to store materials. After several phases, the shelves in the library which looked ample quickly filled up, and the size of the meeting room certainly limits the number that can attend a function.

Educational materials are collected and stored in a user-friendly manner in the library. The collection includes, among others, textbooks of countries of origin of refugees and of those who receive them; works on educational psychology and methodology; sections on issues which are the focus of JRS, among them, education of girls, peace education, environmental studies; relevant topics such as literacy, development, health issues. Samples of programmes for distance education and those designed for out-of-school children are also available.

The outreach of the Resource Base took the shape of a monthly Newsletter in which several books were reviewed. JRS projects were then able to request the purchase of materials that they found suitable for their projects. A website[11] was also created in order to make available book lists, newsletters and project profiles to JRS personnel and co-workers form other organizations.

A person: Education Resource Person for Africa

I had the privilege to begin the Africa education project as Resource Person. It is not often that one starts a project with so much at one's disposal: a wealth of experience, past and present; committed JRS field personnel who describe themselves as *passionate about education*; a core group of refugee teachers and administrators working closely with JRS staff and eventually assuming positions of responsibility; the support of JRS as an organization; a realistic budget that enabled the project to be fully operative as soon as it began. Most of all, there was a tangible desire to work together, to talk with and to learn from each other on the part of persons involved in JRS education projects.

---

[11] www.jrsafricaeducation.org

Visits to the field and meetings of JRS personnel have been at the heart of the project. At the request of Mark Raper SJ, a first meeting was convened in 1997 in order to discuss and draw up the *Guidelines for the Involvement of JRS in Education in Africa*. The Guidelines have subsequently been revised and refined according to new insights and evolving situations. Guidelines for Scholarship Programmes and Criteria for Projects have also been elaborated, field-tested, and reworked.

Other meetings took place for interest groups, for instance, for persons in charge of programmes for Early Childhood, for those involved in peace education projects, an approach to new teaching/learning methods for teachers. Participants were expected to share the contents of the workshop on their return to the field. Each meeting provided the opportunity for input as well as for professional and friendly exchanges. Networks grew from reality, not from theory.

As Resource Person I had the opportunity to work closely with other NGOs and UN organizations, for instance, preparing the Thematic Study on Education in Emergencies for the World Education Forum in Dakar, participating in meetings on Peace Education sponsored by UNICEF and UNHCR, taking part in the Interagency Consultation in Geneva that gave birth to the Interagency Network on Education in Emergencies (INEE). These opportunities to interact with persons of other organizations who shared the same concerns and work together to face challenges and find solutions were fruitful because the input received from field projects made collaboration a reality at a wider level.

In my experience, it was the visits made to the field that gave the project its reason for being. It was not just a question of doing evaluations or needs assessments. These were visits to persons equally passionate about education. It was there, in the field, in conversation, thorough observation and interaction, that ideas and challenges flowed both ways. Yes, it was a way to bring the Resource Base to the field. But, most importantly, the occasion of each visit made me aware of the persons for whom we were working in Nairobi, and gave me a better sense of materials needed, and the energy to search for them. Setting up channels for networking among persons and projects working along the same lines or facing similar challenges was undoubtedly my greatest joy.

In the six years that I spent as Resource Person, I saw the project grow in ways that responded to concrete needs and realities. And it had to be so, as the overall situation of refugees and displaced persons in Africa changed dramatically in those years. It was necessary to start new projects in new refugee situations – at that moment, in Guinea. But the process of repatriation to Liberia, Burundi, and Angola had begun to gather momentum. By the time I finished, the task on hand focused on developing strategies and taking practical steps for *education for repatriation*, both for the people who had stayed home and for refugees who would return.

The six years went quickly, not without hitches or difficulties at times, but always with wonder and gratitude for the commitment to education on the part of the people with whom I interacted, and for the common effort in which we engaged through the Africa Education project in order to prepare the ground for hope to take root.

Don Doll SJ/JRS   Nimule secondary school, southern Sudan

An experienced educator once said that for many refugees, living in a camp offered an opportunity to study in better conditions than at home. Considering the tough living conditions, the despair of so many refugees, and their frequently bleak prospects for the future, such an opinion sounded cynical and at least questionable. But after eight years working in camps in Southern Africa, I fully subscribe to this opinion.

Formal education is a real answer to the needs of refugees. It makes sense in the context of reality in a camp where refugees often have nothing to do but hang around, their sense of responsibility dulled from having to depend totally on others for their most basic needs. Many refugees arrive in huge camps from villages, so living in anonymous circumstances is something new, as is the disruption of traditional family patterns.

Due to its long-term nature, a school offers opportunities for the future. And this is of incredible importance, because the future has to do with living, with having aims and purpose. Apart from basic needs for food, shelter and health care, people have three other needs which cry out to be met: the need for togetherness, to have work or a trade, and to have a structured life. A school can meet all three needs. First, it offers work. Not only for tutors, but also for students, it becomes a workshop of learning. A well-run school is a place for togetherness. Its schedule and activities structure the day as well as the life of those who attend.

Going to school may fulfill a dream of both teachers and students in camps. War has destroyed their lives to an extent, but now they show they are not defeated.

François Chanterie SJ[12]

---

[12] François Chanterie was involved in JRS programs in Malawi, DR Congo and Angola.

FROM ETHIOPIA TO NAIROBI
Bernadette Mangan LSA

Sr Bernadette worked with JRS in Ethiopia between 1996 and 1998.
From 1999 onwards, she has been the Personnel Officer in JRS East
Africa.

My first introduction to JRS was in 1991 in Tigray, northern Ethiopia. At
that time I was working as a nurse mainly engaged in Primary Health
Care with my own community in Edaga Hamus. As our house was on the
main road between Makele and Adigrat we very often welcomed passers-
by to share our hospitality.

It was on one such occasion that I became acquainted with JRS. Mark
Raper SJ and Mike Evans SJ, then JRS East Africa Regional Director, made
several support visits to the JRS teams in Adigrat and Hawzaen and to the
JRS workers who had been seconded to work with the Daughters of Charity in Monoxito, Makelle and Alitaena.

In 1996, having completed our 10-year commitment to the people of the
Adigrat Diocese I applied to work in JRS and was invited by Mike Evans SJ
to return to work in Ethiopia. I signed a two year contract and proceeded
to Addis Abeba. I was seconded to the Daughters of Charity to work in
Alecu, Dembidollo, South Western Ethiopia. JRS was fairly active in Ethiopia at that time with projects in Hawzaen, Debre Zeit, Addis Abeba and
Gambella, with several members seconded to Makele, Alecu, Monoxito
and Alitaena.

In 1999 I was invited to become the first Personnel Officer in JRS East
Africa. Priority was given to understanding and living the JRS vision and
mission. The document drawn up at the Pastoral Workers meeting in Harare
in 1998 was a valuable starting point and tool which we used as a resource document in all our orientations.

Interpersonal relationships are difficult at the best of times, but in teams
which comprise persons of both sexes, of various cultural backgrounds, of
various age groups, priests, brothers, religious sisters and lay persons
and of different religious persuasions we can expect to have problems

218

from time to time. I have learned over the years that what may begin as problems may end up being opportunities of growth for all concerned.

Meanwhile, in Ethiopia the projects of Hawzaen and Gambella were handed over to the local community to run, as they no longer met the criteria for JRS direct involvement. The project in Debre Zeit closed having completed the objective set at its inception.

Restructuring of the Refugee Community Center in Addis Abeba took place and the setting up of a new project in Kaliti began. The latter was to address the need of the displaced widows and orphans sent from Eritrea after 1991. Endless meetings took place with the representatives of the government of Ethiopia as this was to be a joint project.

Many southern Sudanese were in the camps of Finudo and Sherkole in Ethiopia and in Kakuma Kenya. Others were in the camps of northern Uganda and great credit is due to the JRS workers who worked tirelessly in setting up schools and training teachers to run them. Many refugees were given scholarships and their progress was monitored and encouraged so that today many of those who began their education in the Ugandan camps are now ready to take an active role in the repatriation of their people in southern Sudan.

In 2001 John Guiney SJ succeeded Stephen Power SJ as Regional Director. He had previously worked in Tanzania as project director in Kakonko so he was familiar with the needs of the region. After his initial visits to the projects with Stephen, he prioritized what he saw as the immediate needs. He appointed a Regional Advocacy Officer and he separated the Regional and Kenya Country office staff.

In 2003 an external evaluation of the Regional Office took place, this addressed the issues of the regional office staff and their function in relation to all the projects in the region. During that same year JRS Eastern Africa was host to a Human Resources Consultant sent by the International Director in order to compile a Human Resources Manual.

Also in 2003 an International Meeting of all Country Directors was held in Nairobi. This was a valuable exercise in that they were encouraged to become more involved in each project and to visit the field more often rather than working too much from their offices.

When I look back on my time in JRS, I am profoundly touched by the lives of some of our young staff who died young, among them Samuel, Hadish, Abeba, Simon, James, Bekelech, John Loboi. These were people who in the midst of their own suffering were concerned about the refugees and displaced and because of their youth we never thought that death was so close.

Our lives are coloured by our encounters with others we meet on our journeys. For what JRS has meant and means to me I wish to say a special Te Deum.

The JRS driver, John Loboi was killed in an ambush on a JRS car in northern Uganda, together with other four people. John was laid to rest on 13th May 2003 in his home in Lobone, South Sudan. John, 24, leaves behind a wife and two children.

The incident took place on 12th May, as John was driving back to Lobone from Kitgum, northern Uganda. The car was ambushed and hit by a rocket-propelled grenade at about 4.30pm. The attackers, suspected to be members of the Lord's Resistance Army (LRA) looted the items before setting the car on fire.

Aden Raj, JRS Country Director in Uganda
12 May 2003

ADVOCATING ON BEHALF OF REFUGEES IN ZAMBIA
Raúl González SJ

Raúl González worked in Zambia between 2000 and 2002 as Advocacy Officer, after being part-time coordinator for JRS Latin America. In 2002 he worked in the International Office. Refugees from Central and Eastern Africa made their way to Southern Africa with the ultimate goal South Africa. Many got stuck in Malawi, Zambia, Zimbabwe and in South Africa. Xenophobic sentiments have emerged at a time when most of Africa is democratizing. The result has been the adoption of anti-refugee policies and practices by governments. It is in this context that JRS started projects for refugees living in urban areas in Zambia and South Africa in 1997.

When I joined the team of JRS Zambia in January 2000, I carried with me what I had known about the JRS in Latin America. Two years as regional coordinator there made me learn how advocacy work should be part of the accompaniment and service, right from the grass roots. The peculiarity of JRS Latin America as far back as the 80's was that, even in countries with a poor rule of law and immersed in conflicts that generated refugees, the teams always planned their advocacy work trying to influence the legislation and local policies, not limiting themselves to particular cases or situations. They did so participating in the local policies on displacement, directly or campaigning with other local church or human rights organisations and universities.

I arrived in Zambia asking myself whether it would be possible to do advocacy work on the general conditions which affect refugees, in an African context and in Zambia itself. As happens in Latin America, the possibility of accompanying refugees depends on the autorization of the host country. And contrary to Latin America, much of the staff of JRS is expatriate, which complicates things if we talk about participating in local policy and about a sensitive issue. My questions did not find easy answers.

Much of the advocacy work of JRS Zambia at the beginning of 2000 was linked to the limitation of refugees' rights. The most poignant problem was the detention of refugees who were living in urban contexts. The situation became more serious when government policies started to consider refugees as rejected and dangerous people.

221

Before 2000, JRS Zambia had developed advocacy work denouncing, at times with other agencies, the 'official version' on the treatment of refugees. Formation of the Zambian population had taken place in the areas affected by influxes of refugees, as well as involving the local church in aid to refugees.

Our strategy was presented to government officials, UNHCR and other agencies, in a meeting where we were invited to discuss the rights of refugees. We presented ourselves as an international organisation, and also as a work of a Province of the Society of Jesus, present in Zambia and Malawi for a long time. We were there to support the efforts of the local church, not to do a different work. Our objective was to have a refugee law which would facilitate integration of refugees in the long term.

The response of the churches and local organisations was excellent. A programme together with the diocese of Lusaka turned out to reduce significantly the detention time of refugees who were held for immigration reasons. Both the Catholic Secretariat and the Catholic Commission for Justice and Peace participated in lobbying initiatives to change the negative impact of refugee policies. The Jesuit Center for Theological Reflection published our proposals and supported our plans. The Catholic radio of Lusaka, Yatsani radio, broadcasted programmes on refugees. The local church also paved the way to its broad network of contacts with other churches. We met with the Christian Council and the Evangelical Fellowship, and a team of pastors started raising awareness among the Christian population.

With Catholic Relief Services, we organised workshops on refugee issues for Zambian people in several towns and villages with large influx of refugees, principally those close to the borders. These workshops were organised in the parishes and many people attended: government officials, local chiefs, leaders of local organisations, Catholics and people from other confessions. We offered our knowledge about refugees, their rights, their resources, and we dialogued with the Zambian communities about their vast experience in welcoming refugees. So the answer to my question was clear. It is possible to develop a grass roots advocacy work in countries with large influxes of refugees, even if they are very poor. My contribution had been to offer the strategic vision of JRS Latin America on advocacy.

Many things helped develop this work. Despite the changing of personnel, there was no discontinuity in the job. I was replaced by Michael Gallagher SJ, a person with much more experience than I, who continued and expanded with great quality the initiatives already put in place. This continuity is decisive so that a long term work such as advocacy is really fruitful. Our work just reinforced the efforts already in place to build a more humane country. The local church, civil society and the Jesuit province have promoted justice and peace initiatives for a long time, so we only included the refugee issue in their agenda. A decisive element was the inclusion of Zambian staff to the advocacy work. People like Nshimbi Kabamba, Lillian Lupiya or Ruth Nambeya learned quickly and developed many delicate initiatives in a better way than the expatriates. They facilitated relationships and communication problems with the local authorities. Today, the policy officer in Zambia is a Zambian expert on refugees.

When I finished my mission in Zambia in mid 2002, I was called to set up a global advocacy strategic plan in the international office. I could witness that besides Latin America and Zambia, strong local advocacy work was also being done by JRS in other countries.

My memories go to cases in which we succeeded and others in which we failed. Together with the feelings every refugee leaves in the heart, I deeply thank the Zambians committed to faith and justice who accompanied and supported us in many ways. And of course, the strong conviction about local policy work as being crucial to the mission, complementary to the international efforts and as a way to serve refugees.

Internally displaced in southern Sudan   Don Doll SJ/JRS

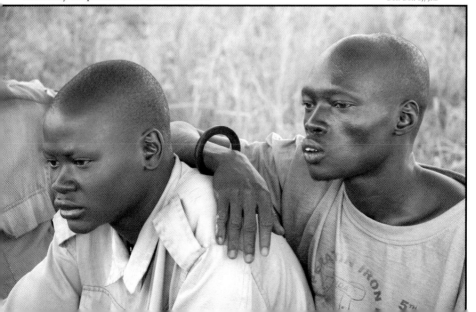

Focussing on our strengths
John Guiney SJ

In 2001, John Guiney succeeded Stephen Power as Regional Director for East Africa, after working for many years with JRS in Tanzania.

The founder of JRS Tanzania and present Moderator of the Provincials of Africa and Madagascar, Fr Massawe, noted at the opening commemoration of the JRS Jubilee in Nairobi that we do not celebrate 25 years of JRS. We instead, commemorate our existence and weep because of the existence of so many refugees. We can only celebrate, he noted, when JRS will no longer be needed in our world.

When I joined JRS in Eastern Africa it was in a state of expansion due to the assassination of President Ndadaye in Burundi in 1993, the 1994 genocide in Rwanda, and the change of regimes in DR Congo. There was a massive displacement of Grands Lacs refugees into Eastern Africa. To compound matters, the Somali situation was still unresolved and the Ethiopia/Eritrea conflict together with the situation in the Sudan continued to be a protracted problem.

Also at the time I began work in JRS in 1997, there were significant changes regarding infrastructure: Financial systems were being put in place to help reporting, accountability and funding. Systems and processes for recruitment of personnel were structured in the region. Orientation of new workers to JRS and their accompaniment was beginning to be considered a priority with the appointment of a Personnel Officer. Local capacity building took place while maintaining the international character of the organisation. JRS was seen as being in the forefront in collaborating with the laity in the service of refugees: 80% of people working in JRS East Africa are lay people and the vast majority from Africa.

A major development in the past years in JRS East Africa is the presence of an active Regional Advocacy Officer with an emphasis in building up advocacy in the projects and countries where we are involved. In East Africa, to give refugees back their voice we have to start at grass-root level. Another development has been the emphasis on education as an instrument of protection, development and hope. We have developed effective programmes to include girls and people with disabilities. The *girls affirmation programme* in all our educational projects is a major innovation and has helped hundreds of girls to complete their primary and secondary education.

We have also recognised that peace making and conflict resolution is an integral part of education. Education and peace building is a tool to understand the past, live in the present and prepare for the future. In order to build peace we have to understand what war is about, deal with the past and develop skills of conflict management and resolution. A secure and friendly environment must be provided to people in refugee and IDP camps to effectively deal with and overcome the trauma of war. This space is the community, within schools, literacy groups, women or civil society groups where people can tell their story, be listened to and understood, as well as acquire skills to deal with present and possible future conflict. Education goes beyond school and peace education; formal and non-formal education is inseparable.

This type of education is all the more important because innocent civilians, in particular innocent women and children, are really the main victims of wars. I think of a moral genocide such as in northern Uganda, where over 1.6 million are displaced and where over 15,000 children are being used by LRA (Lord Resistance Army) as sex slaves or soldiers. The brutalisation of women in conflict has challenged JRS to be courageous and creative in responding to their protection and promoting their inherent rights and dignity.

A challenge for JRS is how to remain light in our administration and yet continue to be good professionals, ready to move on with the refugees, learning from the past and focussing on our strengths[13].

---

[13] Interview with John Guiney, Rome, May 2005.

Returning home to Angola after a long exile

Joe Hampson SJ

1998 saw renewed wars both in Angola and in DR Congo. JRS Southern Africa grew in response given the huge refugee flows towards Zambia and Namibia, and within Angola. Joe Hampson replaced Peter Balleis as Regional Director in 1999. Since the end of the war in Angola in 2002, the main focus of JRS Southern Africa has been the repatriation and reintegration of Angolan forcibly displaced people. In May 2005 Joe was replaced by Joanne Whitaker RSM.

In 1993 Mark Raper SJ came to visit me in Zimbabwe to discuss the setting up of a new JRS Southern Africa region, and to request the services of Peter Balleis SJ to be the regional director there. At that time I was Peter's Provincial in Zimbabwe. My answer then was that JRS was not needed. I said to Mark 'you are duplicating what Imbisa (bishops' conference) refugee desk is doing'. So Mark had to persuade me about the added value of JRS, and the special way that it provides services. And he did. Years later, in 1999, I started working as JRS regional director in Southern Africa. At that time there was great pessimism about Angola, yet JRS was very involved in that country through a structure of small teams, depending mainly on international volunteers. Though small and with a family atmosphere, it was a tremendous witness to the power of JRS presence.

Savimbi's death in February 2002 was a major development in the region. Nobody was able to anticipate the cease fire and the end of the war that came a few weeks after the death, bringing 30 years of armed conflict to an end. There was finally an open horizon for rebuilding Angola. Zambia, Congo and Namibia were the host countries for Angolan refugees. A repatriation process started, and is still going on now.

A trend during these years has been the growing poverty in Southern Africa, making it very difficult for these host countries to welcome refugees. But despite growing poverty, neighbouring countries have shown openness to receive refugees, which I think is a fine example to offer to more developed countries. Some positive developments in my time with JRS have been the fact that it became more African in its staff, giving us more grounded information about certain issues, and helping JRS within the region; we have also developed human and material resources and logistics to allow us to do more. What we still lack is a sufficient capacity to reflect on and evaluate what we do, in spite of this expansion.

A dilemma during my work as regional director has been how to improve the quality of our service to refugees, and how to reward sufficiently our own people who work so hard in their jobs. The exit strategies have also been a source of dilemmas. It is easier to start a project than to close it. When you start there is a creative energy, and to close it means going a bit against the philosophical current of JRS, which is to accompany refugees. Advocacy and protection are problematic issues in our region, where civil society and mass media are weaker and where there is sometimes little or no culture of human rights. So we are faced with the challenge of how to work with local governments on issues of protection, yet keeping some kind of relation with them.

For the future I feel JRS has to become smaller within our region, and focus on the issues that link repatriation and reintegration to longer term development. The line with development work is not always so easy to understand. Take Angola, where we are now in the second year of the repatriation phase. Officially, the projects in Luau and Cazombo will finalise at the end of 2005 from a refugee point of view, but we will stay one year more to help with reintegration. After this, do we create a local structure, like in Cambodia or El Salvador; do we hand it over to the diocese, or do we find another partner who can sustain the impact that JRS already made?

With the repatriation to Angola going ahead, there remain some problems which are more intractable, such as protracted refugee situations in Somalia and Burundi. Many small groups of refugees from these countries are abandoned in urban contexts. There is a growing alienation of refugees who end up in cities like Johannesburg, Harare, Lilongwe, Lusaka or Luanda. The work in urban areas is an even bigger challenge for JRS since our historical experience has been more oriented to camps, and most governments are reluctant to face up to the realities of refugees in urban settings – they are usually dismissed as illegal migrants, or simply ignored.

In 2005, Joanne Whitaker RSM took over from me and became the first non-Jesuit Regional Director. The focus in the Southern Africa region continues to be the repatriation and reintegration of Angolan refugees[14].

[14]Interview with Joe Hampson, Rome, May 2005.

A COMMON DREAM: GOING BACK HOME
Stefano Canu

Stefano Canu has worked with JRS during the last 17 years, first in Rome (Centro Astalli) with refugees mainly from Africa and the Middle East and later in Africa. In 1999 he went to northern Uganda, where he worked as Project Director with Sudanese refugees. He later joined JRS teams in Angola, where he worked with the internally displaced people.

I have had the chance and the honour of working for many years with African refugees in many countries and under different circumstances: in urban areas, in camps and settlements, or with internally displaced people. These refugees often came from different contexts, cultures, languages and traditions. Many situations therefore, but with one common aspect: the strong and desperate desire to go back home, regardless of whether lived in Rome, London, or a remote village in Uganda or Sudan.

Refugees living in an urban context might want a good job, or a documentation which enables them to live in safety. A refugee based in a camp or a settlement might hope a better future for him, his family, or access to safe water and free school for the children.

But the first priority is to go back home, to the place they were born, in dignity and safety. The elders long to be buried near their village. Their children, many born in exile, dream of seeing, for the first time, the valleys, the towns, the colour of the sky which are only part of their imagination, thanks to the tales of their parents.

Once I was told a story of a refugee who lived in Rome. Although he seemed happy, well settled, with a fairly good job and valid residency papers in his wallet, there was something wrong with him. He used to say: *"You know, now I got this travel document, issued by the local government, where it is written that I am free, free to travel, to go on holiday. I have never been free in my life. So this is good, really. But, you see, this document is saying also something else... Right here it is written that I really cannot go everywhere. But there is in fact a small limitation, a small country in the world. Unfortunately this is my country. I will never have the chance to go there again, because I am a refugee."*

228

Granting refugee status to somebody is a way to: return his dignity, ensure him protection, give him freedom. But it is not the solution to the problem. A refugee shall always live with great pain, and this suffering shall never be resolved by the possibility of getting a job, healthcare or an education for his children. A refugee is a prisoner of the world, he can go everywhere except the place to which he would really like to go.

I was tempted to write about the harsh conditions of life facing refugees in Europe, the difficulties they confront integrating in the Western society, or the terrible cold during the winter, while they sleep wrapped in Caritas blankets. I could also mention the cries of mothers in Africa when they lose their babies because there is not enough money for medicine. Or about rebel attacks during the night, the looting and burning of villages, and the impoverished who are robbed of what little they had. This is also a part of the life of a refugee.

But I would like to share a happy moment. In 2003, the first UN convoys were bringing Angolan refugees back from Zambia. Some of them had never been in their country before, since they were born in exile. Some did not even speak the national language, Portuguese. They were poor, carrying just some of the crop they had harvested and some poultry. While they were crossing the border, all of them started shouting, crying, clapping... A real explosion of joy. A big crowd was waiting for them on the other side of the border. These Angolans welcomed them with great emotion and happiness.

Refugees left their houses back in Zambia, the land they had been cultivating for decades, and some relatively stable security. They decided to return to Angola, with a small kit, a tent and utensils for the first phase of their return journey. But no clear plan for the future, starting again from scratch but at home. This is what they wanted more than anything else in the world.

St Francis used to pray asking God to give us the strength to accept what we cannot change. I hope instead that something changes one day for refugees, that their dreams become reality and that all of them go back home.

Sudanese refugee in Nimule, Southern Sudan

If we look for sources of optimism in Africa, we will not find
many. Optimism does not come out of suffering. The suffering
of Africa, however, is in itself a source of hope. The suffering of
the people, their struggle, the witness of the widow, the people
themselves, because they have suffered so much, can formulate a hope for the future. There are many hopeful signs, though
they are not to be found in the circles of power, but among the
people we work with. It is the deep voice of Africa which we
have to listen to in order to find hope for Africa and the rest of
the world.

> Extract of JRS statement after the symposium
> *Africa on the Threshold of the 21st Century*, organ-
> ised by the Institute of Human Rights at Deusto
> University (Bilbao), Alboan and JRS, in April 2000.

Centro Astalli in the early eighties, Rome, Italy

Chapter Four

EUROPE

In the early 80's in Rome, thousands of foreigners, especially Eritreans and Ethiopians displaced by war and famine at home, were left homeless in the city without shelter against the winter cold. So it was not surprising that Michael Campbell-Johnston and Dieter Scholz, the two Jesuits who had worked with Fr Arrupe to lay the foundations of JRS world-wide, began to assist these homeless foreigners. Centro Astalli in Rome is one of the oldest JRS projects.

Following the fall of the Berlin Wall in late 1989, the much-feared mass migration to the West did not occur. But soon after, conflict enveloped the region of the former Yugoslavia, which quickly fragmented in the early 1990s into six smaller states. Savage local battles led to great loss of civilian life and the forced displacement of hundreds of thousands of people. Neighbours and former friends were turned into enemies by the exhumation of ancient grievances recounted in terms of ethnic or religious differences. Impulsive acts of violence created rifts that will still take generations to heal.

For JRS, some challenges in the Balkans were totally new, some familiar. The first core teams were partnerships including personnel from outside the region with experience of JRS and people from within the local communities who had local knowledge, languages and networks of contacts. Based on deep friendships and trust, strong cooperative activities were developed with both Muslim and Serbian Orthodox communities.

Eastern European countries have for many years provided a back door route into Western Europe for asylum seekers whose journeys began in such places as Sri Lanka, Sudan or Somalia. Many were stranded subsequently in societies facing difficult circumstances. Over the years since 1989, JRS has extended its roles in these countries, building on early beginnings in places of great need such as Romania.

Western European authorities frequently fail to distinguish between a migrant and a refugee, despite continuing developments in international law

EUROPE

designed to protect people in both categories. At the present time, punitive and seemingly xenophobic measures dominate the responses of western governments to the influx of asylum seekers. Alongside their many partners, JRS teams offer food and shelter to new arrivals, provide employment counselling, visit those in detention centres, provide information and public education, and help formulate just and appropriate policies.

Deeper questions about the nature of society itself are raised by the arrival of asylum seekers. In Europe, JRS engages in exploration of such issues as, 'Why should something as arbitrary as one's birthplace determine where one is allowed to live?' 'Do entrance restrictions and borders stand as barriers to a more equal world, forcibly protecting the privileges of those who live in the least crowded, richest and safest states?' On the other hand, 'Do not governments have a responsibility to preserve unique cultural communities of people who share common practices and understandings?'

This chapter details the organisational growth of JRS in Europe and South East Europe, and offers an international perspective as seen by JRS staff working in the International Office in Rome.

ORIGINS, EXPANSION AND CHALLENGES
Josep Sugrañes SJ

Josep Sugrañes witnessed the beginnings of JRS. He was International Associate Director at the International Office in Rome between 1992 and 1997 and helped set up JRS in Latin America and francophone Africa.

In a certain sense, my relationship with JRS starts with its beginning. I was one of those called by Fr Arrupe for a meeting in September 1980 where the main lines of service of the JRS were established. Of that meeting I especially remember the interest and love of Fr Arrupe in giving a response to this great human problem, both with the charism and the means the Society of Jesus possessed.

Fr Arrupe asked me to start a JRS *antenna* in Spain. But he wrote later to ask me to wait. I learned, from other channels, that Spanish provincials were not quite sure about this initiative. Because of this, I think JRS had its birth mainly in the anglophone and central European Society, even if later on other Jesuits of different geographical areas joined in.

In reality, a more formal relationship with JRS started for me in 1992, when, while I was working in Chad, Mark Raper asked me to give him a hand as his associate in Rome. This was how for five years, until 1997, I followed particularly the areas of Latin America and francophone Africa, as well as helping in the international office while Mark was away.

In 1992, JRS had the following operational centres: East Africa and Southeast Asia, as well as works in El Salvador, Mexico and Hong Kong among others.

During my five years of work with JRS, under the direction of Mark Raper many offices and operations started in many more regions. In Europe activity in ex-Yugoslavia began while the war in the Balkan region was still going on. In Africa, teams were organised in Liberia and Angola, and then because of the genocides in Rwanda and Burundi JRS started working in those countries, as well as in Congo (ex-Zaire) and Tanzania. In Latin America, the El Salvador office was closed after the civil war ended, and

235

more energy was put into Mexico to give a response to the plight of Guatemalan refugees. A national office opened in Colombia to offer services to internally displaced people there. In a few years the JRS regions had multiplied: three in Africa, two in America, two in Asia, two in Europe.

At the same time the Pedro Arrupe Tutorship was launched in Oxford and the advocacy work in New York, Geneva and Brussels took shape.

This speed of growth demanded that JRS adapt to the new circumstances. So in those years the focus was:

- To adapt the JRS international office in Rome to the new dimensions of JRS, carefully seeking the balance between an excessive centralisation of services and an international office which would only act as a channel of communication between regional offices. This meant creating and strengthening the projects, communication and human resources departments.
- An international council of JRS was created with the aim of providing advice to the International Director in his decisions and projects.
- We worked on the essential documents of JRS: the "Charter" and "Guidelines", which adapted its structure to the changes due to growth and defined its place in the Society of Jesus.
- Recruitment of volunteers and their formation was strengthened through courses and exchanges.

Overall, I think that in this way we tried to respond to several important challenges. The first one, of course, was to be faithful to the JRS mission, which also meant faithfulness to the refugees, their dignity demanding a service in companionship and compassion and our responsibility to be their voice in international fora.

Another challenge was the change from being a rather 'charismatic' JRS to another where charism was balanced with a measured dose of structure which did not drown the richness of human relationships.

The latter was connected to the efforts to maintain unity despite diversity within JRS. The roots of the diversities were obvious: different country situations, different working conditions, and a variety of origins among the volunteers. Because of this, JRS could not have a unique model, and unity had to be strengthened through the visits of the international director and exchanges between regional directors.

I feel that despite some tensions, the mission of JRS was carefully discerned. In other words, given that the huge dimension of the refugee phenomenon could not all be covered by JRS, we had to make decisions not only about quality and quantity considerations, but also involving the kind of activities we did and the places where we were to be present.

I have always considered this period of my life as a real privilege.

JRS Germany

Refugee in Germany

JRS Europe: Organisational development and main events between 1988 and 2000

Eddy Jadot SJ

Eddy was engaged in the set up of JRS in Europe since its beginnings. The JRS Europe Region was officially established in 1994, with its office in Brussels. Eddy was JRS Regional Director in Europe until 2000, when he was replaced by John Dardis. He was JRS Country Director in Belgium until 2003 and now works as Spokesperson for JRS South Asia in Brussels and in a JRS programme with migrants in detention.

Preliminaries to the start of JRS Europe: 1988-1992

At the beginning of 1988, seven years after Fr Pedro Arrupe established JRS, I first got involved in refugee ministry at the local level in South Belgium. At that time, there was no JRS network in Europe, although a number of Jesuits were serving migrant workers and refugees in some European countries and a few pioneers of JRS in Europe were already at work with asylum seekers, like the team of Centro Astalli in Rome and Brother Bernard Elliott in London to mention only two examples. In February of that year, an informal *Consultation on Refugees and Asylum Rights* was jointly convened in Brussels by OCIPE Jesuit, John Lucal, and Michael Schultheis of the JRS International office: 24 Jesuits from Western Europe shared their experiences, leading to two recommendations: to support the work already performed, and to get Jesuit European Provinces structurally more involved in refugee service. A seven member *European Jesuit Advisory Group on Migrants and Refugees* was then entrusted with the implementation of the plan.

On February 14th, 1990, Fr General P.H. Kolvenbach's letter, confirming the mandate given by his predecessor to the whole Society of Jesus, increased the motivation of a number of European Jesuits to commit themselves to migrants, asylum seekers and refugees. 55 Jesuits from Western Europe – among them Mark Raper SJ, at that time International Director – participated in a seminar in the South of France. European Provincials were requested to implement Fr Kolvenbach's appeal, according to five topics defining specifically a JRS identity: face-to-face service with refugees, ethical reflection and research on the root causes of people's displacement, public awareness and advocacy for refugees, links with the JRS in the third world and participation in refugee NGO platforms.

A few months later, in April 1991, Fr Ignasi Salvat, then President of the Conference of European Provincials (CEP), approved the plan proposed above, and urged European Provincials to appoint a person in their Province to liaise with the JRS.

Individual contacts were then taken with Jesuit Provincials in 1991 and 1992. They aimed at proposing how to make JRS present in the Provinces, taking into account the diversities between them. Two options were therefore envisaged with each Provincial; either a light presence through a contact person representing JRS and keeping Jesuits informed about JRS developments and requirements in the world and in Europe; or a small JRS country team conducting various activities benefiting refugees. The JRS Europe office main role was to offer a support to JRS country offices, helping to define and implement a common identity with regard to JRS Europe commitments.

In March 1992, Mark Raper and myself reported to the CEP Assembly in Dublin, respectively on the developments of JRS in the world, and on the visits made to the Provincials of Spain, Germany, Great Britain, the Netherlands, Switzerland, France, Austria, Hungary, Ireland, Italy, Portugal, Belgium. Later on contacts were to be taken also with Luxembourg, Malta, Greece, Sweden, and Romania. Jesuit Provincials showed their interest and their willingness to efficiently address national refugee issues in an interprovincial approach and cooperation with JRS Europe in the areas of a common reflection, research, and advocacy. In most of these countries, JRS teams were established, or contact persons appointed.

Right from the very first European meeting of JRS country offices in December 1992, when 13 Jesuit Provinces were represented, direct service to asylum seekers and refugees was not proposed as the only task. It was indeed clearly stated that JRS Europe commitments should also include collaborating with other NGOs, engaging in research and getting involved in advocacy activities through contacts with national and European policy makers.

Major developments in JRS Europe from 1993

In September 1993, the meeting of an enlarged Advisory Board[1] of the European coordinator in Frankfurt was an important step forward to launch a formal platform of country JRS offices. Two main decisions were taken:

1. A constitution of JRS Europe as an *International Non-Profit Association* was to be drawn up, which later on was recognized by the European Union (EU). Having a public status made it then possible for JRS Europe to comply with the requirements of several institutions: the EU itself, and Refugee NGO platforms like ECRE (European Council on Refugees and Exiles, of which JRS Europe is one of the 120 member NGOs) and Caritas Europa. It was also a condition for possible access to European Commission funding.

2. The main objectives of a JRS Europe office were discussed and approved:
   • to regularly inform Jesuit European Provincials and JRS country teams
   • to be available to local Churches and help them to getting actively committed to refugees
   • to coordinate activities of JRS country offices, mainly those that would require a common approach (for example in advocacy work at EU level)
   • to keep contacts with the EU institutions
   • to liaise with other Refugee European NGOs
   • to keep regular links with and give support to other regions of JRS, in the areas of advocacy, recruitment of personnel and funding
   • to remain in touch with Jesuit academics and higher educational and social institutions, mainly with a view to develop research projects.

JRS Europe and Research

In the early 90's, the last objective listed in the main goals of JRS Europe began to be implemented with a study commissioned to JRS by the UNHCR Regional Office in Brussels. A legal research, conducted by Professor Jean-Yves

---

[1] The members of the Board were: JRS International Director Mark Raper and his assistant Josep Sugrañes, CEP President Philip Harnett (Ireland), Stjepan Kušan (Croatia) who would soon be JRS Southeast Europe Regional Director, Josep Ricart (Catalonia), Jean-Yves Grenet (France), Jörg Alt and Michael Hainz (Germany), Jan Stuyt (Netherlands), Jef Van Gerwen (Northern Belgium).

Carlier of the Université Catholique de Louvain, on *Who is a Refugee*[2], was jointly entrusted by JRS Europe to both Belgian Jesuit Colleges FUNDP (Facultés Universitaires Notre-Dame de la Paix, Namur) and UFSIA (Universitaire Faculteit Sint-Ignatius, Antwerpen). Several research assistants made a study by country, covering Switzerland, USA, Canada, and 12 EU member states: Austria, Belgium, Denmark, France, Germany, Greece, Italy, Luxembourg, the Netherlands, Portugal, Spain and the United Kingdom.

In the second half of the 90's, another research was undertaken. Three individual studies were made on Irregular Migrants issues, in Germany, Spain and

Bernard Elliot SJ with refugee friends   JRS United Kingdom

---

[2] Jean-Yves Carlier and Dirk Vanheule, Klaus Hullmann, Carlos Peña Galliano, The Hague, Kluwer Law International, 1997. A second volume was published: Jean-Yves Carlier and Dirk Vanheule, Editors: *Europe and Refugees: A Challenge?*, with the contributions of the conclusive Colloquium held in Antwerp on 21st April, 1995, after the research was completed.

the United Kingdom[3]. A synthesis report, commissioned by the JRS, was written by Professor Matthew J. Gibney, and produced by the Refugee Studies Centre (RSC), University of Oxford, as a RSC Working Paper: *Outside the Protection of the Law: The Situation of Irregular Migrants in Europe* (December 2000).

Significant events between 1994 and 2000

JRS Europe Office in Brussels
At the end of August 1994, during the Annual General Meeting of JRS Europe coordinators in Louvain, two main decisions were taken:
• Mark Raper formally established JRS Europe as a Region of the JRS, with an office to be opened in Brussels in November 1994.
• The Assembly unanimously approved that, as a first important link with JRS worldwide, JRS Europe should be active in promoting the International Campaign to Ban Landmines (ICBL), with a first goal in view: to support the ICBL by advocating in each European country and requesting individual governments to sign and ratify the Ottawa Treaty. The first two Assistant Regional Directors – and Policy officers – of JRS Europe, Ward Kennes and Lena Barrett, were involved in this common international project of JRS.

JRS Country Offices
Thanks to the support received from most Jesuit Provincials, and to the commitment of many lay persons, other religious and Jesuits, the JRS European network became increasingly present, often joining hands with other refugee NGOs in partnership projects at the service of asylum seekers and irregular migrants. By the end of 2000, there were JRS contact persons, sometimes with small size programmes, in Austria, Belgium, France, Greece, Luxembourg, the Netherlands, Spain and Sweden. Bigger JRS teams were conducting various types of projects in Italy, Germany, Ireland, Malta, Portugal, the United Kingdom and Romania. From its early years, JRS Europe, as a member of ECRE, also focussed on policy and advocacy regarding the main legal issues of refugees in Europe. In several countries, JRS teams kept tight links with other regions of JRS.

---

[3] The three studies were: in Germany: Jörg Alt, *Illegal in Deutschland: Forschungsprojekt zur Lebenssituation "illegaler" Migranten in Leipzig*, JRS Europe/Von-Loeper-Literaturverlag, 1999; in UK: P. Anderson, *In a Twilight World: Undocumented Migrants in the UK*, available at http://www.geocities.com/Paris/Chateau/5532/Twilight.htlm, 1999; in Spain: Ruiz Olabuénaga, Ruiz Vieytez and Vicente Torrado, *Los inmigrantes irregulares en España: La vida por un sueño*, Serie Derechos Humanos, vol. 4, Universidad de Deusto, Bilbao, 1999.

Each year, an Annual General Meeting (AGM) of JRS Europe country directors and teams was held: in London (1995), Zagreb (1996), Sant Cugat (Barcelona) (1997), Bad Saarow (Berlin) (1998), Monte Cucco (Roma) (1999), Rodizio (Lisbon) (2000).

This latter AGM in Portugal began with a *Seminar on Advocacy*, facilitated by Amaya Valcarcel. Mr Bill Seary, a private consultant and previously a member of the Executive Secretariat of ECRE, was the main resource person. JRS workers highlighted the need for regular training, so from 2000 onwards seminars on several issues were held at these annual meetings.

Challenges and Signs of Hope

Due to the general context in Europe at the end of the 90's, with the increase of xenophobic attitudes, coupled with the priority given by most governments to security, a challenge for JRS has been to remain faithful to its original inspiration, giving priority to *forgotten refugees*, trying to promote their rights and speaking out on their behalf.

Dilemmas were there, when JRS workers had to discern in which areas they had to get involved, such as: which is our priority, a direct service with refugees or advocacy on their behalf? Strictly to maintain the original mandate received from Fr Arrupe of caring for asylum seekers and refugees, or to give our attention to other categories of migrants in need?

The main signs of hope have come, in my view, from asylum seekers and refugees themselves. Many JRS workers, such as those visiting detention centres in several European countries, have often felt that they were receiving much more from these sisters and brothers than providing for them the needful. JRS workers developed such a high esteem for them, on account of their capacity of reacting with peace and goodness despite their fears and distress. For many of us, being *friends in the Lord* – among ourselves and with refugees – is certainly not a slogan.

WELCOMING REFUGEES IN IRELAND
Frank Sammon SJ

Frank has worked with refugees in Ireland since 1990, as Coun-try Director. He was first involved in assisting Indochinese refu-gees who arrived in Ireland, and then refugees fleeing from other conflicts.

Beginnings

I began to be involved in JRS about the year 1990 when four of us met in Dublin to address some of the issues facing the Vietnamese Boat People – several hundred of whom had come to Ireland as Programme Refugees.

Michael Pelly (an Irish Jesuit who had returned from Hong Kong) had been working with the Vietnamese people in Ireland for almost ten years by this time. Tom Casey and Ashley Evans (both Irish Jesuit scholastics) met with Michael and me, and we raised a number of strategic issues about the Vietnamese community in Ireland. In fact Michael had drawn up several detailed and well-researched reports on the needs of the Viet-namese people in Ireland which he had presented to the government agen-cies most directly responsible for the lives of these refugees. Out of those meetings several developments occurred: Tom Casey wrote an article for Studies on Fortress Europe; Ashley Evans became a founder member of the Irish Refugee Council and went on to work with the Khmer people in Cambodia, and I came to be involved in JRS.

Michael Pelly had introduced us to a group of refugees in Ireland and had helped us appreciate the difficulties they faced at that time. In the coming years, I met some of the Vietnamese families in Dublin – sometimes cel-ebrating the Eucharist in their homes in Dublin's northside and attending other events like their New Year celebrations or some big event taking place among the Vietnamese community in Ireland. This was a time in Ireland when the total number of asylum-seekers applying for Conven-tion refugee status in Ireland totalled 39 in a single year. By the year 2000, that number had risen to 10,000 per year – and is now about 4,000 per year and Ireland was learning to think about putting in place the arrangements that were needed to allow large numbers of immigrants to settle and make their home in Ireland. One memory I have of these days is a general recollection of attending meetings of the Irish Refugee Council in Dublin and in Ennis as Church groups and NGO's worked at setting up an organisation that would be close to the experience of refugees and voice their needs – especially to government and in the Irish media. Over the coming years, the Irish Refugee Council (IRC) seemed to be in a state of perpetual financial crisis. However gradually and especially through the generosity of a major funding agency the IRC was able to be more certain of its financial viability, and was able to play an important role in Irish society.

Journeys

A second memory I have is that of making connections with a wider Jesuit network of people and projects involved in the JRS. Our links with the needs of refugees can be captured in two opportunities I had to travel to refugee projects in 1997 and 1998.

I travelled with Mark Raper (International director) to visit JRS in Liberia in December, 1997. Miriam Therese O'Brien and Nuala Cole, both St Louis Sisters from Ireland, were working with the JRS project in Danane, Cote d'Ivoire. The project had developed a range of programmes, health, education, income-generating and many others. The one day that we travelled back into Liberia was one that will remain with me in a special way. We travelled back to see the many places in Gbarnga, Liberia, which had been destroyed in recent military activity. Franklin Siakor showed us all the places that had been part of the diocesan compound. The national pastoral training centre had been destroyed for the second time. But through it all, the team had managed to keep going. What incredible courage, and staying power they showed! What amazing gifts the project managed to work at with people who had been uprooted and forced to flee from their own homes. And the generous welcome Mark and I received those days was very special.

In July and August of 1998, I travelled to JRS East Africa and had an opportunity to visit the JRS projects – in Nairobi, in Kampala, in Adjumani. Then I travelled down to see the refugee camps in Western Tanzania. Here John Guiney brought me to see how JRS was present through its different programmes – a radio project (Radio Kwizera), pastoral programmes, educational programmes.

These two visits to East Africa and West Africa allowed me learn from the refugees and to understand better the lives of the JRS team and of the refugees living in the refugee camps. During these visits we met with Jack Otto SJ, who was setting up the JRS links to bring the internet connection even to the remotest places!

These visits to JRS in Africa were just short visits. Mostly I was participating in JRS in Europe. The meetings every October helped bring together our JRS network and to share our lives and our vision of JRS in Europe. Usually too it was a great chance to meet the JRS International team from Rome.

The Jesuit Mission Office – Margaret Walsh and Kevin O'Rourke in a special way – had helped the work of JRS over these years and continued to work with the Agency for Personal Service Overseas (APSO) in recruiting personnel to take on different roles in JRS worldwide.

New beginnings

In recent year JRS in Ireland began to take a fresh look at the lives of refugees in Ireland when John Dardis, as JRS Europe director, drew up a funding proposal to access a European Refugee Fund which was offering funds for projects involved in the work of integration. Building on a strong Jesuit connection around the parish of St. Francis Xavier in Gardiner, Street, Belvedere College and the Jesuit Centre for Faith and Justice the funding proposal outlined a project that would work with local community groups and individuals to address issues of integration.

Our JRS Community Links project began to organize a programmes of activites that would help refugees, immigrants and local people come together and get to know one another better. These social events in Dublin – at the Mosque in Clonskeagh, at celebrations for Christmas and Eid, in a Summer Project for family groups – helped us meet people coming to Ireland from many, many places. Nadette Foley, Ann Horgan, Majella Dennehy and a great group of volunteers helped us organize some wonderful social occasions. As the song says: "Dublin can be heaven, with coffee at eleven, and a stroll in Stephen's Green". Yes! Dublin can be heaven, but it also can be very tough going for the refugees and for the local communities; little by little the work of intergration takes place. Often it is through a child like Thomas Starrs, aged about nine, that I learned about the basic hospitality of Dublin people. That was a lovely learning experience for us!

JRS – Looking at the bigger picture

Brian Grogan recently spoke to me about his going to work for the fledgling JRS in 1981 when he was planning a sabbatical time after completing a seven year appointment in the Jesuit Community, Milltown Park. Brian met Pedro Arrupe, our Jesuit Superior General in Rome, and Fr Arrupe asked Brian to spend some months in Ethiopia learning about the needs of refugees. These were the early days of JRS. As often happens our JRS ministry is one of presence in situations where people are uprooted and are forced to rebuild their lives from nothing. Part of our JRS vocation is to share in those feelings of powerlessness and not knowing what the next day will bring.

THE PEDRO ARRUPE TUTORSHIP IN OXFORD
Maryanne Loughry RSM

*Maryanne Loughry was the JRS Pedro Arrupe Tutor in Oxford be-
tween 1997 and 2004. She has for years led formation programs for
JRS workers, interpreting and teaching how the Ignatian vision can
be applied to refugee service. From her post in Oxford, Maryanne
engaged in advanced training for refugee workers at all levels, building on her own field experiences with the Vietnamese and later with
the Palestinians.*

As JRS evolved it was evident that JRS personnel needed to be more informed about the issues shaping refugee life. At Oxford University Dr Barbara
Harrell-Bond had established a Refugee Studies Centre (known in its early
days as the Refugee Studies Programme) which facilitated practitioners
reflecting on their experiences working with refugees in an academic environment.

Very early in the life of Refugee Studies Centre (RSC), JRS volunteers came to
Oxford to write, study and participate in a variety of RSC courses. When
RSC established an international summer school in refugee studies, JRS
was one of the significant refugee organisations to have staff both attend
and teach on this annual course. Each year between six and ten JRS volunteers would come from different parts of the refugee world to study refugee
law, politics, ethics and the psychology of displacement for four weeks.
Many of these JRS volunteers went on to become JRS Regional and country
directors.

As JRS developed its relationship with RSC some JRS volunteers came to
take up different posts at RSC. Through the Ford South-East Asian fellowship, Patricia Pak-Poy, Paul White, Tang Lay Lee and I came to stay at RSC
for three months at a time in the early 1990s, writing up our experiences of
the Indochinese refugee camps and the issues that surrounded them.

In 1995 Dr Harrell-Bond established with JRS and the Jesuit Private Hall at
Oxford, Campion Hall, the Pedro Arrupe Tutorship. This post had as its
main objective that the Tutor would serve as a bridge between the RSC and
JRS and the operational world of humanitarian organisations, both non-

governmental and inter-governmental. It was also desirable that the Tutor would be able to take part in teaching and student activities, and to participate in research and the academic life of the Centre and the University.

The first Arrupe tutor was Rick Ryscavage SJ (1995-1997) and I was the second (1997-2004). Both of us assisted JRS with its research projects, in-service training and were active members of the JRS International team.

Also in 1995, aware of the many volunteers who were not able to take up this opportunity, JRS started its own 'in-service training', inviting staff from RSC as well as experienced JRS staff to contribute to the course. The first of these trainings was conducted in 1996 at Centre Christus in Kigali, Rwanda. The in-service training, while not replacing the RSC summer school, provided a venue for larger numbers of JRS staff to reflect on their refugee work.

After one of the in-service training sessions run by Maryanne with support from Marg Moore, one of the Jesuits wrote these words which are implicitly a tribute to the programme Maryanne and Marg had directed:

It is at times hard to see what keeps this extremely mobile, diverse and at times apparently loose organisation together. It cannot be a strong organisational structure because it does not have one, at least compared to the enormous organisational structure of the UN and other organisations. At this JRS in-service seminar, I spent three weeks with 35 other JRS workers. I went away with a feeling of unity. The group kept its diversity in work and outlook but an inner bond of unity had grown.

Mark Raper SJ
Mercy and the National Interest, Keynote address for the National Conference of Mercy Refugee Service, 22nd November 2002. The Academy, Melbourne.

EUROPE

Sarajevo after the bombings

Brother against brother in South East Europe

Stjepan Kušan SJ

Stjepan Kušan was Croatian Provincial between 1987 and 1993. He coordinated the Jesuit work for refugees between 1991 and 1993. JRS was officially set up in the Balkans in 1993 and since then, Fr Kušan has been JRS Regional Director. From 1998 untill 2002 he was part of the Council of the JRS International Director.

Armed conflicts in South East European countries brought terrible suffering for the whole region throughout the 90's and on the threshold of the 21st century. The disintegration in 1991 of the Socialist Federal Republic of Yugoslavia initiated a massive exodus of the people. The scale of the exodus from Bosnia was without precedent in modern Europe. From a pre-war population of just over four million inhabitants, it is estimated that every second person was in some way victim of the 'ethnic cleansing' policies. About one million people were displaced within the borders of Bosnia. Another million were refugees abroad: approximately 400,000 in other republics of former Yugoslavia and 600,000 elsewhere. Member States of the European Union sheltered many of these refugees, namely Austria, Germany and Sweden.

Support for Bosnians displaced by war had begun in 1992 by German and Austrian Jesuit students. From a base in Nuremberg, Fr Martin Maier sent supplies regularly to Bosnia. JRS officially opened an office in Zagreb, Croatia, in August 1993, with two members: Jan Stuyt SJ, from the Netherlands[4], and myself, a Croatian. Years before, Fr Stuyt had worked as legal consultant with Vietnamese and Cambodian asylum seekers in Southeast Asia.

From the beginning, the new JRS team worked with the local networks of Jesuits in Belgrade, Sarajevo, Montenegro and Croatia to serve the huge number of refugees in collaboration with many other agencies. A scholarship programme started for Serbian, Muslim and Croatian children. A hostel was opened where children of the various ethnic groups could live together. A legal assist-

---

[4] See 'From Accompaniment to Advocacy', by Jan Stuyt SJ, in this chapter.

In the early 1990s, the fighting raging in Bosnia-Herzegovina was of such ferocity that the UN created several enclaves or 'safe areas'. We now know that this policy was a disastrous failure, since the UN and NATO were not prepared to protect these enclaves. One enclave was at Srebrenica where 7,500 Muslims were slaughtered, another at Zefa, and a third, near the town of Velika Kladusa, was referred to as the Bihac pocket. This territory in the north of Bosnia, holding 180,000 people, was wedged between the secessionist Serbian controlled Krajina region of Croatia, and Bosnian Serb territory, and accordingly between the Croatian Serb army and the Bosnian Serb militia. The Bihac leader, Fikret Abdic, was either installed by the Serbs or had done a deal with the Serbs in order to keep the Bihac pocket safe. When the Bosnians finally took control of the Bihac pocket in August 1995, Abdic and the other leaders did deals and left to safety elsewhere, but a large group of people crossed into Croatia and lived for several years in a refugee camp of tents. Our JRS team, young German and Croatian men and women volunteers, went to assist them and set up a primary school and many other activities.

When I visited the camp about 18 months later, in early 1997, the number of refugees had diminished to a couple of thousand, since those who could had slipped home, and the most acceptable refugees had been selected for resettlement in third countries. The agencies assisting them were also reduced to just the Red Crescent Society and JRS. The teachers at the little school prepared a lunch, at the end of which, the principal of the school, whom I shall call Vildana, a blue-eyed and fair-haired Muslim woman, said to me: 'When all those people and agencies came to help us in the beginning, the last group that I expected to stay with us Muslims was the *Jesus* Refugee Service. Now I see that not only did you stay with us, but you love us.'

Somewhat foolishly I replied: 'But is it not true that we are brothers and sisters, and do we not have the same Father, the same God?' Vildana looked at me, or rather through me, for what seemed like five minutes, as she digested this. Finally, and with immense surprise, she concluded: 'Yes!' It was a radiant moment of warmth in an environment created by years of betrayal, terror and distrust.

What gave Vildana, after all the violence, terror and betrayal that she had lived through, much of it at the hands of Christians, whether they be Orthodox Serbians or Catholic Croatians, the ability to recognise that our Christian God could be any match for her great God, her Allah Akbar? Only the lived faith, which means faith in practice, the constant love of those young volunteers who stayed with her people, could give this experience of solidarity. The volunteers were attentive to the needs perceived by the refugees themselves. Through daily encounters and conversation they became kindred spirits with one another. Once the normal barriers had been broken down by meeting face to face in trust, a new realisation was possible. Surprise enables new connections, gives new hope and energy, and introduces a readiness for change.

Mark Raper, *The Church as an agent of hope*, 2004

ance project was started at Osijek, just metres from a Serbian front line. Fr Tomislaw Slokar and Sr Liberia Filopovic, based in Sarajevo, joined the team.[5]

Just after the signature of the Peace agreement in December 1995, it was hoped that up to 850,000 persons would return to their homes in 1996, but from early 1996 until end of 1999 347,500 refugees returned to Bosnia from abroad and almost 300,000 internally displaced went back to their lands. In the Dayton agreement, among other things, it was agreed that everybody was free to return to the place of origin in Bosnia. It was hoped too that the majority of the refugees would return massively. But it did not happen. One of the major obstacles of the return of refugees was – and still is – that they have no home to go back, first because of the huge number of devastated houses, and because their lands were occupied by others[6].

The Kosovo Crisis

At the end of 1998, when problems in Kosovo were already causing forced displacement of ethnic Albanians, JRS set up a base in Shkodër, Albania with the help of the Italian province. A presence was maintained there until September 1999. At the height of the crisis, between March and July 1999, some 17 persons from different countries joined the JRS team. This team worked predominantly in Shkodër and Kukes. Its main task was to strengthen the capacity of Caritas Albania in key roles of co-ordination.

In Shkodër, the team managed the Arre e Madhe camp on behalf of Caritas Albania. The camp hosted some 800 refugees, mostly vulnerable people, who were provided with emergency health care, food and accommodation. From that base, assistance was given to many others in Shkodër. In Kukes, JRS provided medical and pastoral care to the many new arrivals.

When the Kosovars started a mass and quick return to Kosovo, JRS witnessed that those who were more vulnerable were left behind in Albania, without the supporting networks of friends and relatives. This included a number of elderly refugees, sick and handicapped people, and single mothers with children. JRS changed its activities according to the changing events and helped these vulnerable refugees to return home.

---

[5] Taken from JRS South Asia 20th Anniversary book and *Servir n.1*, November 1993.
[6] Comments from Fr Kušan to *JRS experience in dealing with Repatriation*, Amaya Valcárcel, 1999.

In April 1999 JRS set up an office in Skopje, Macedonia, and started its work in Kosovo, Macedonia, Montenegro and Serbia. This was done with the material and human resources support offered by European Provinces and a number of friendly aid organisations. The programmes included first aid assistance to newly arrived refugees, education and psycho-social support. JRS also assisted refugees who were hosted by local families.

Peace talks held in Rambouillet in February 2000 failed to ease fast-growing tensions and Serb repressions against ethnic Albanians in Kosovo. On 24 March, NATO launched an air war against Yugoslavia. Within days, 848,100 ethnic Albanians fled or were expelled from Kosovo, including 444,600 to Albania, 244,500 to Macedonia and 69,900 to Montenegro, telling stories of Serb atrocities.

In Montenegro there were two categories of refugees: Those who had arrived before the NATO intervention and those who fled during that time. JRS set up an education and teacher training programme with special attention to traumatised children.

At the beginning of June, Yugoslavia accepted a peace deal requiring the withdrawal of all forces from Kosovo and the entry of UN peace-keepers. Within three weeks, 600,000 refugees flooded back to the destroyed province in what amounted to one of the fastest returns in history. The refugees, followed by a host of humanitarian organisations, returned to destroyed villages and cities, to a territory which had no functioning civil government. Around 200,000 Serbs and Roma fled Kosovo when the Albanian Kosovars returned, and those who remained in the province were subjected to persecution.

JRS workers in Macedonia visited Kosovo a number of times following the return of the ethnic Albanians, taking food and other supplies for the Missionaries of Charity in Pec, one of the most badly damaged towns. The destruction wrought by the NATO bombings against Serbia left a country depleted of resources, evoking a post-war Europe picture. A steadily worsening political situation – characterised by nation-wide protests against Slobodan Milosevic – was matched by a swift economic decline.

The tragedy of the Serbs and Roma people who fled Kosovo is that they were mostly unwanted, unwelcome and unable to travel freely within Serbia. Together with HOCS (Humanitarian Organisation of Orthodox Christians in Switzerland), JRS organised assistance for the refugees in two camps near Belgrade, and set up an office there to coordinate JRS activities in the North and South East of Yugoslavia.

Meanwhile, Bosnia's political structures and Bosnians themselves were still overwhelmingly divided along ethnic lines, preventing the successful return and reintegration of refugees and displaced people. The Kosovo crisis added an extra burden to this situation. JRS was asked by the Bosnian government to help the most vulnerable Kosovar refugees in Sarajevo. In collaboration with the Franciscans and Caritas, JRS assisted them distributing food parcels to the Kosovars and to the Serbs who escaped mobilisation. The international attention on Kosovo caused that many humanitarian organisations left Bosnia – after four years of work – for Kosovo.

JRS continued its projects in Bosnia, namely assistance to land-mine survivors, soup kitchens and accompaniment of elderly people. JRS teams also rebuilt some houses in the central Bosnian town of Borovica, making it possible for a large part of the village population to return home.

The variety of the situations challenged JRS to become a promoter of peace and reconciliation by serving people across the front lines and selecting workers among different ethnic groups in the conflict.

Kosovo Emergency

WFP/Di Lauro

Refugees from Yugoslavia have gone back home to Croatia over the past years in a steady flow, struggling to start life almost from scratch. Due to unresolved property rights, some returnees had to wait in transition camps until their status was cleared. The return of refugees allowed for reconciliation work and ecumenical collaboration with the Serb-Orthodox church in Croatia. In order to foster reconciliation, JRS organized seminars in communications and trust-building.

The road ahead

On 12 July 2003, JRS officially marked ten years of service in Southeast Europe. The teams engaged in a process of sharing lessons learnt and set up a strategic plan for the following three years.

Statistics released by UNHCR in mid 2003 drew attention to the still massive number of refugees and displaced people in the region. Though the conflict in the former Yugoslavia has come to an end and media attention has long since passed on to other areas of the world, there are still over one million people who officially remain displaced in the Balkans.

In creating JRS, Fr Arrupe has changed the image of Jesuits. We are no longer seen as people locked up in universities, working with our minds, but bringing Jesus close to people in great need. My memories go to the collective centres where refugees were held during the ex-Yugoslavia crisis in the early 90's. These were not refugee camps, but bankrupt companies or disused factories. People used to sleep together in small rooms. I remember a lady who was close to her 26 year-old son. She told me "He will never be able to marry. He does not have a place where to bring a woman". Stories like this one deeply touched my heart[7].

---

[7] Interview with Fr Kušan, Rome, May 2005.

In recent years some millions of refugees have returned home. Some went willingly, as had many Mozambicans and Cambodians. Some went freely but with caution, as had the Guatemalans. Over a million Rwandans and a hundred thousand Bosnians had no choice about their rushed return to their country of origin. All, I am sure made this journey home with trepidation if not outright fear. Reintegration into society after a time of conflict is a very human and messy process. It takes time. Burying the dead and mourning them takes time. The wounds of grief take time to heal. Discovering and coming to terms with the truth takes forever and is sometimes never achieved. Establishing justice appears to be even rarer, especially when the economic and legal systems have been destroyed. But reconciliation cannot even be imagined before these other steps have been in great part planned and commenced if not achieved. Unless it is imposed by force as in Bosnia, reintegration can take generations and reconciliation even longer. The steps of the path to reconciliation, namely naming the truth and seeking justice, must be taken first.

Mark Raper SJ, *Those who travel under duress*, 2000

Stjepan Kušan SJ with refugee woman in Borovica, Bosnia

Mark Raper SJ/JRS

Showing love and care
to those most in need

John Dardis SJ

John Dardis was JRS Europe Regional Director between 2000 and 2004. In 2004 he was appointed Irish Provincial and was replaced by Jan Stuyt SJ. In 1995 he helped set up a radio station in the refugee camps in Eastern Tanzania.

I arrived in Rwanda in 1995, a year after the genocide had taken place there. It was my first placement with JRS. Over 800,000 people had been killed and the effects of war and of hatred between the different groups had been devastating. It had left scars on the countryside and also on the consciousness of the people. As the plane landed and we taxied in to the terminal, everything looked normal. However, I later realised that beneath the surface there was so much going on. As we drove through Rwanda and over the border into Tanzania to the refugee camps we were stopped several times at checkpoints. I was amazed at the courtesy shown, even by people who had been so traumatised and by soldiers still tense after the fighting.

Our mission was to build a radio station which would serve both the refugee communities in Western Tanzania and the non-governmental organisations. As the weeks went by we tackled problem after problem. We were building a radio station which would have a potential audience of a million people. For me this was extraordinary. Dublin, where I come from in Ireland, also has a population of about a million people with many, many radio stations all competing for listeners. Here, we were the only station for hundreds of kilometers. Again, the significance of what we were doing, and the ability to make a real difference was what struck me.

Faith as cornerstone

One day, visiting a camp, several young men approached me and said "We were seminarians back in Rwanda, but had to leave. Now we want to read the Bible more, we want to develop our faith. Can you help?" And so we met and we had a simple discussion about faith together. It was in blazing heat, under a straw roof, in the barest of conditions in a remote refugee camp. Yet it

259

is one of the places where I feel I met God in a profound way in my life. Here were people who had suffered enormously, had lost everything. Yet their desire to reach out to others, to dream, to say that survival is more than just food and water but involves something much more profound, this desire was still there. In the middle of death, hatred and genocide, people were saying "We won't buy into that culture – we want to live as Christians where we serve each other and suffer with and for each other."

Refugee camps are strange places and it can be the survival of the fittest which dominates. Taking part in a UNHCR census of the refugee population I remember one woman coming up to my table. She had stood in a line for hours. Her previous ration cards showed seven members of her family. She stood before me with three children. 'Where are the other three?' I asked her. 'They died' she said. Just like that. No long explanation. No effort to get extra rations for her surviving children or in any way beat the system. 'They died'. The remark haunts me even today. The dignity of it. The defeat behind it. The brutal honesty. In Africa life is often simple. It is about the profound issues of life and death. In the West we have the money and resources to dress those basic issues up. In so doing perhaps we escape the most basic truths of our existence.

JRS and Political change

Coming back to work in Europe the refugee situation is entirely different. It is not so much situations of mass influx following disaster but a steady trickle of people in from developing countries as they move northwards from Africa, or westwards from the countries of the former Soviet Union.

When I worked at political level in Brussels at the EU institutions, visiting Members of Parliament and talking to the EU Commission, it seemed a very different world from the killing fields of Rwanda or from those bare camps in Tanzania. Sometimes it seemed so sanitised and far away. I had to remind myself: it is the same world. Those killing fields still exist. The bare camps with abject poverty are still there.

This brings me to a key aspect of the JRS mission and one which we need to improve. As an NGO and as an Order within the Catholic Church our most valuable asset is not large-scale logistics or huge funding campaigns. What is most valuable about JRS is our on-the-ground contact with people in the most remote areas. How can we bring their stories to the heart of the European Parliament, the European Commission and even the Council?

Who is a refugee?

Visiting a Detention Centre in Berlin and meeting people who are detained because they had failed to get the necessary papers I sensed the ambiguity of what being a refugee in Europe is. The international community wants to limit the meaning of 'refugee' so that countries will not have to accept "too many". Of course we cannot expand the meaning of 'refugee' until it includes practically everybody. However, the Church understanding of 'refugee' is so wide and so compassionate. The Church says it is not just people who have been suffering persecution, but also people who have suffered economic deprivation[8].

In Lisbon I met a refugee who had fled from his homeland. I saw the way in which this had traumatised him and yet I was struck by how easy it was to relate to him. It is the human that counts most, and the human, with the grace of the Holy Spirit, which redeems. This is the call to the JRS. To humanise all those situations which have been dehumanised. That is a real strength of JRS, based on the Jesuit and Ignatian tradition. We enter situations that are broken and full of pain. And by simple human presence, by seeing the dignity of each person and believing in their potential, we see beyond the appearances, we see the person as God does.

'Continue to believe in the refugees'

I left the JRS in 2004 with grateful memories for the many wonderful people I had worked with and for. I think of Mark Raper who first invited me to go to Rwanda, of Fratern Masawe who was the founder of Radio Kwizera and a dear friend, of Eddy Jadot who worked so tirelessly to establish JRS in Europe, of Stepan Kušan my co-European director. Of course John Guiney my fellow Irish man in JRS and all the other Regional Directors and of Lluís Magriñà who supported me in my work in Brussels. There are so many others including all the Country Directors of Europe. I wish JRS well and say to you to continue to believe in the work you do, continue to believe in the refugees. That is the way to transform our world, by showing love and care to those who are most in need.

---

[8] *Refugees: A Challenge to Solidarity,* document on refugees of The Pontifical Council for the Pastoral Care of Migrants and Itinerant People and Cor Unum, Vatican City 1992.

Refugees having supper at Centro Astalli, Rome, Italy

WHAT I LEARNED FROM REFUGEES
Francesco De Luccia SJ

Francesco joined Centro Astalli (JRS Italy) in 1995. He was Country Director until 2005 and is still part of the Centro Astalli Foundation.[9]

Although Centro Astalli was founded in 1981, I first started working there ten years ago. Without a doubt, it has been one of the most significant experiences of my life. When I began to meet asylum seekers and refugees I was struck by the strong sense of dignity that they possess. You might think that when life has been harsh, one has the right to be rude and aggressive. I have found the majority of refugees whom I have known to be surprisingly gentle and polite. They possessed a kind of inner strength.

Often addressed aggressively by members of the police and the Italian public, they felt deeply offended because they did not understand why. They expected the same kindness and politeness that they offered. When they had to sleep rough, they considered it unbearable. This was not because of the physical conditions that they endured but because of the denial of their humanity. Very often I was told by refugees: "If you were in my country, you would have never slept outside during the night. Surely someone would have taken you into his or her house".

It is ironic that many Europeans consider their continent to be the birth place of concepts such as individual rights. Unfortunately, it does not apply to those who are not European Union citizens even when they live here. If you are not in possession of a residence permit your fundamental rights are suspended and you are not entitled to housing, education, employment or healthcare. Resident permits have become the pre-condition to be considered as a person. Of course once refugees have got their papers they still have a lot to do to rebuild their lives. But without them, often they are referred to as 'illegals' and their humanity is denied. I was taught that it was God, not the head of the police force, who created human beings! Perhaps my old teachers were wrong.

---

[9] Taken from *Servir n.34*, March 2005.

Centro Astalli has served and still serves thousands of refugees and migrants arriving in Italy. It relies on the solidarity of so many people who offer their time, energy and skills to support and defend basic human rights. Every year some one hundred and fifty people volunteer for Centro Astalli providing services day and night. The volunteers do not do this kind of job by chance. Theirs is a conscious decision based on the conviction that refugees and migrants suffer discrimination and deserve support to overcome the obstacles they face. Many refugees' lives have changed because of the commitment of volunteers and others. Our guests have had the opportunity to see how committed JRS staff and volunteers are to the principles of solidarity and justice.

I have learned a lot in 10 years. I have learned that to have lost material possessions and even family and friends, does not mean that one loses one's dignity. Refugees are often in need. However, they frequently have a clear idea of what it means to have respect for oneself and others. A great lesson!

I have come to understand that refugees who come to Italy or other European countries are very often highly motivated with a strong desire to rebuild their lives. They are aware of the risks of trying to get to Europe, as many have lost relatives and friends trying to reach Europe's shores. They also understand that they are considered a threat to the wealth and welfare of Europeans and expect life to be tough. Nonetheless, refugees are people who have not given up on the future, and often want to make sure that their children are granted access to the basic human rights that they were denied.

I have also learned that society still needs the solidarity of the volunteers, and the role played by organisations, like JRS, whose mandate is to accompany, serve and advocate the cause of refugees, is extremely important. I have learned from refugees that society still needs people to stand up to public opinion and the political institutions; to demand that the human rights of all are respected and to try to build bridges with newcomers.

FROM ACCOMPANIMENT TO ADVOCACY
Jan Stuyt SJ

Jan Stuyt is Regional Director in JRS Europe since September 2004. He joined JRS in 1989, first assisting Indochinese refugees in different Asian countries and later in the Balkans. Back to Europe, the main focus of his work is advocacy on behalf of asylum seekers and migrants in detention.

Working with the boat people

From 1989 to 1993 I worked for JRS in South East Asia. At that time there was a huge number of boat people coming from Vietnam and large camps for Cambodian refugees in Thailand. My years with the Vietnamese were a time of happiness, learning, great friendships and fulfilment. I often wondered whether or not I was gaining more from the refugees in terms of my own personal growth, than the other way around.

At that time JRS was a small organisation, operational in several parts of Africa and in South East Asia. Usually JRS did not have projects of its own, but worked under an umbrella group of national organisations like the Catholic Church in Thailand or the Malaysian Red Crescent Society in Malaysia. JRS has for many years been a member of the Burma Border Consortium. The lawyer's project for legal assistance to Vietnamese asylum seekers in Hong Kong was one of the few projects in Asia where JRS operated completely under its own name[10]. A large group of Australians were active in JRS Asia Pacific and quite a number of Jesuits in formation from Western Europe. In Pulau Bidong I worked in a team of three Malaysians, four expatriates and seventy refugees.

I lived and worked in camps for the Vietnamese in Battaan in the Philippines, and Pulau Bidong and Sungai Besi in Malaysia. As coordinator of the lawyer's project, I later went to Hong Kong and Bangkok. It was the time

---

[10]See Chapter One, "The 1989 Comprehensive Plan of Action for Vietnamese Asylum Seekers", by Paul White.

of the first American war in Iraq, in reaction to the occupation of Kuwait by Saddam Hussein. Expatriates from the USA and Europe in mainly Moslem Malaysia were warned not to walk around by themselves and to keep a low profile, especially during Ramadan.

The camps were in a reasonably good state. In the Philippines the camp hospital offered the best medical care for miles around and the presence of refugees with comparatively rich relatives, sending remittances from overseas, was certainly a boost for the local economy. It was not difficult to raise money for small projects in the camps; for the distribution of clothing or an income-generating project. The Vietnamese boat people who arrived before the middle of 1989 were easily resettled in the USA, Canada, Australia, France and other Western countries.

It was for me a great time: I felt needed and I could use all my talents both in terms of practical work and as a pastor. Sometimes I wondered: how much impact did it all have? Probably not too much; others would have done much of what I achieved sooner or later. But I keep thinking that my presence was significant for two or three Vietnamese, who in turn meant a lot to their communities. If my being there made a difference it was because I enabled some key people in the Vietnamese community to become leaders. Life in the camp was demanding, but for me full of meaning. I talked to the camp leaders, the different religious leaders (also the Buddhist and the Kao Dai) and I had regular contact with the internal security, as well as the Catholics working in the kitchen, in sanitation, in the camp schools and in the hospital.

I worked for two years in Malaysia for the Malaysian Red Crescent Society as a social worker. The authorities knew that I was a Catholic priest and allowed me to continue my pastoral work on the side, as long as I limited myself to ministering to the Vietnamese and did it outside of my "9 to 5" job as community worker. The pastoral work was important for me, and for the Vietnamese. My predecessors in the camps had done a good job: the Jesuit priests and brothers before me had established a reputation for dedicated, unselfish presence. Since large gatherings of refugees were usually not allowed in the camp the daily religious services took on a special importance as an expression of Vietnamese culture and coherence. They were also a place where people could express the pain of the recent past and their uncertainty about the future. It was a privilege to have a key role in the liturgy of the Catholic refugees. The presence of the so called "seminarians", refugees who had finished their studies in the seminary years ago, but whose ordinations were not permitted by the Vietnamese government, assured Vietnamese leadership from within the community. I established friendships with fellow workers and with refugees, that have lasted until today. I was very well aware that it is more difficult to work in the suburbs of Amsterdam or Paris with immigrant adolescents, than to work with the leaders of the Vietnamese communities in the camps.

To Sarajevo

When the time had come for me to return to Europe, the war broke out in Yugoslavia and I was asked to help launch a JRS office there. Generous donations from Germany and the presence of a very open minded Croatian Jesuit, facilitated the beginning of JRS in Croatia and Bosnia[11].

In Asia the presence of JRS workers had helped the refugees to organize their own life in the camp, notably by starting schools in the camps run by the refugees themselves and by supporting their churches and temples. In Croatia and Bosnia our presence was important in influencing the host communities. The war was still going on; refugees lived in open centres and in private accommodation. The divisions ran between ethnic groups and according to religion. In the raging conflict the local relief organisations always risked being partial or helping their only their own friends. JRS as an international organisation could promote dialogue, organise meetings between ethnic groups and moderate partiality. It would be an illusion to think that we could prevent it, the conflict being so near and the wounds so recent. But thanks to the quality of the local staff the efforts to promote the broader view were not always in vain. After Zagreb and Osijek in Croatia we established activities in Sarajevo, Bosnia, and after the war, in Serbia, Macedonia and Kosovo. Once again it showed the strength of being part of an international Church: we were strong and assertive locally, but at the same time kept an international perspective.

[11]See in this chapter "Brother against brother in South East Europe", by Stjepan Kušan SJ.

UNHCR/A.Hollmann

A Muslim funeral in Sarajevo

A bureaucrat in Brussels

Fifteen years ago, in 1990, there was no JRS Europe to speak of. There was no common approach and no exchange between the different Jesuits working with refugees and asylum seekers in Europe. Centro Astalli in Rome was receiving migrants, individual Jesuits in several countries were visiting foreigners in detention, and there was much discussion over whether to establish a JRS in Europe. The list of possible future tasks of JRS Europe included: ethical reflection, support for workers overseas and cooperation in NGO coalitions serving refugees. Following the fall of the Berlin wall in November 1989, Europe was excited by new prospects. However much has changed in the world since 1990: There were the attacks of 9/11 in New York and of 3/11 in Madrid. Xenophobia is on the rise all over Europe, the immigration authorities are much stricter, the number of migrants has increased dramatically and administrative detention of migrants and even asylum seekers has become common practice in many countries of the European Union.

In this climate JRS Europe tries to coordinate what is being done by Jesuits and their co-workers in several countries. A JRS office that coordinates the work in Europe was opened in November 1994 after three years of preparation. A common focus in many countries is the issue of detention of migrants and asylum seekers. Since I came to Brussels in 2004, I have had to get used to a new style of work. In our office we give time to study and analysis and we try to influence policy makers and journalists in Brussels. I no longer have the gratifying direct contact with refugees, and the climate in which we work is now very negative towards the presence of strangers in our midst. It is much harder to find funding for this kind of work. The joy of working in Brussels is the contact I have with colleagues and friends in JRS and other NGOs: a remarkable group of generous and devoted people, always maintaining high standards in their work.

Of the threefold mission of JRS (to serve, to accompany and to advocate) there is no accompaniment and no direct service in the European Regional Office. However there is more advocacy and there is certainly more professional advocacy. In the globalisation era we will need highly qualified people to continue this apostolate on behalf of forcibly displaced people.

JRS... AN ONGOING LEARNING EXPERIENCE
Hilda Serrano

*Hilda has worked in the International Office in Rome since 1985.
She has witnessed the broad organisational development of JRS
throughout the years.*

I came to JRS in 1985 from another office in the Jesuit Curia. Not by a personal choice, but for administrative reasons. I knew that Father Dieter Scholz
was the director, the office was at the third floor of the Penitenzieri building
and that the then JRS secretary, Barbara Gross, kept busy most of the time
the only photocopier available for all. The first impact was not easy. Major
concerns at that time were in Asia and Ethiopia; names of places and people were difficult to write and pronounce, geography was a real challenge.
German almost became my first language, but I never managed to grasp it,
and above all, I did not have an idea of what JRS was all about. During these
years, I have learned by doing. The JRS mission with refugees and displaced has become very clear.

The core of the JRS mission have been realised right by my desk through
visitors, correspondence, phone calls, staff meetings, liturgies, coffee
breaks...

International directors, and assistants to the directors at different times,
with whom I have shared this experience, have been: from 1985 to 1990,
Dieter Scholz and Michael Schultheis (1986-1988); from 1990 to 2000, Mark
Raper and Josep Sugrañes (1992-1997); since 2000, Lluís Magriñà, Carlos
Esteban Mejía (2003) and Stephen Power (2004 onwards).

The first group of refugees I got to know in Rome came from Northern Africa, and they were hosted at a religious house near the Curia. Dieter visited
them regularly and they were followed very closely by Ermelina, an Italian
lady, who cared for them. She died rather unexpectedly and her funeral was
a very sad experience. They cried as if they had lost their real mother. I still
see, now and then, one of these men. He talks about how different refugees
who arrive now to Rome are. He says there is a real generational gap among
refugees: different behavior, expectations, tolerance. He does not recognise
himself in them.

270

When Michael Schultheis joined as associate director, we started the *JRS Exchange*, an A3 paper with a circulation of ten photocopies, containing news on what was going on at JRS worldwide.

Mark Raper, among other things, started *Servir* as official newsletter from the international office. Myron Pereira SJ, from *Jivan* in India, came for a month to Rome to work with Anthea Webb, for the production of the first issue. When Myron left the first issue was ready and Anthea had a chance to unpack her suitcase and start settling in Rome.

Josep Sugrañes introduced a formal methodology for the accounting in the office. A proper programme was used for main currencies and the voucher system started. I entered a new world made of numbers, reconciliations of accounts and exchange rates. With the Euro, exchange rates are minimal, but reconciliations and the voucher system are still well in place. Josep also introduced the use of electronic mail in our daily work: step-by-step instructions on how to prepare and send messages, were at least seven pages long. We have come a long way regarding the use of electronics for communications. Now JRS has internet, intranet, websites, domains, satellite phones... and most important, real experts to follow this even from far away.

Our aim in the International Office is to be of assistance to the regions and facilitate their work with refugees. Some regions are more autonomous, others are followed more closely. Annual Regional Directors' Meetings, visits to the field by international staff, workshops on specific topics at country level and constant communication with the regions have proved to be essential elements in the services we can offer.

Unfortunately, farewell parties have been frequent. Tears of laughter during their preparation were mixed with those of sadness for the departures. JRS people (staff, volunteers, refugees) are a source of inspiration. They are faithful friends regardless of time and distance.

Having met Fr Pedro Arrupe and knowing JRS, I would dare to say that the founder and his creation resemble each other. Fr Arrupe was a small man of slim build, never too busy to stop in the hall for a greeting. Seeing his fragile outward appearance, one may have been surprised by his strong side, revealed in his firmly held convictions and tenacity in following a cause all the way through (incredible are his memories about the Hiroshima tragedy) He was alert to issues not so evident to many, a perspective which pushed him to do what he could if it was worthwhile for those most in need. For Father Arrupe, becoming *men for others* through love, justice, service, deep prayer and discernment, was a priority. He left a mark in all those who had met him.

In a way, JRS is the same. It is a small organisation with a light administrative structure but with a true commitment to its mission. Making the best possible use of its limited human and financial resources, it manages to reach and help many refugees and displaced people worldwide. JRS leaves a mark in all those who have been in touch.

JRS came into my life unexpectedly but at the right moment. Things have not always been simple but I feel it has accompanied me, served me and pleaded my cause, as it does to refugees and displaced. It has also "empowered" me with a new set of tools to read, evaluate and act differently on events in my life; happy and sad ones. On counting my blessings, having been adopted by the JRS family, is an important one.

Don Doll SJ/JRS

Hoping for a brighter future

HIS HOPE HAD NOT BEEN IN VAIN
Jenny Cafiso

Jenny Cafiso worked as Programmes Officer in the JRS international office in Rome between 1995 and 2003. She was responsible for planning, reporting and evaluations of JRS programs around the world, with a special focus on West Africa and Latin America.

In August of 1995 I accepted a four month contract with the International Office of JRS. There were four people on staff. I had a rather vague job description with the title of Programs Officer. At that time I had no idea that I would end up spending the next eight years with JRS in what proved to be a transformative experience at a an intellectual, spiritual and personal level.

When I joined I did not realize the breadth and scope of the organisation and even though I had worked for many years in the field of international development and had lived in Peru, I did not imagine the stories of suffering and courage I would hear from refugees in every continent, and the situations of war, violence, poverty and injustice I would see in the most remote and difficult areas of the world. Over the years I assumed the mission and ethos of JRS and became part of its growth as I was deeply moved and challenged.

I got a first glimpse of the mission and character of JRS in my first trip overseas with JRS. One of the responsibilities I had was to be the contact person for the Liberia team. At that time – 1995 – the team working in Liberia was being supported from the international office and was deeply immersed in the Liberian reality. The JRS team like the refugees were victims of the war that had plagued that country over many years. They lived as internally displaced people in Liberia and later as refugees in Guinea and Côte d'Ivoire.

In a visit to a refugee camp of Liberians in Guinea I sat in a straw hut hearing the stories of the refugees. I was so overwhelmed by what I heard, by what I saw and in particular by the lack of future prospects, that the only thing that I found myself asking was if there were many incidences of suicide in the camp. The refugees looked around and they could not think of anyone. When I asked why, none knew, but one person ventured a guess "I think it is because we are never alone".

What I found remarkable was that in the midst of all of that despair you would find so many with hope and the desire to live. The experience of the flight from their home brought many to help each other. There were remarkable acts of courage and solidarity. In the refugee camps they had to work hard to keep the family alive. The presence of JRS, inside Liberia and in exile, helped them not feel alone.

Vision and mission

When I started, JRS was an organisation with a light and decentralized structure: it had a very small international office, few and very small regional offices, minimal administrative costs and procedures. Like many other organisations of this type, it had been built thanks to the charisma, vision and commitment of a few people who had had life changing experiences working with refugees and had dedicated a lot of their lives working with them.

The organisation had a clear identity, a method of work which reflected a vision, mission and character. These were reflected in the types of projects chosen, the places in which JRS worked and for how long it stayed, in the language used, the style of living and working. Key guiding principles were: hospitality, compassion, personal relationships with refugees, presence, community, service, advocacy rooted on experience, strong roots in Ignatian spirituality.

Charisma or Procedures: conflicting priorities?

As the reality of forced displacement grew, the situations to which JRS responded become more numerous and more complex, the number of projects multiplied and the commitment of the Society of Jesus to this work through JRS was affirmed as a long term one. The organisation grew and developed accordingly.

While its core mission and structure remained the same, there was an articulation of the mission, a consolidation of practices, expansion into new areas of work, greater prominence given to advocacy and research. We developed and approved the Charter and Guidelines, we implemented financial accounting systems in most regions, we instituted the practice of an annual external financial audit for all our projects overseas, developed a procedure and format to formulate project proposals and reports, we started to have regular external evaluations of our projects, we instituted regular team meetings, annual regional meetings, we developed personnel procedures, designed and implemented a data base of all our projects around the world which recorded the activities, beneficiaries, personnel and funding for each of our projects, as well as a data base of our funding agencies, we established an office in Geneva, we obtained ECOSOC status at the UN, we participated actively and took leadership in international campaigns to ban landmines or against the use of child soldiers. This was matched by an increase of staff in the international office and the regional offices. By the time I left in 2003 there were 11 people in the international office and nine regional offices had between two and six people on staff.

Some people feared a bureaucratization of the organisation and a potential loss of its style and vision, and particularly of the personal and direct method of work. The experience of our first external financial audit was a frustrating and painful experience for many people. Some members of our teams felt these requirements were donor driven and did not fit with the character of our organisation.

There is no doubt that the implementation of all the changes above meant that in the short term more time and energy had to be spend doing office work. It is also true that with the institutionalization of the organisation, with projects lasting longer and offices becoming more 'permanent", personnel can become 'stale' and can lose the vision, passion and commitment which is usually found in a volunteer organisation.

This is part of the 'normal' and necessary growing process of any organisation which lasts more than a few years. Unfortunately the reality of forced displacement has increased in size and complexity. Until there are significant changes in the world order, a redressing of disparities and the creation of more just relations within and among nations, war, violence, and conflict will continue and with it the mass movement of people.

In order for JRS to maintain its capacity to respond to the reality of mass displacement in all its new complex manifestations it has to reflect on its history, the lessons it has learned, the experience it has accumulated. Today the contribution of organisations like JRS which have been around for 25 years or more, is not only their charisma and vision, but also their experience. The way of proceeding can not be reinvented in every new situation. The challenge for an organisation like JRS is to have the structure, know how and experience to be able to respond to new emerging realities while still maintain its character. It is a difficult balancing act which I believe JRS has so far managed to achieve.

Refugees or Migrants

Since the days when JRS began, the reality of refugees and the nature of JRS work has changed significantly. While the first JRS teams worked largely with refugees living in camps, JRS now works also with internally displaced people, with refugees in urban areas, people in detention, undocumented migrants and economic refugees. A consideration of the causes of displacement inevitably reveal a complex relationship linking displacement with war and violence and in turn with poverty, and in turn still with international political, financial and commercial relations.

Consequently, the question of the JRS mandate was discussed and debated repeatedly, particularly in Latin America, North America and Europe where the people who seek refuge have left their countries for a variety of reasons and often do not fit the U.N. definition of a refugee. The discussion was also influenced by the capacity of the Society of Jesus to respond to the world phenomenon of migration which it has identified as one of the key issues in the social sector.

In the case of JRS Europe it was resolved that JRS would continue to work with all forced displaced people without distinction. In the case of Latin America, it was decided that a new service, Jesuit Migration Service would be set up which would work in conjunction, but separately from JRS. I suspect the topic will be discussed again and new answers found as the reality changes.

Local insertion and international presence

JRS favors the empowerment of refugees. It does so by focusing on training to develop skills which they can use when they go back home, and especially through education of the young people. In its hiring practices it will give priority to refugees, then to local people and only lastly to international workers. At the same time it holds on to its principle and practice of ensuring that there is significant presence of international volunteers and staff. The way these principles which may seem to be conflicting, have been lived out in JRS have not only differed depending on the region in which we worked, but also changed over time.

276

As JRS' presence in the region becomes more long term and consolidated, the number of long term local staff increases. Local staff offers a more in-depth knowledge of the local culture, politics, history of the country and of the people, which is hard for international staff to have, unless they are present for a long time. One of the challenges for JRS in this area is ensuring that local people increasingly assume leadership positions in the organisation.

Over the years the importance of the international character of the personnel was also affirmed. The presence of international personnel can give some protection in refugee situations and it can contribute to the formation and education of people in the west.

The experience of JRS showed that it is important to be rooted locally, while fostering in all our teams an appreciation of the international scope and impact of JRS. It sought to practice decentralization without creating self contained local teams.

Relationship with funding agencies

JRS developed over the years a privileged relationship with funding agencies especially in Europe and particularly with the Caritas network. It was a relationship of trust and long term commitment, which allowed JRS to work with flexibility and over the long haul. With some Caritas agencies we negotiated long term "block grant" agreements based on common objectives, shared values, and broad and long term strategic objectives, rather than project by project decisions. The relationship built over the years is one of partnership and not only funding. This allowed JRS to develop institutionally, especially in Africa, to set up regional offices, to institute regular meetings of the staff, to develop strategic plans and to develop those procedures which allowed for the work to take place for the long term.

Traditionally some Church personnel were accustomed to receiving financial and other support on an individual basis, based on trust and personal contacts. Now there are restrictions and procedures for the transfer of funds, some imposed by governments, but also by the desire on the part of organisations to be accountable to donors, to be transparent, to show good stewardship of our resources.

Laity and religious in JRS

JRS was set up as a collaborative effort of Jesuits, other religious and laity who wanted to serve refugees. It assumes that we share a common project, a vision and a commitment and responsibilities. It has operated this way since the beginning in projects around the world. In a talk to JRS staff, Father General, Peter Hans Kolvenbach, said that JRS is first and foremost a service to refugees and only secondly a Jesuit institution. What unites all who work with JRS is a commitment to refugees.

As a result JRS is often cited in the Society of Jesus as the best instance and practice of collaborative relationship between laity and religious. Over the course of my years at JRS I shared a commitment to the refugees with many other lay people, religious and many Jesuits. The deeper the commitment, the closer our relationship with the refugees, the easier it was to work together. Many Jesuits and lay people I worked with were not only colleagues, but friends.

This road however has not been at all smooth. Changes still need to happen in procedures such as hiring process, assignment of responsibilities, ac-countability expected, to name a few, in order to reflect our belief that we are partners in a common mission where each of our contributions are respected and appreciated. There is still some way to go before everyone accepts that we are all called to compassion independently of our status.

The long patient view

In one of my visit to Zambia I met Felix, a refugee from Rwanda. We traveled together in a jeep for several hours, talking, laughing and singing. And so it was that I heard the story of Felix who had been forced to flee with his wife and young children to escape the fighting in Rwanda. They took refuge in Congo, only to get caught in the war that broke out there. He was forced to flee again, but this time he lost track of his wife and young children. He ran for many days, was captured and beaten with a friend by rebels, saw his friend die, he was thrown in a river for dead, but managed to survive and eventually ended up in a refugee camp in Meheba.

When I met him he had been there three years alone with no news of his family. But just a few days earlier he had heard on the radio someone from Canada sending a greeting across the waves to his wife. He managed to contact the Radio station and found out that his wife and children were back in Rwanda alive. He was happy to know they were well, but saddened that they could not be together as neither was allowed to travel. But he lived in hope. Two years later I returned to Zambia and while I was there Felix's wife and children arrived in Zambia and he was seeing them for the first time. He brought them to see me. The joy in all their faces seemed to wipe away all the tears and pain of the past. His hope had not been in vain.

It was an amazing story of pain, loneliness, hope and joy. I have always remembered his story because it exemplifies the story of many refugees. I am grateful to JRS for giving me the opportunity to meet Felix and others like him. All that we do has to be for them. That has to continue to be our guiding light.

Refugee from Sudan

Don Doll SJ/JRS

Communicating JRS
Hugh Delaney

Hugh Delaney worked in the JRS office in Brussels in 2001. In 2002 he moved to the International Office in Rome, where he worked as Information Officer until 2004. In 2005 he was in charge of a JRS education program for Sudanese refugees from Darfur in Eastern Chad.

JRS first came to my attention at the end of 2001 when I was working in Brussels on projects related to the European Union, including EU immigration and asylum policy. In Brussels, I had met the JRS director for Europe, a fellow Dubliner by the name of John Dardis, and we would meet occasionally for lunch or for a chat. On one such occasion John said to me: "Hugh, do you know that there is a position being advertised for a Communications officer with JRS in Rome, but you wouldn't be interested in that". I'm still not sure today if John threw in the second part of his sentence because he really believed I wouldn't be interested or just to see my reaction. Rome, I thought to myself, of course I'm interested. I can admit now that it was the prospect of living in the Eternal City that first caught my interest but as I learnt more about the organisation, the more I wanted to become part of it.

Since then, I have worked for JRS in different settings and in different functions: over two years at the International Office in the role of communications co-ordinator; some time in Brussels working on projects and funding; a spell in Dublin where I helped out as a volunteer with JRS Ireland on bits and pieces including work on the newsletter; and now in Chad, in Central Africa where I am currently working on an education project in two camps for Darfur refugees.

The JRS International Office was in a state of transition when I joined at the very beginning of 2002. The International Director, Lluís Magriñà, had been in the position for about one year, a relatively short period of time, and was in the process of formulating new plans for the organisation. One of the plans was to appoint an assistant director to back up the work of the Director, and within one year of my arrival there was also the appointment of a new Advocacy Co-ordinator, Programmes Officer, and Human Resource Co-ordinator.

The changes at Rome reflected both the changing needs of the JRS field operations vis a vis the international office, as well as a determined effort at the centre to make the organisation as professional and efficient as possible.

Sometimes it's hard to link all the pieces of JRS together, and this is one of the roles of the office in Rome. Communications is a key area in this respect, through the publication of Annual Reports, regular news bulletins and the website which all highlight JRS' work with refugees in different settings.

Some of my worst and best memories of my time at Rome involve trying to put together the Annual Report and posting it out by a certain deadline. Detailed reports would arrive in from all the JRS projects throughout the world, in various languages including Spanish, Portuguese, French or English, depending on the region and country. The task at hand involved ploughing through these thick reports and trying to boil it down to one page for each country for the global report. Deciding what to leave in and out often led to arguments and exchanges both within the International Office and also with the country or project concerned.

Seeing the final product always made the effort worthwhile. When the global report arrived back from the printers, Stefano Maero, the technical side of the Communications team in the International Office, and I would have to lug the thousands and thousands of reports up and down narrow and windy stairs in the Jesuit building to arrive at the posting office from where they would be sent around the world. During my time there we developed a better system of posting whereby the reports would be sent directly to a shipping agency which would label each package and send it off. No more carrying reports around with Stefano.

During my first year with JRS I visited Eastern Africa to attend a meeting in Nairobi and to see some of the JRS projects in operation. One of the places I visited was Kakuma camp in the desert lands of Northern Kenya, home to nearly 100,000 refugees from several countries including Sudan, Uganda, Ethiopia and Somalia. Many of the refugees had been there for up to 15 years and the size and misery of the place made a big impression on me. After only a short visit I was relieved to be able to escape from the place, and I left full of admiration for the JRS staff who spend two years in the camp and who are making a real difference to the lives of many refugees there. When you have visited a place like Kakuma you never see things quite in the same way again.

The annual meetings between the JRS Regional Directors and the International Office staff in Rome was always an important time to communicate, to socialise and to plan. It was an occasion to remind the regional directors what services the international office could provide to the field and for the regional directors to make requests and suggestions in relation to how JRS worked. It was also a time for me to encourage the directors to send regular reports from the field so that I would have enough information to do my job of communicating in Rome.

The shoe is now on the other foot for me as I am currently based in Eastern Chad, working in two camps for the Darfur refugees, assisting with education. Now the international office relies on me to send them reports, and I am anxious that the news I do send it put to good use. Having been on both sides of the fence, it is easier for me to see how this two way relationship works, between the centre and the field projects. It is a relationship that has developed since I first started working for JRS and one of the most important keys to its success is good communication within the organisation.

Voices of refugees in Geneva
Christine Bloch

*Christine Bloch has been the JRS Representative in Geneva since
1999, when she replaced Elisabeth Janz. She works in close collaboration with the regional advocacy officers and the Advocacy Coordinator at the international office. JRS has learnt over the years that the
credibility and impact of its advocacy work comes from listening to
the voices of the refugees and enabling them to reclaim their rights.*

Before joining JRS I worked with minority representatives and brought their
voices to UN Human Rights fora. I first thought that the new task with JRS
should not be so different – bringing refugee voices to UNHCR decision-making bodies. However, it has proven to be much more difficult. Firstly, refugees
hardly ever have access to these decision-making processes. Secondly, even
NGOs who might help bringing these voices are not always present in the
meetings, where key decisions such as conclusions for UNHCR Executive Committee are drafted. Thirdly, many of the NGOs working with refugees are not
doing advocacy work so as not to bring their operations in jeopardy, which
means that very few are trying to bring these voices in. Most often decisions
regarding refugees are made without the refugees, and even without their main
advocates. So some of the main advocacy issues in Geneva focus on ensuring
that refugees become more active in decision-making processes.

Something I find imperative in order to carry out a credible lobbying and
advocacy work in Geneva is to go to the field and speak to the refugees and
JRS workers staff. Otherwise, how can one even begin to think we are bringing the voices to Geneva? Only when you have listened to the refugees can
you begin to imagine what their lives are like. These are the experiences I can
bring back to the decision-makers.

The first proper consultations between UNHCR and refugees took place in
UNHCR's consultations with refugee women in 2001, in response to issues
raised in the consultations with refugee women at local, regional and at
headquarter levels. These included issues on registration, documentation,
food distribution, health, education, physical safety and security, participation in peace building and decision-making, and opportunities for skills development and income generation. When the consultations finished in

December 2001, the High Commissioner for Refugees announced his intention to pursue five commitments to refugee women to enhance their rights and to implement concrete measures to improve their protection. However, in 2004 there were still big gaps in the implementation of these commitments despite the fact that these are the priority of the organization.

One of the big events in Geneva during the time I have been here were the UNHCR's Global Consultations on International Protection. These consultations were UNHCR's response to the European Governments criticism of the 1951 Convention and its Optional Protocol for being out of date. The consultations were reviewing the applicability of the 1951 Geneva Convention with regards to areas that governments had said it was lacking in dealing with such as mass influx situations, the asylum/migration nexus and maintaining the civilian character of asylum. Again the voices of refugees were very absent apart from a young refugee girl, who came to speak about protection of refugee children, airing concerns that no one had actually been debating. However, the final outcome of the consultations – the Agenda for Protection – does include refugees' right to participate in decisions concerning their lives, especially for refugee women and children.

Last spring I was participating in some very difficult discussions on irregular secondary movements of refugees. Often when such discussions take place it becomes a battle over a word. In such situations I always try to bring in experiences from the field, striving to give a human face so that refugees are at the heart of these discussions. Though government representatives do not always agree with the proposal we are suggesting, they always find it important when we try to link the discussions to the realities in the ground.

The latest initiative I have been involved with is to ensure that the voices of refugees are heard when UNHCR and NGOs are planning their activities. The initiative has been baptized *"Gender, age and diversity mainstreaming"*. The thrust of the initiative is to undertake participatory assessments directly with refugees prior to planning activities for the future, and to include refugee representatives directly in the planning process for UNHCR's budgets. It is to ensure that refugees of all gender, different age groups, – including the young and the elderly – and from different ethnic groups or nationalities are consulted in the assessment process, and to ensure a more human contact between the refugees and the humanitarian workers. Though we do not see many refugees in Geneva, at least they are increasingly more *visible* by being included in the plannings of UNHCR and NGOs.

Our first task is to accompany the people. Living with them as they live we will more likely hear and experience their stories, hopes and responses to their situations. We can be present *without a flag*, like yeast. Let us remain open to peoples' changing needs in precarious situations, attending too to the life of the spirit in them. Our simple aim is to support them as they try to reconstruct their lives; to denounce with them the forces that destroy. The people live in uncertainty, so let us be flexible. Being an international body, we can communicate to the world what is hidden, what people suffer, often silently. Let us question why masses of people are forcibly displaced. Let us constantly question our way of being present. Let us discern our way of service.

Extract from a reflection made by JRS workers during the summer school at Oxford, 1993

Kosovar refugee in Albania

Jack Iacuzzi SJ/JRS

EPILOGUE

Commemorating the past and looking to the future

In November 1980 when Fr Pedro Arrupe called on Jesuits to establish the Jesuit Refugee Service, there were only 16 million refugees in the world. JRS was to be a new apostolate for the Society and opened new paths of service and learning with the refugees.

Today, 25 years later, with 50 million forcibly displaced people worldwide, the context in which we work has changed dramatically. The Berlin Wall has fallen and with it states which were once of strategic importance. Forced migration is taking place in a rapidly changing world where the old certainties are often out of date. Wars and conflicts are ending, while others are erupting. The geopolitically important issues and areas of the world are not those of yesterday.

JRS has tried to remain faithful to Fr Arrupe's original vision while trying to adjust to the new scenarios of forcible displacement. Over the last five years many more are the internally displaced within countries than with those who manage to cross the borders. The traditional refugee camps still give shelter to millions of refugees but many are also those who end up in urban areas. These groups are often more isolated, anonymous and difficult to trace. Migrants who end up trapped in detention centers is unfortunately a growing trend. The debate over the nexus between migration and refugee flows is on the table.

However, JRS cannot be expected to respond to the needs of all people on the move. Although the debate on exactly who is within the mandate of JRS will continue, it is clear that JRS has to restrict itself to those who are forcibly displaced.

Working with internally displaced people is more difficult due to often volatile security situations and the social and political conditions. This work will need even more collaboration of JRS with local organizations.

Advocacy, communications and programme strategies have been developed and continue to evolve to serve the most forgotten in places ignored by governments, NGOs and the mass media. Our scope of action covers 53 countries, with contact persons in other 20 countries. JRS employs more than 1,000 staff – lay, Jesuit and other religious, to meet the needs of over 450,000 refugees and IDPs with the specialisations it has developed in education for refugees and in particular types of pastoral care.

A very clear sign of hope is our work in education, as understood in a broad sense. We offer primary and secondary education to some 150,000 students; basic literacy, vocational training and income generating activities to adult refugees in the hope that they are self reliant once they go back home.

To do all this we need to constantly develop our capacities to analyse our own needs. Understanding what these rapid changes mean to forcibly displaced persons is the challenge we must continually face. With this knowledge we will be able to judge whether we advocate locally, regionally or internationally in Washington, Brussels or Geneva. Whether we must speak out on our own or seek alliances with others as we often do with the likes of the International Campaign to Ban Landmines and the Coalition to Stop the Use of Child Soldiers.

Throughout these 25 JRS has learnt many things:
It is relatively easy to become involved in works, but less easy to remain flexible and prioritise where and when to stay and where and when to move on to new situations. We need to go back and again to renew the original vision of a flexible JRS, ready to move where people are most in need. This requires a light administration, but also adopting more professional approaches.

JRS' most valuable resource has been its staff, many very excellent lay people and other religious who work together with the Jesuits in every part of the world.

The work on JRS requires a high degree of availability, JRS workers need to be ready to go to even the most difficult situations. It also requires a high degree of availability as an organisation in the need to be flexible and responsive both in addressing the work to do but also in the people with whom it needs to do it with.

There are many examples of availability and rapid response in this book. With the years, JRS has developed the work with non-Christian groups. JRS has Muslim or Buddhist workers. This has been most efficacious for our work, in particular in areas such as Aceh, and it could only be very close to the heart of what Fr Arrupe would have wanted.

We seek to form alliances and build capacities, both within JRS and in the organisations with whom we work.

JRS mission statement established in General Congregation 34 is clear and very well-accepted. It is this mission: to serve, accompany and advocate, of which we must not lose sight. We find strength and energy in the belief that we are sons and daughters of the same Father, and that the Spirit sends us to live as brothers and sisters.

This history is a work of love. Despite being kept in the shade of injustice and evil, refugees are a witness to the light of God. While there are refugees JRS will continue to have a history. Let's make that history one of which we and the forcibly displaced can be proud.

Lluís Magriñà SJ
International Director
Rome, September 2005

Going to school in Nimule, south Sudan

A JRS CHRONOLOGY

November 1979   Fr Pedro Arrupe SJ sends a letter to Jesuit Major Superiors seeking support to provide relief to the Indochinese *boat people*. Fr Arrupe was overwhelmed by the immediate offers of help.

1980   An estimate six million refugees world-wide and an estimated four to five million displaced.

September 1980   Fr Arrupe calls a Consultation in the Jesuit Curia to consider the possible response of the Society of Jesus. Decision to set up a service to co-ordinate Jesuit refugee work. This was to be called the Jesuit Refugee Service (JRS).

November 1980   14 November: The birth of JRS is announced. Michael Campbell-Johnston SJ takes responsibility for JRS, which forms part of the Social Secretariat of the Society.

Early 1980's   The work of Jesuits in many countries is pulled under the umbrella of JRS. The countries where work with refugees was active at this time included: Vietnam, Laos, Thailand, Malaysia, Hong Kong, Indonesia, Philippines, Cambodia, Ethiopia, Sudan, El Salvador.

1980   Centro Astralli is founded in Rome to provide food and shelter for Eritrean and Somali refugees. It is set up in the basement of the same building where St Ignatius and his companions had helped the victims of the 1538 famine. This is the longest running JRS project.

     The war in Guatemala starts displacing the population towards Mexico (through 1982, one million people are displaced).

August 1981   Last talk of Fr Arrupe to JRS workers in Bangkok. He suffered a cerebral stroke on the flight back to Rome.

1981   Angelo D'Agostino SJ is appointed to take responsibility for refugee concerns in Africa.

1982   Work in Ethiopia begins with the displaced and people affected by the Ethiopia-Somalia war and later by the Wallega famine.

     Mark Raper SJ is appointed to co-ordinate JRS in Asia Pacific.

1983   Civil war breaks out in Sudan for the second time since independence (1956).

     Forced displacement in Sri Lanka due to violent reactions by the ethnic Singalese to armed campaigns by the Jaffna Tamils.

     Diakonia, the newsletter of JRS Asia Pacific, appears. It publicised refugee issues and the work of JRS with them for Jesuit publics.

     Frank Moan SJ is appointed as refugee co-ordinator for the American Jesuit Assistancy.

1984 JRS separated from the Social Secretariat. Dieter Scholz SJ became its first director and Mike Schultheis SJ first associate director.
JRS starts a program of accompaniment for refugees of El Salvador and Guatemala.

1985 First meeting of Regional Directors takes place in Thailand. The Bangkok regional office is set up.
Mercy Sisters set up Mercy Refugee Service, an important event for JRS recruitment policies.

1986 JRS starts working in Khartoum, Sudan, with the internally displaced people.

1987 Projects established in Malawi to support the many refugees fleeing Mozambique and Angola.
Repatriation to El Salvador starts (through mid 1991).

1988 Mike Schultheis SJ appointed JRS Director for Africa. The war in Mozambique creates huge refugee flows towards Malawi.

1989 An estimated 15 million refugees, and up to 30 million internally displaced people world-wide.
Establishment of the Resource Base for Refugee Education in Nairobi.
Appointment of Tom Steinbugler SJ as Regional Director of JRS Asia Pacific.
The Comprehensive Plan of Action for the resettlement of Vietnamese Asylum Seekers (CPA) is signed by many Western and Asian countries and UNHCR. JRS starts a legal project to assist *boat people* with their resettlement claims in Hong Kong and the Philippines.

May 1990 Mark Raper SJ is appointed International Director.

1990 Mike Evans SJ is appointed first regional director in East Africa. Mike Schulteis SJ moves to Malawi.
War in Liberia starts, displacing over a million people within and some 700,000 as refugees outside the country. War in Liberia starts, displacing over a million people within and some 700,000 as refugees outside the country.
First visit of a JRS team to Cambodia. Cross border operation and a JRS presence in Cambodia start.

1991 Disintegration of the Socialist Federal Republic of Yugoslavia. Massive exodus, particularly in Bosnia and Herzegovina.
JRS initiates the MOLU education project (Mozambican Open Learning Unit) in Malawi.
The split in the Southern Sudanese rebel movement, the SPLA, causes flight into Northern Kenya. Kakuma camp is formed and JRS starts working there.

Siad Barre regime collapses in Somalia. Refugees flee to Kenya and Ethiopia.
JRS officially starts working in Mexico to assist Guatemalan refugees in Chiapas, Campeche and Quintana Roo.

1992   Signing of peace accords in El Salvador in January. The Aristide *coup d'etat* in Haiti raises the number of Haitian refugees to Dominican Republic. JRS starts working in Dominican Republic.
JRS Europe formed by bringing together the work with refugees of the Jesuits across Europe.
Mike Schultheis SJ moves out to take up a particular concern for the Mozambicans based in Malawi. Michael Evans SJ is appointed Regional Director for East Africa.
Peace accord in Mozambique. JRS starts repatriation programs and reintegration work in Mozambique.
JRS is set up in Liberia under the direction of Myriam O'Brien SSL, with direct coordination from the international office.
Huge refugee flows from Sudan into North Uganda.

1993   JRS is established in Croatia, Bosnia, Nepal, Liberia, Uganda, Kenya, Mozambique, Peru, Zambia and Somalia.
JRS withdraws from some programs in Malawi, Sudan, Thailand, El Salvador. War in Burundi starts after the assassination of Melchior Ndadaye, producing huge refugee flows.
Vincent Mooken SJ is appointed first Regional Director of South Asia (spilt from JRS Asia Pacific).
Cambodian refugees start returning home.

1994   JRS joined other international agencies to work with the survivors of the massacre in Rwanda, with projects in Burundi, Rwanda, Tanzania and Zaire (DR Congo). The JRS Grands Lacs region is set up with Mateo Aguirre SJ as Regional Director.
JRS joins the International Campaign to Ban Landmines.
Armed conflict starts in Chiapas, Mexico. Legal incorporation of the *Servicio Jesuita para el Desarrollo* (former JRS) in El Salvador. Michael Campbell-Johnston SJ returns to El Salvador replacing Peter O' Driscoll. Rob McChesney SJ is appointed Director of JRS USA. JRS is set up in Colombia.
JRS Europe starts under Eddy Jadot's direction. The regional office is set up in Brussels and JRS expands to other European countries. Regional meetings start.
Tom Steinbugler SJ hands over to Quentin Dignam as Regional Director in JRS Asia Pacific. Down scaling of JRS programs with Indochinese and withdrawal of JRS as these camps are closed.

1995   South Africa Regional Office established with Peter Balleis SJ as Regional Director. Withdrawal from Mozambique. Set up of Radio Kwizera in Tanzania.
Dayton peace agreement in December 1995. Repatriation to Bosnia starts.

Barbara Harrell-Bond establishes with JRS and the Jesuit Private Hall at Oxford, Campion Hall, the Pedro Arrupe Tutorship. Rick Ryscavage is appointed as first Tutor, until 1997.
First JRS in-service training seminar in Kigali.
Jesuit Service Cambodia starts development work with Cambodian returnees, while continuing to assist refugees.
JRS and Caritas set up an education program for the Bhutanese refugees in Eastern Nepal. Bombing and exodus from Jaffna, Sri Lanka.
Carlos Esteban Mejía appointed coordinator for Latin America region.

1996 JRS establishes a permanent presence in Geneva with the appointment of Elisabeth Janz to represent JRS at the UN and to ensure that JRS has a voice in key committees and NGO networks.
A Communications Audit takes place, an evaluation of JRS communications capabilities around the world.
Forced repatriation of Rwandans from DR Congo and Tanzania.
Set up of JRS Angola. The campaign to ban landmines in collaboration with JRS Cambodia becomes part of JRS mission in Angola.
JRS starts working in Tamilnadu, India.
Richie Fernando SJ is killed in Banteay Prieb, Cambodia.

1997 An agreement is signed finalising the first stage of the return process for Guatemalan refugees in Mexico. JRS Mexico ends its work with Guatemalan refugees but continues to assist displaced from Chiapas.
JRS USA starts the Detention Centre Project.
Carlos Esteban Mejía is replaced by Raúl González SJ as coordinator for Latin America.
Tun Channareth, a JRS Cambodia worker and a landmine survivor receives the 1997 Nobel Peace Prize on behalf of the International Campaign to Ban Landmines.
Steve Curtin SJ takes over from Quentin Dignam as Regional Director in JRS Asia Pacific.
JRS begins the Africa Education Project to enhance the quality of education. Stephen Power SJ replaces Joseph Payeur SJ – who had replaced Mike Evans in 1996 – as Regional Director in East Africa.
JRS Southern Africa begins the work with urban refugees in Zambia and South Africa. JRS Grands Lacs sets up its office in Bujumbura. Work starts in Rwanda with Congolese refugees.
JRS starts to work with Burmese refugees in the Thai-Burma border camps.
Closure of Sie Khieu, the last camp for Indochinese in Thailand.
Maryanne Loughry RSM replaces Rick Ryscavage SJ as the Pedro Arrupe Tutor in Oxford, until 2004.

1998 Renewed wars in Angola and the *African war* in DR Congo. JRS Southern Africa grows in response given the huge refugee and IDP flows in Zambia and Angola. Outburst of war between Ethiopia and Eritrea. First meeting of pastoral workers in Harare.

JRS joins with a group of five other leading NGOs to form the Coalition to Stop the Use of Child Soldiers, campaigning to draw attention to the estimated 300,000 child soldiers worldwide.

1999   Africa Resource Base opened to provide resources for the development of education for refugees across Africa.
Christine Bloch replaces Elisabeth Janz as JRS Representative in Geneva.
JRS establishes a presence in East Timor and West Timor working to support refugees and facilitate their return. Karl Albrecht SJ and Tarcisius Dewanto SJ are killed in September.
War and displacement in Angola. New projects in Namibia and Zambia start.
JRS is set up in Macedonia, Kosovo, Montenegro and Serbia. Stjepan Kušan SJ is appointed Regional Director.
End of the Guatemalan refugee repatriation operation in June.

April 2000   A symposium on Africa is organised by JRS at Deusto University, Bilbao.

2000   An estimated 22 million refugees and 30 million internally displaced people worldwide.

October 2000   Lluís Magriñà SJ replaces Mark Raper SJ as International Director.

2000   On 3rd October, Br Antoine Bargiggia, a JRS worker, is killed in Burundi.
JRS faces out from Congo Brazzaville as reintegration of refugees grows.
Andre Sugijopranoto SJ appointed Regional Director in Asia Pacific. JRS is set up in Ambon, Indonesia, and later in other islands such as Aceh and Medan, Sumatra.
Chepe Núñez SJ is appointed regional director in JRS Latin America and the Caribbean. Due to increased violence in Colombia, JRS expands its work within Colombia and to Ecuador, Panama and Venezuela, and later on to Costa Rica and Brazil.

2001   An estimated 21 million refugees and 25 internally displaced people worldwide. UNHCR's Global Consultations on International Protection. First UNHCR's Consultations with refugee women, Geneva.

November 2001   Mateo Aguirre SJ is replaced by Joaquín Ciervide SJ as Regional Director in the Great Lakes. Mateo re-launches JRS activities in West Africa and sets up a JRS region there with the establishment of a project in Guinea and later on in Liberia and Ivory Coast.

2001   John Guiney SJ replaces Stephen Power SJ as JRS East Africa Regional Director.

2002	JRS hands over its activities in East Timor to the Jesuits and local church groups. A peace agreement is signed in Angola. Repatriation and reintegration of Angolan refugees and IDPs start.
July 2002	JRS gets a consultative status at ECOSOC.
August 2003	JRS is officially registered at the Vatican State as a foundation and recognised by the Italian State.
2003	International Meeting of all Africa Country Directors in Nairobi. Assassination of the Apostolic Nuncio in Bujumbura. PS Amalraj SJ replaces C. Amal SJ as Regional Director in South Asia. Ken Gavin SJ is appointed JRS USA Country Director.
December 2003	JRS gets an observer status at the International Organisation for Migration (IOM).
2004	Peace agreement in Sudan. Crisis in Darfur and set up of JRS in Chad. Two million displaced by the tsunami in December. JRS increases its response in Sri Lanka and Indonesia.
2005	Joanne Whitaker RSM replaces Joe Hampson SJ as Regional Director in Southern Africa. Andre Sugijopranoto SJ is replaced by Bernard Arputhasamy SJ as Regional Director in Asia Pacific. Alfredo Infante SJ replaces Chepe Núñez SJ as Regional Director in Latin America.
August 2005	Peace agreement in Burundi.
September 2005	First international meeting of Regional and Country Directors of Africa and Asia in Nairobi.

Sudanese refugee in Gulu, Northern Uganda

ASIA and the PACIFIC

NEPAL

INDIA

HONG KONG

VIETNAM

THAILAND

PHILIPPINES

CAMBODIA

SRI LANKA

MALAYSIA

SINGAPORE

INDONESIA

EAST TIMOR

AUSTRALIA

■ Currently working
□ Formerly working

AMERICA

CANADA

USA

MEXICO

HAITI

DOMINICAN REPUBLIC

HONDURAS   JAMAICA

GUATEMALA

EL SALVADOR

VENEZUELA

PANAMA

COLOMBIA

ECUADOR

PERU

BRAZIL

Currently working
Formerly working

AFRICA

GUINEA
CÔTE
D'IVOIRE
LIBERIA
CHAD
SUDAN
ETHIOPIA
CONGO
UGANDA
KENYA
RWANDA
DEMOCRATIC
REPUBLIC
OF CONGO
BURUNDI
TANZANIA
ANGOLA
MALAWI
ZAMBIA
ZIMBABWE
MOZAMBIQUE
NAMIBIA
SOUTH AFRICA

■ Currently working
☐ Formerly working

EUROPE

IRELAND

UNITED
KINGDOM

GERMANY

BELGIUM

SLOVENIA

ROMANIA

CROATIA

BOSNIA-
HERZEGOVINA

SERBIA

MACEDONIA

PORTUGAL

ITALY

SPAIN

MALTA

Currently working
Formerly working